THE RISE OF PRISON LITEF
SIXTEENTH CEN

Examining works by some of the most famous prisoners from the
early modern period, including Thomas More, Lady Jane Grey,
and Thomas Wyatt, Ruth Ahnert presents the first major study of
prison literature dating from this era. She argues that the English
Reformation established the prison as an influential literary sphere.
In the previous centuries we find only isolated examples of prison
writings, but the religious and political instability of the Tudor reigns
provided the conditions for the practice to thrive. This book shows
the wide variety of genres that prisoners wrote, and it explores
the subtle tricks they employed in order to appropriate the site
of the prison for their own agendas. Ahnert charts the spreading
influence of such works beyond the prison cell, tracing the textual
communities they constructed, and the ways in which writings
were smuggled out of prison, and then disseminated through script
and print.

RUTH AHNERT is a lecturer in Early Modern Studies in the School
of English and Drama at Queen Mary, University of London.
Her work focuses on the literature and culture of the Tudor period,
with a specific emphasis on religious history, prison literature, and
letter writing. Recent and forthcoming publications examine prison
scenes in early modern drama, trial narratives, and Protestant
letter networks. Dr Ahnert serves on the Council of the Society for
Renaissance Studies, and is co-editor of the society's *Bulletin*.

THE RISE OF PRISON
LITERATURE IN THE
SIXTEENTH CENTURY

RUTH AHNERT

CAMBRIDGE
UNIVERSITY PRESS

CAMBRIDGE
UNIVERSITY PRESS

University Printing House, Cambridge CB2 8BS, United Kingdom

Published in the United States of America by Cambridge University Press, New York

Cambridge University Press is part of the University of Cambridge.

It furthers the University's mission by disseminating knowledge in the pursuit of
education, learning and research at the highest international levels of excellence.

www.cambridge.org
Information on this title: www.cambridge.org/9781107040304

© Ruth Ahnert 2013

First published 2013

Printed in the United Kingdom by CPI Group Ltd, Croydon CR0 4YY

A catalogue record for this publication is available from the British Library

Library of Congress Cataloging-in-Publication Data
Ahnert, Ruth.
The rise of prison literature in the sixteenth century / Ruth Ahnert.
pages   cm
Includes bibliographical references.
ISBN 978-1-107-04030-4 (Hardback)
1. Prisoners' writings–History and criticism.   2. Prisoners in literature.   I. Title.
PN494.A38 2013
809′.8920692–dc23   2013014365

ISBN 978-1-107-04030-4 Hardback

Contents

Illustrations

Acknowledgments

This book began as an undergraduate essay set by Colin Burrow during the final year of my English degree at the University of Cambridge. I quickly realised that the topic of sixteenth-century prison writers could not be addressed adequately in a weekly essay, and decided to make it the focus of my doctoral research. I was fortunate enough to be supervised for my PhD by Daniel Wakelin, who was not only an astute and rigorous reader but also a kind and sage mentor. He has had a profound effect on the way I approach texts, and the book is what it is because of him. The development of the thesis into the book was also crucially shaped by the advice of my examiners, Brian Cummings and Jason Scott-Warren, and it has benefited from numerous other careful readers, including Linda Bates, Aisling Byrne, Helen Cooper, Joanna Craigwood, Sarah Howe, Joe Moshenska, Bill Sherman, Paul Strohm, Diane Vincent, James Wade, Edward Wilson-Lee, and the two anonymous readers from Cambridge University Press. Mary Flannery read more than her fair share of the manuscript, as well as providing other crucial support throughout the duration of this project through friendship and food. Any remaining faults are, of course, my own.

Many others offered helpful comments at conferences and through other forums, including Jerome de Groot, Genelle Gertz, Kathleen Lynch, Molly Murray, Bill Sheils, and Rivkah Zim. Audiences at meetings of the Renaissance Society of America, the Sixteenth Century Society and Conference, the Society for Renaissance Studies and at the Religious History of Great Britain 1500–1800 seminar (Institute of Historical Research) asked useful questions and provided thought-provoking comments. I am indebted to Tom Freeman for sharing his incomparable knowledge of Foxe's 'Book of Martyrs' (and cinema) with me over numerous dinners in Cambridge. Colleagues at Murray Edwards College, Cambridge, and Queen Mary, University of London, also provided prudent advice, support and friendship. I am especially grateful to Tamara

Atkin, Shahidha Bari, Michèle Barrett, Julia Boffey, Warren Boutcher, Andrea Brady, Jerry Brotton, David Colclough, Mark Currie, Markman Ellis, Heather Glen, Alfred Hiatt, Lisa Jardine, Gwilym Jones, Raphael Lyne, Leo Mellor, Joad Raymond, Christopher Reid, and the late Kevin Sharpe. Evelyn Welch has been an inimitable mentor during my time at Queen Mary, helping me to think big, but also to know when to let a project go. Special thanks to my editor, Sarah Stanton, for seeing the potential of this book, and for responding so quickly and efficiently to all my queries, and to Fleur Jones, Rebecca Taylor, Jessica Murphy, and Hilary Hammond for overseeing the various stages in the production of the volume.

I would not have been able to undertake this project if it were not for the financial support of various institutions. Early research for the project was made possible by grants, studentships and fellowships from Murray Edwards College, Cambridge, the University of Cambridge and the Arts and Humanities Research Council. A postdoctoral research fellowship funded by the Society for Renaissance Studies enabled me to undertake the research for Chapter 5. And a grant from the Marc Fitch Fund paid for the reproduction of the images found in the following pages. I am most grateful to all these institutions. I must also thank the librarians and archivists at the British Library, Cambridge University Library, Emmanuel College Library and the National Archives, especially Helen Carron at ECL. Annie Heron at Hampton Court Palace helped me track down images of graffiti to illustrate Chapter 2. Portions of Chapter 2 were first published as 'Writing in the Tower of London during the Reformation, ca. 1530–1558', in 'Prison Writings in Early Modern Britain', *Huntington Library Quarterly*, special issue 72 (2009), edited by William H. Sherman and William J. Sheils; I am grateful to the editors of this journal for permission to reprint revisions of that material here.

First books have a long history of debts, and I'd like to take the opportunity here to thank my sixth-form teacher, Anita Gentry, who saw my academic potential and persuaded me to apply to Cambridge to study English. Friends and family have supported me and offered much needed distraction throughout the process of writing this book, especially my parents Judith and Graham Roberts, my brother Lewis Roberts, my grand-mother Joan Roberts, and my mother-in-law and father-in-law, Bridget and Frank Ahnert. The person who would have been proudest of this book, but sadly did not live long enough to see it, is my late grandfather Lewis Myall Roberts. I would also like to remember Jemima and Leslie Windscheffel here. However, my greatest debt of all is to my dear husband, Sebastian, who has helped me in more ways than I can count. This book is for him.

Abbreviations and references

When quoting from early printed books, I provide semi-diplomatic transcriptions: superscript letters are lowered; contractions are expanded and supplied letters italicised; thorn and *y* are replaced with *th* and terminal *-es* graph with *-es*. These have been silently expanded. Deletions in the text are signalled with <xxx>, lost letters and words with {...}, interlineations with /xxx\ and editorial insertions with [xxx]. Titles from early modern printed books have frequently been truncated for brevity. The following abbreviations are used for books, journals or libraries that are cited frequently:

BL	British Library, London
CW	*The Complete Works of St Thomas More*, 15 vols. (New Haven, 1963–97)
ECL	Emmanuel College Library, Cambridge
EETS OS	Early English Text Society, Original Series
HLQ	*Huntington Library Quarterly*
LM	*Certain most godly, fruitful, and comfortable letters of such true saintes and holy martyrs of God* (otherwise known as 'Letters of the Martyrs'), ed. Henry Bull (London, 1564)
LP	*Letters and Papers, Foreign and Domestic, of the Reign of Henry VIII: Preserved in the Public Record Office, the British Museum and elsewhere (in England)*, ed. J. S. Brewer et al., 21 vols. (London, 1862–1910)
MED	*Middle English Dictionary*
ODNB	*Oxford Dictionary of National Biography*
OED	*Oxford English Dictionary*
Rerum	*Rerum in Ecclesia gestarum* (Basle, 1559)

STC	*A Short-Title Catalogue of Books Printed in England, Scotland, and Ireland and of English Books Printed Abroad, 1475–1640,* compiled by A. W. Pollard, and G. R. Redgrave, 2nd edn, revised and enlarged by W. A. Jackson, F. S. Ferguson and K. F. Pantzer, 3 vols. (London, 1976–91)
TAMO (1563)	*The Unabridged Acts and Monuments Online* or *TAMO* (1563 edition) (Sheffield: HRI Online Publications, 2011). www.johnfoxe.org [accessed 18 December 2012]
TAMO (1570)	*The Unabridged Acts and Monuments Online* or *TAMO* (1570 edition) (Sheffield: HRI Online Publications, 2011). www.johnfoxe.org [accessed 18 December 2012]
TAMO (1583)	*The Unabridged Acts and Monuments Online* or *TAMO* (1583 edition) (Sheffield: HRI Online Publications, 2011). www.johnfoxe.org [accessed 18 December 2012]
TNA SP	The National Archives, State Papers

Latin biblical quotations are taken from St Jerome's *Nova vulgata Bibliorum sacrorum editio* (Vatican City, 1979); English biblical quotations are taken from Miles Coverdale's *Biblia the Bible* (Cologne?, 1535). I have used Coverdale's translation (rather than William Tyndale's, for instance) because it is this version that provides the source for the Psalm translations of Thomas Smith and Henry Howard, the earl of Surrey, amongst others. References to Psalms are by the Vulgate numbering.

Throughout this book, whenever a particular work was printed in more than one of John Foxe's and Henry Bull's publications (*Rerum*, *TAMO* (1563), *TAMO* (1570), *TAMO* (1583), and LM), reference will be made only to the earliest work in which it appears. However, if a holograph or early manuscript version of this work survives, reference will be made to that manuscript alone.

Introduction

> Freedom is a simple productivity application that locks you away
> from the internet on Mac or Windows computers for up to eight
> hours at a time.[1]

This marketing blurb for a new piece of computer software proposes a
paradox. Imprisonment provides freedom, and constraint leads to productiv-
ity. It is true: the software helped me finish this book. Apparently, I am not
alone: its website is filled with testimonies from famous authors who regularly
make use of the programme to free themselves from online distractions.
However, it is also a truism. The idea that social dislocation and physical
restraint provide the necessary conditions for expansive and poetic thought
has been suggested by figures as diverse as the twelfth-century abbot, Peter of
Celle, and the twentieth-century philosopher, Gaston Bachelard.[2] Recently,
too, there have been a spate of journalistic articles examining the ways in
which people are increasingly seeking forms of self-incarceration in order to
make time and space for writing and uninterrupted thought.[3]

There is good evidence for such arguments. Some of history's most
influential writers, thinkers, and political figures wrote from prison,
including St Paul, Boethius, Marco Polo, Walter Raleigh, John Bunyan,
the Marquis de Sade, Oscar Wilde, Lady Constance Lytton, Adolf
Hitler, Dietrich Bonhoeffer, Ezra Pound, Antonio Gramsci, Martin
Luther King Jr, Nelson Mandela, and Gerry Adams, to name a few. Many
other writers drew on past experiences of incarceration in their writings,
such as Primo Levi and Aleksandr Solzhenitsyn. The idea that prison is a
kind of crucible for literary production is, however, contentious and

---

[1] http://macfreedom.com/ [accessed 18 December 2012].
[2] See Peter of Celle, 'On Affliction and Reading', in *Selected Works*, tr. Hugh Feiss (Kalamazoo, MI,
1987), 137–8; Gaston Bachelard, *The Poetics of Space*, tr. Maria Jolas, revised edn (Boston, MA, 1994).
[3] See for example Tony Perottet, 'Why Writers Belong Behind Bars', *New York Times* (22 July 2011),
available from www.nytimes.com [accessed 18 December 2012].

I

overly idealistic. It ignores that fact that for many prisoners, subjected to particularly harsh or regulated conditions, it was extremely hard to find either the opportunity or the means to write. Accounts of detainees at Guantánamo Bay testify to the fact that, before they were allowed writing materials (which were provided for short periods of time and under strict watch), one of the few means by which prisoners could write was on Styrofoam cups, on which they wrote poems with pebbles or dabs of toothpaste.[4] Nevertheless, the fact that prisoners under the strictest of surveillance still found a way to write goes some way to explaining why periods of prolonged or excessive persecution often result in bodies of new literature – even though they might subsequently be censored, suppressed, or destroyed. The sixteenth century was one such period.

This book argues that the sixteenth century was a watershed in the development of prison literature as a supra-genre in England. In the centuries prior to the Reformation, we find only isolated examples of English literature produced during incarceration. By contrast, the religious and political instability of the Tudor reigns, especially during the period between the late 1520s and Mary I's death in 1558, provided the conditions for prison literature to thrive. England witnessed unprecedented levels of religious persecution during the Reformation: fifty-three Protestants were put to death for heresy in England and Scotland in the period 1527–46, and at least two hundred and eighty-two perished under Mary I.[5] Catholics suffered incarceration and execution during Henry VIII's reign for failure to recognise their king as supreme head of the Church in England. Neither was Edward VI's Protestant reign without its religious casualties: a number of Protestant separatists were burnt for heresy, and certain high-profile Catholics languished in jail for much of the reign. Moreover, the scheming and schisms of Tudor courtly politics led to the arrest and execution of various important Tudor statesmen, including Thomas More, Thomas Cromwell, and Edward Seymour, not to mention two of Henry's wives. Those involved in subverting Mary and Elizabeth's claim to the throne on Edward VI's death were also put to death, including the nine-day queen Jane Grey, her husband Guildford Dudley, and his father John Dudley, the Duke of Northumberland.

These religious and political prisoners, unlike the majority of the detainees during this period, were not only literate but had powerful motivations to write. These motivations were as diverse as the causes for

---

[4] Marc Falkoff, *Poems from Guantánamo: The Detainees Speak* (Iowa City, 2007), 3.
[5] See Brad Gregory, 'The Anathema of Compromise: Christian Martyrdom in Early Modern Europe', PhD thesis, Princeton University, 1996, 13.

which individuals were imprisoned. Political careers and, indeed, lives depended on prisoners writing to vindicate themselves, or elicit sympathy and support from influential parties; public figures recognised that their reputations must be maintained, even when facing the scaffold. Religious prisoners were confident that their cause was validated by a stoic endurance of imprisonment and execution. Rather than appealing for freedom, Catholic prisoners' writings reflected their private devotions and prayers; and Protestant prisoners sought to encourage their co-religionists at home and in exile, to teach and guide them on doctrinal issues, and to ensure unity of belief. Unsurprisingly, these circumstances and impulses resulted in works of literature that covered a vast range of genres and forms: from trial narratives to Psalm translations, dialogues, religious polemics, pastoral guidance, poems, love lyrics, humanistic translations, prayers and meditative guides, letters of appeal, letters modelled on St Paul's, marginalia, and graffiti.

In the past the diversity of written outputs, as well as the different reasons for the prisoners' incarceration, has prevented scholars from writing about sixteenth-century prison literature as a coherent body of work. The scholarship that has touched on this topic has tended to constitute case studies on individual texts and authors – most frequently Thomas More, Thomas Wyatt, and Henry Howard, the Earl of Surrey. The other point of access to incarcerated authors has been through sixteenth-century martyrologies, such as John Foxe's 'Book of Martyrs', although these collected documents are rarely talked about as prison literature per se. This book, by contrast, argues that the imprisonment of the author is a far more important organising principle than other generic headings under which a work might be placed, and that a comprehensive analysis of sixteenth-century prison literature reveals trends that remain hidden in more genre-specific studies of works produced inside and outside the prison walls. To date, the only book-length study to tackle early modern prison literature as a discrete body of work is the special issue of *Huntington Library Quarterly* edited by William H. Sherman and William J. Sheils.[6]

The trends that emerge in prison literature written in the middle years of the sixteenth century are noticeably distinct from the examples we have from the Middle Ages or from other obvious medieval models for martyr writing. Scholarship on fourteenth- and fifteenth-century prison

---

[6] 'Prison Writings in Early Modern England', special issue, ed. William H. Sherman and William J. Sheils, *HLQ*, 72 (2009).

works – such as Thomas Usk's *Testament of Love*, James I of Scotland's *The Kingis Quair*, Charles d'Orléans' *English Book*, George Ashby's *A Prisoner's Reflections* – consistently emphasises the influence of Boethius' *Of the Consolation of Philosophy*, which was written by the sixth-century Roman senator while awaiting execution.[7] This dialogue, which represents a fictionalised version of the author in conversation with Lady Philosophy, led to a series of prison writings that were concerned both with self-presentation and self-justification.[8] But although Boethius' dialogue continued to be translated and printed in the sixteenth century,[9] aside from Thomas More's *A Dialogue of Comfort against Tribulation*, there is a notable lack of Boethian-influenced prison works.[10] Another form of writing we might have expected to influence religious prisoners is the body of medieval devotional literature that taught its readers how to practice a kind of vicarious martyrdom through meditation on Christ's suffering, such as Thomas à Kempis's *Imitatio Christi*, the *Meditationes vitae Christi*, which is believed to have been written by Bonaventure, Richard Rolle's *Meditations on the Passion*, and Ludolph of Saxony's *Vita Christi*. These various meditations on the life of Christ enjoyed widespread popularity, and More recommends two of them (*Meditationes* and the *Imitatio Christi*) in his famous polemic, *The Confutation of Tyndale's Answer*, which was written while he was still lord chancellor. Unsurprisingly, several of More's Tower works show the influence of this earlier tradition, as do the writings of Recusant prisoners

---

[7] See, Joanna Summers, *Late-Medieval Prison Writing and the Politics of Autobiography* (Oxford, 2004); *The Kingis Quair and other Prison Poems*, ed. Linne R. Mooney and Mary Jo Arn (Kalamazoo, MI, 2005); *Charles D'Orléans in England, 1415–1440*, ed. Mary-Jo Arn (Rochester, NY, 2000); Robert Epstein, 'Prisoners of Reflection: The Fifteenth-Century Poetry of Exile and Imprisonment', *Exemplaria*, 15 (2003), 157–98; A. C. Spearing, 'Prison, Writing, Absence: Representing the Subject in the English Poems of Charles d'Orléans', in *Chaucer to Spenser: A Critical Reader*, ed. Derek Pearsall (Oxford, 1999), 297–311; Julia Boffey, 'Chaucerian Prisoners: The Context of *The Kinges Quair*', in *Chaucer and Fifteenth-Century Poetry*, ed. Julia Boffey and Janet Cowen (London, 1991), 279–316; and Diane Marks, 'Poems from Prison: James I of Scotland and Charles d'Orléans', *Fifteenth-Century Studies*, 15 (1989), 245–58.

[8] Summers, *Late-Medieval Prison Writing*, 22–3.

[9] See *The boke of comfort called in laten Boetius de Consolatione philosophie* (Tavistock, 1525); *Boetius de consolationae philosophiae: The boke of Boecius, called the comforte of philosophye* (London, 1556). Elizabeth I's translation can be found in *Elizabeth I: Translations, 1592–1598*, ed. Janel Mueller and Joshua Scodel (Chicago, IL, 2009), 45–368. Chaucer's English translation was printed by William Caxton in 1478, and was included in editions of Chaucer's works from 1532.

[10] Martin Buzacott also argues that Book 2, metre 4 of Boethius' *De consolatione* is an analogue for Thomas Wyatt's 'Who lyst his welthe and eas Retayne' ('A Boethian Analogue for Sir Thomas Wyatt's "Who List his Wealth"', *Notes & Queries*, 31 (1984), 163–4); however, the passage in question clearly derives from a chorus in Seneca's tragedy *Phaedra*, from which the poem's Latin refrain is also taken.

later in the sixteenth century and seventeenth century. For such Catholic writers, these works were a bastion against Protestant heresies being imported from the Continent. By contrast, Protestant writers rejected the medieval model of meditative inwardness in favour of new and reconditioned forms that better suited their evangelical agenda, such as the prison letter and trial narrative, which allowed them to minister actively to Protestant communities outside the prison instead of focusing on their own imminent demise. They were not the only group to innovate. In the middle years of the sixteenth century we also see the Psalm paraphrase become a typical form of prison writing, adopted primarily by political prisoners, despite having no explicit association with prison before these decades.

The fact that the flourishing of prison literature in the sixteenth century has not met with sufficient or sustained critical investigation means that the established history of Tudor oppression needs to be rewritten. Geoffrey Elton's work in particular did much to establish the Tudor state as monolith: he argued that Henrician England witnessed a 'revolution in government', characterised by the centralisation of bureaucracy and revenue and a new effective campaign of state propaganda.[11] Whether this revolution of government is seen (as in the case of Whig and Marxist historians) to be an emancipating and progressive move away from the feudal and Catholic power structures, or (as in the case of the 'revisionist' historians) to be a repressive system imposed on the unwilling masses, it is clear that this centralising impetus had a crucial impact on the freedom of speech and on literary production.[12] This corollary has been the basis of new historicist approaches to sixteenth-century literature – which have argued that literary activity was shaped by an essentially repressive framework – as well as James Simpson's groundbreaking volume *Reform and Cultural Revolution*.[13] The latter argues that 'concentrations of power that simplify institutional structures also simplify and centralize cultural practice, by stressing central control, historical novelty, and unity produced from the top down'.[14] However, as other scholars have begun to point out, the idea of a single, centralised literary sphere is not borne out by all the

---

[11] See especially, G. R. Elton, *The Tudor Revolution in Government: Administrative Changes in the Reign of Henry VIII* (Cambridge, 1953).
[12] See David Loades, 'The Theory and Practice of Censorship in Sixteenth-Century England', in his *Politics, Censorship and the English Reformation* (London, 1991), 96–108.
[13] See, for example, Stephen Greenblatt, *Renaissance Self-Fashioning: From More to Shakespeare* (Chicago, IL, 1980; reprinted 2005), 9.
[14] James Simpson, *Reform and Cultural Revolution: 1350–1547*, Oxford English Literary History 2 (Oxford, 2002), 558.

textual evidence. If, along with Thomas Freeman we hail prison literature as one the most 'characteristic cultural forms' in England during this period (which, in terms of volume, is no exaggeration), then we can see that literary innovation was not being produced from the top down.[15] Quite the reverse, the very structures that sought to enforce the centralisation of discursive space – exile, imprisonment, and execution – forced multiple new spheres of literary resistance and dissent into existence.

History has shown that when unreasonable strictures are placed upon freedom of expression, proscribed voices are likely to emerge elsewhere in oppositional sites, or what have been described as 'counter-public spheres'. Most contemporary conceptualisations of the public sphere are based on the ideas expressed in Jürgen Habermas's book *The Structural Transformation of the Public Sphere*, which presents this sphere as necessarily inclusive: 'a public sphere from which specific groups would be *eo ipso* excluded was less than merely incomplete; it was not a public sphere at all'.[16] This inclusivity, however, has been much criticised in recent years by scholars such as Nancy Fraser, who identifies the ways in which marginalised groups excluded from a universal public sphere form their own spheres or 'counter-publics'.[17] A counter-public sphere is, by definition, a site of resistance: it is an arena for hearing proscribed voices, expressing proscribed ideas, and entertaining an alternative reality to the existing order. Gerard Hauser argues that prisons are one such counter-public sphere, especially when they house political prisoners: for while imprisonment 'removes the activist's voice from the epicentre of evolving events', it also simultaneously 'bestows a perverse imprimatur, since one presumes the state would feel no need to remove the political prisoner from society were he or she unimportant'. As a result, he argues 'the prisoner's messages acquire an aura of authority to direct thought and action against the existing order'.[18] While Hauser's examples are

---

[15] Thomas Freeman, 'Introduction: The Rise of Prison Literature', in 'Prison Writings in Early Modern England', ed. Sheils and Sherman, 133–46 (133).

[16] Jürgen Habermas, *The Structural Transformation of the Public Sphere: An Inquiry into a Category of Bourgeois Society*, tr. Thomas Burger and Frederick Lawrence (Cambridge, MA, 1991), 85.

[17] Nancy Fraser, 'Rethinking the Public Sphere: A Contribution to the Critique of Actually Existing Democracy', in *Habermas and the Public Sphere*, ed. Craig J. Calhoun (Cambridge, MA, 1999), 109–42. For a related argument about the early modern public sphere (and specifically the post-Reformation public sphere), see, Peter Lake and Steven Pincus, 'Rethinking the Public Sphere in Early Modern England', in their edited *Politics of the Public Sphere in Early Modern England* (Manchester, 2007), 1–30.

[18] Gerard A. Hauser, 'Prisoners of Conscience and the Counterpublic Sphere of Prison Writing: The Stones that Start the Avalanche', in *Counterpublics and the State*, ed. Robert Asen and Daniel C. Brouwer (New York, 2001), 35–58 (38).

mostly restricted to twentieth-century Polish prison writings, his conclusion also holds true for the sixteenth century – despite the prevailing image of Tudor state control.

The Rise of Prison Literature in the Sixteenth Century narrates the emergence of the prison as an important and influential literary sphere. The chapters that follow not only discuss explicit narratives of opposition and the rallying of dissident communities against the dominant powers, but also the more subtle tricks by which prisoners appropriated the site of the prison for their own agendas. In order to show how the prison might be deemed a counter-public *sphere*, Chapters 2 to 5 are arranged spatially, each one dealing with a wider group of people and a wider geographic area. Following an initial chapter outlining the history and administration of sixteenth-century prisons, Chapter 2 focuses on the individual prisoner and how his or her actions and writings can be interpreted as clandestine tactics used to express autonomy from within disciplinary structures. Chapter 3 examines how writings were employed to create prison communities, both in a structural sense (in terms of forming ties) and in an ideological sense (through the transmission of ideas about community). Chapter 4 addresses how incarcerated writers imagined counter-publics extending beyond the prison, and the organisational structures by which texts were actually transmitted. And finally, Chapter 5 challenges the idea that the print publication of prison writings metaphorically liberated these texts: while it is true that print allowed prisoners' works to circulate to a much wider readership than was possible through manuscript circulation, they became subject to a range of textual shackles, such as paratexts and silent editing. The function of this arrangement is to show the spreading influence of prison literature in this period. Prison writing was not a niche cultural practice. It may have taken place in marginal locations, but the texts emerging from prisons in the middle decades of the sixteenth century had a crucial impact on the literary, religious, and political landscapes in England.

CHAPTER ONE

The sixteenth-century prison

The title page of the 1539 'Great Bible' – the first royally commissioned Bible in English – provides a powerful piece of propaganda about Henry VIII's spiritual and temporal power over English society (Figure 1). This stratified composition has Henry sitting at the apex handing down Bibles to Thomas Cranmer, on the left, and Thomas Cromwell, on the right. In the middle register Cranmer distributes the volume to the clergy; and, presumably, in the bottom register the newly Englished Bible forms the basis of the priest's exhortations to his congregation. Henry is thus the distributor of God's word on earth, and everyone gives thanks to him proclaiming 'VIVAT REX', and 'GOD SAVE THE KYNGE' – everyone, that is, except for the imprisoned figures in the bottom right-hand corner of the title page. The illustration thus creates an image of centralised authority: it not only celebrates the magnanimity and power of the monarch, it also provides the English people with a warning that only authorised forms of speech and writing are permitted. Dissident elements – those who would not acknowledge Henry's Supremacy or conform to orthodox Christian belief – would be silenced and contained within the prison. In this way, the title page suggests that the Henrician prison was in the service of the monarch, and that it was a successful and suitable means of ensuring control over the public realm.

This image of the prison is, of course, a myth. A large body of literature, including writings of resistance and dissident texts, emanated from the prison in Henry's reign and those that followed. And the penal theory and administration of the sixteenth-century prison was a good deal more complex than this image allows. It is, nevertheless, an important starting point. Firstly, this title page puts prison back in the picture of pre-modern penal history. Michel Foucault's narrative of the emergence of the modern prison in his seminal *Discipline and Punish* has had a significant impact on how the early modern penal system has been studied. Foucault represents the eighteenth century as a crucial turning point in penal legislation, which

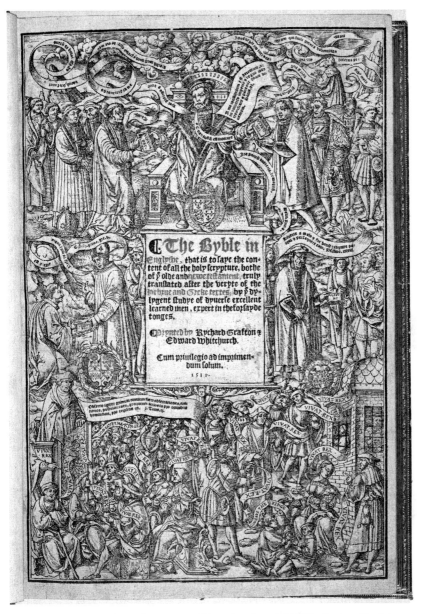

Figure 1 Title page from the 'Great Bible', Miles Coverdale's *The Byble in Englyshe* (London, 1539).

established prisons as the dominant method of punishment in the modern era. 'At the beginning of the nineteenth century ... the great spectacle of physical punishment disappeared; the totured body was avoided; the theatrical representation of pain was excluded from punishment'.[1] Before the eighteenth century, Foucault claims, pubic inflictions of torture and executions were the state's primary methods of demonstrating its power, and the prison was merely a holding place. However, not only is this picture of the European penal system reductive, it has also diverted eyes away from the pre-modern prison. The popularity of this work explains why the study of prison literature is only now emerging, while interest in the tortured body in Renaissance literary culture has already attracted a number of studies.[2] The second reason that the image of the prison on the title page of the 'Great Bible' is an important point of departure for our understanding of the contemporary prison is that it propagates a myth that utterly misrepresents the administrative reality of these early modern institutions. While this piece of propaganda suggests that incarceration was closely allied with Henry's policy of centralisation, the truth was that the administration of sixteenth-century prisons more accurately resembled the privatised rail system instituted in England during the 1980s under Margaret Thatcher: the system was decentralised, utterly disorganised, and driven by market forces rather than any ideological framework.

The early modern prison system – if it can be called a system at all – might best be described as an 'antipanopticon'.[3] Jeremy Bentham's famous design for the panopticon prison, discussed at length by Foucault, models the idea of centralised power. The cylindrical building, with its central inspection tower, was divided into individual cells that stretched from the tower to the outer walls to allow windows at either end. The occupants of the cells would thus be backlit, isolated from one another by walls, and subject to scrutiny both collectively and individually by an unseen observer. Such a design, as Foucault writes, makes the prisoner an 'object of

---

[1] Michel Foucault, *Discipline and Punish: The Birth of the Prison*, tr. Alan Sheridan (London, 1977; reprinted 1991), 14.

[2] See for example Cynthia Marshall, *The Shattering of the Self: Violence, Subjectivity, and Early Modern Texts* (Baltimore, MD and London, 2002); Elizabeth Hanson, *Discovering the Subject in Renaissance England* (Cambridge, 1998), 24–54; Stephen Greenblatt, 'Mutilation and Meaning', in *The Body in Parts: Fantasies of Corporeality in Early Modern Europe*, ed. David Hillman and Carla Mazzio (New York, 1997), 221–42; and Jonathan Sawday, *The Body Emblazoned: Dissection and the Human Body in Renaissance Culture* (London, 1995), 54–84.

[3] For use of this term, see Michael Collins, 'The Antipanopticon of Etheridge Knight', *PMLA*, 123 (2008), 580–97; and Molly Murray, 'Measured Sentences: Forming Literature in the Early Modern Prison', in 'Prison Writings in Early Modern England', ed. William H. Sherman and William J. Sheils, *HLQ*, special issue, 72 (2009), 147–67 (152).

information, never a subject of communication'.[4] As such, the design prevents prisoners adopting proscribed behaviour, plotting together, or influencing one another. By contrast, early modern prisons lacked a consistent design. Usually the prison building comprised a series of group cells, lacking any systematic order, and there was little provision for surveillance.[5] This, however, was just the physical manifestation of various more profound inconsistencies that riddled the administration of prison houses in this period, and which made it almost impossible for the government to oversee them. The following pages will provide an introduction to this complex penal system in order to suggest that the volume of prison literature produced in the mid-Tudor period, and the forms that it took, cannot be attributed solely to the religious and political climate of these years. The disjuncture between governmental policy and the administration of individual prisons provided important openings and opportunities for literary production and dissemination.

An antipanopticon

In order to grasp the lack of coherence in the early modern carceral system, it is important to understand its ideological differences from the modern British system. Regardless of individual attitudes concerning the use of corporal and capital punishment or the standard of living occasioned to prisoners, the vast majority of people would agree that the function of the modern prison is punitive. By contrast, Foucault's followers maintain that this was not the case for the premodern prison, which, instead, was primarily used as a custodial and coercive measure. According to this thesis, early modern prisons were used to detain those awaiting their trial or sentence, and to force prisoners to yield to the demands of their captors. This is true up to a point, but Foucault's emphasis on the eighteenth century as the point at which the prison began to be used punitively rather oversimplifies the matter. There were examples of imprisonment being used as a punishment in its own right in the Middle Ages,[6] and Krista Kesselring has shown the incarceration was used increasingly as a legal penalty in the Tudor period. Members of Tudor parliaments were especially keen on this mode of punishment, and prison sentences were applied to a range of offences

---

[4] Foucault, *Discipline and Punish*, 200.
[5] Norman Johnston, *Forms of Constraint: A History of Prison Architecture* (Chicago, IL, 2000), 33.
[6] Ralph Pughe, *Imprisonment in Medieval England* (Cambridge, 1968). See also Seán McConville, *A History of English Prison Administration*, vol. 1, *1750–1877* (London, 1981), 3–4; and John Bellamy, *Crime and Public Order in England in the Later Middle Ages* (London, 1973), 162–6.

including forgery, foreign trade, usury, owning prohibited books, or attending religious services other than those sanctioned by law. Statutes mandated increasingly severe penalties for repeat offenders, and there were a number of statutes in the reigns of Henry VIII, Edward VI, and Mary I that called for life imprisonment. The latter was most commonly suggested for religious offences that bordered on treason, such as preaching against the monarch and using prophecy to incite insurrection.[7]

The sixteenth century also saw the first attempt to use imprisonment as a social corrective. The first house of correction, on the site of Bridewell Palace, was established in 1553. Like its imitators, the Bridewell tended to house people from the lowest echelons of society and it employed hard labour, rigorous discipline, and beatings to correct them. Unlike modern prisoners, inmates were not guilty of serious crimes but rather of the delinquent kinds of behaviour that arise from poverty: idleness, disorderliness, unlicensed begging, and vagrancy. Admittance to such institutions was used primarily as a short sharp shock, and inmates were not, at least originally, sentenced to fixed terms. These two Tudor developments – the use of the prison both as a punishment and as a corrective – show that key individuals and bodies were beginning to develop new penal theories and ideologies that foreshadow the kinds of developments Foucault sees occurring a century and a half later. But, because these sixteenth-century changes were so piecemeal and divergent in nature, they merely contributed to the fragmentation of a system that was already riven by conflicting penal theories.

Even when the prison was serving its most common function, as a holding pen, the length and nature of this detainment could vary widely. The emphasis on corporal and capital punishment meant that criminals might very well be sentenced and hanged or flogged on the same day that they were charged.[8] By contrast, prisoners could be held for prolonged periods on the filing of an indictment; and in some unusual cases prisoners were never charged at all. One extreme example of this is Edward Courtenay, who, regarded as a serious dynastic threat, was imprisoned in the Tower 1538 at the age of 12 and would remain incarcerated for fifteen years. While the other religious and political prisoners discussed in the following pages did not suffer such long periods of incarceration, their terms in prison would often stretch to months and years before they were charged, during

---

[7] K. J. Kesselring, *Mercy and Authority in the Tudor State* (Cambridge, 2003), 29. See also, Pieter Spierenburg, *The Prison Experience: Disciplinary Institutions and their Inmates in Early Modern Europe* (New Brunswick, NJ and London, 1991), 135–70.

[8] McConville, *History of English Prison Administration*, 118.

which time the authorities sought to make them submit to their demands. In the case of religious prisoners, such submission usually meant recanting (the ideal outcome), or incriminating themselves or their fellow believers.

Protestant prisoners during the reign of Mary I were often held for extended periods while increasing pressure was applied through formal and informal heresy examinations and off-the-record conversations with experienced persuaders. For example, John Philpot was originally imprisoned in March 1554 but was not charged with heresy until 16 December 1555, after he had been examined thirteen times. The extent to which the interiors of the prison were conceived of as spaces of coercion is demonstrated by the woodcuts in John Foxe's famous 'Book of Martyrs'. Of the eight images that depict the interiors of Tudor prison cells, two represent the Protestant martyr John Bradford answering questions. The latter especially, entitled 'The talke betwene M. Bradford, and two Spanysh Fryers' (Figure 2), suggests how intimidating such an experience could be: Bradford is made to appear vulnerable in his seated position as the jailor stands threateningly at his side and the first friar, Alphonso bears down on him, accompanied by the hooded form of King Philip's confessor and a third sinister figure.

Such extended detainment and insistent questioning were clearly designed to wear down the prisoner, making it more likely that they would give in to the authorities or slip up and incriminate themselves. This is how, reputedly, Thomas More was finally condemned of treason. Evidence given by the solicitor general Richard Rich claimed that More, after fourteen months of silence and equivocation, had rejected the king's title as head of the church in England in his presence on 12 June 1535. Other prisoners were treated more cruelly in an attempt to make them capitulate, as in the case of the three Carthusians, William Exmew, Sebastian Newdigate, and Humphrey Middlemore, who were eventually executed, like More, for their refusal to swear to the Act of Succession. According to Maurice Chauncy, a fellow Carthusian and writer of the *Passio Sanctorum Patrum Cartusiana Angliæ*, the men were chained to pillars by their necks and legs while standing in their own excrement, to encourage them to swear to the oath; the only food that they were offered was meat, which their rule forbade them to eat.[9] Another example concerns the Henrician Reformer Anne Askew, who was racked

---

[9] Maurice Chauncy, *Passio Sanctorum Patrum Cartusiana Angliæ* (1570), in *The Various Versions of the Historia aliquot Martyrum Anglorum maxime octodecim Cartusianorum*, ed. John Clark (Salzburg, 2007), vol. III, 36–8.

Figure 2 'The talke betwene M. Bradford and two Spanysh Fryers', from John Foxe's *Actes and monuments of these latter and perillous dayes* (London, 1563).

in the Tower by Thomas Wriothesley and Richard Rich in an attempt to get her to name other members of her 'opynyon'.[10] And in Mary I's reign Edmund Bonner was reported to have held the hand of Thomas Tomkins over a candle to show him what it would be like to burn at the stake, so that he would recant.[11]

While those figures detaining and coercing prisoners were all nominally in the service of king and country, they were not acting on behalf of one unified legal system or court. A number of influential Tudor histories have argued that, following Henry VIII's break with Rome and the 1533 Act in Restraint of Appeals to Rome, common law acquired much of the jurisdiction previously associated with ecclesiastical law. The language of the Act of Appeals is dualistic, and it has been glossed as referring to the

[10] *The Examinations of Anne Askew*, ed. Elaine V. Beilin (Oxford, 1996), 127.
[11] *TAMO* (1563), 1170 (including woodcut illustration).

existence in the body politic of lay and ecclesiastical jurisdictions, which are embodied in competing court systems. The implication is that this act and other legislation of the 1530s resolved such dualism; but in reality such resolution was impossible due to the deep irrationality of English law.[12] Throughout the Tudor period, law remained jurisdictionally heterogeneous, overseen by common-law courts, ecclesiastical courts, equity courts, Duchy courts, Admiralty courts, municipal courts, guild courts, manorial courts, and piepowder courts. Each court had its own sphere of influence, but these jurisdictional areas often overlapped – a sure sign of a fractured and inefficient system.[13] As a result, men and women could be imprisoned, at the command of the monarch, by the Privy Council, the Star Chamber, the Court of Admiralty and High Commission, the courts of record or by the ecclesiastical courts, amongst others.

With a legal system so fragmented, it is unsurprising that the administration of prisons was also diverse. Prisoners could be held in a variety of locations while in custody. In early modern London, these included Bread Street Counter, Bridewell, the Clink, the Fleet, the King's Bench, Ludgate, the Marshalsea, Newgate, the Poultry, the Tower of London, Westminster Gatehouse, the White Lion, and Wood Street Counter. Several of these institutions had initially been established to serve particular courts, or to house specific kinds of criminal, but by the Tudor period these structures had evolved into something more chaotic. For example, the Marshalsea prison was originally built to hold prisoners being tried by the Marshalsea Court and the Court of the King's Bench, to which Marshalsea rulings could be appealed, but its use was soon extended. Other prisons had traditionally detained one particular kind of prisoner – the Counters at Wood Street and Bread Street, for example, customarily housed debtors, and the Tower of London prisoners of state – but like many of London's prisons in this period their occupants, in practice, were made up of a mixture of common criminals, debtors, traitors, and heretics.

---

[12] A. J. Slavin, 'The Tudor State, Reformation and Understanding Change: Through the Looking Glass', in *Political Thought and the Tudor Commonwealth: Deep Structure, Discourse, and Disguise*, ed. Paul A. Fideler and Thomas Frederick Mayer (London, 1992), 231.

[13] See Bradin Cormack, *A Power to do Justice: Jurisdiction, English Literature, and the Rise of Common Law, 1509–1625* (Chicago, IL, 2007), 2–3; and Louis A. Knafla, 'The Geographical, Jurisdictional and Jurisprudential Boundaries of English Litigation in the Early Seventeenth Century', in *Boundaries of the Law: Geography, Gender and Jurisdiction in Medieval and Early Modern Europe*, ed. Anthony Musson (Aldershot, 2005), 130–48.

Moreover, these individual prisons were not built following a single blueprint like the panopticon; rather, most were 'functionally miscellaneous and architecturally haphazard'.[14] Some prisons served various ends, such as the Tower, which was at once a royal palace, fortress, royal mint, repository for the royal jewels and government records, and a holding place for prisoners.[15] Other buildings, not originally designed as prisons, were also utilised as places of custody, including private homes, monasteries, and nunneries. Prisoners to be held under house arrest in the Tudor period include Princess Elizabeth (held at Woodstock), and the Oxford martyrs Nicholas Ridley, Hugh Latimer, and Thomas Cranmer (held at the homes of the mayor of Oxford, at the town's bailiffs, and at Christ Church respectively).[16] Those that were designed as prisons, unlike the socially isolating design of the panopticon, featured group cells, which were intended to be shared by numerous prisoners. This of course gave prisoners ample opportunity to share ideas, conspire, disciple one another, and even enter into communal worship. For example, the pressures of overcrowding in the Tower following Wyatt's rebellion in 1554 and, presumably, some kind of administrative oversight, led to four highly influential Protestant leaders – Nicholas Ridley (former bishop of London), Thomas Cranmer (former archbishop of Canterbury), Hugh Latimer (former bishop of Worcester), and John Bradford (chaplain in ordinary to Edward VI) – to be incarcerated together.[17] This arrangement offered clear opportunities for theological discussion and written collaboration; but the power of these leaders to influence whole prison communities became more apparent when they were lodged with ordinary, less eminent, prisoners. Foxe reports that, during his time in the King's Bench and the Bread Street Counter, Bradford:

> preached twise a day continually, onles sicknes hindered hym, where also the sacrament was often ministred, and through hys meanes the kepers (so well he was beloued) such accesse of good folkes was there dayly to hys lecture, and to the ministration, of the sacrament that commenly his chamber oft time was welny filled.[18]

---

[14] Murray, 'Measured Sentences', 151.

[15] Kristen Deiter, *The Tower of London in English Renaissance Drama: Icon of Opposition* (London, 2008), 27–53.

[16] See Diarmaid MacCulloch, *Thomas Cranmer* (New Haven, CT, 1996), 567, 570; and Carl I. Hammer, 'The Oxford Martyrs in Oxford: The Local History of their Confinements and their Keepers', *Journal of Ecclesiastical History*, 50 (1999), 235–50 (238).

[17] See MacCulloch, *Cranmer*, 560. Ridley mentions his former cell mates in a letter to Edmund Grindal, LM, 52. Cf. ECL, MS 260, fols. 114r–115v (transcript).

[18] *TAMO* (1563), 1242.

What is notable about this report is that the structure of the prison allowed Bradford to continue in his calling as a preacher, to offer pastoral guidance and teaching to a whole community of co-religionists. And crucially, this was made possible by the help of sympathetic keepers. It seems almost impossible to believe that such practices could be allowed to happen, or that they were enabled by the very figures meant to guard the prisoners. However, this is not a stand-alone example. There are numerous reports of prisoners finding solace and community in their prison cells, of Protestant leaders converting other prisoners and preparing their less educated co-religionists for their scaffold speeches as their went to their deaths. Indeed, the formation of counter-public communities was a widespread and continuous problem amongst all kinds of prisoners in this period and later, as Peter Lake and Michael Questier's work on recusant prison communities shows.[19]

One of the most important factors that led to prison guards permitting such activities, as well as to the lack of uniformity in prison buildings and their administration, was the private for-profit status of these institutions. All prison staff, from the governors down to the turnkeys, purchased their position with the hope of recouping their initial investment, not from their salary but rather from the prisoners in their custody.[20] Prisoners would effectively pay rent, which would cover their bedding, food, and drink; additional fees would buy coal and candles, furniture and furnishings, and greater freedoms, such as use of the gardens, admittance of visitors, and even permission to conduct business outside the prison walls (as long as the prisoner stayed in the presence of a keeper and returned to his or her cell at night). Because even the necessities had to be paid for, such institutions could be cruel and squalid for the poor: those without either personal means or sympathetic friends were forced to beg through the gratings of the prison from passers-by for money and scraps of food. The flipside of this was that there was some levity to buy a better experience through legitimate financial means, the prisoner's social capital, or the governors' sympathies or corruption. Prisoners of noble birth would retain their servants and family members in prison, and lodge in more spacious or better-furnished rooms. In the case of the most

---

[19] Peter Lake and Michael Questier, 'Prisons, Priests and People', in *England's Long Reformation, 1500–1800*, ed. Nicholas Tyacke (London, 1998), 193–233.

[20] Thomas S. Freeman, 'Introduction: The Rise of Prison Literature', in 'Prison Writings in Early Modern England', ed. William H. Sherman and William J. Sheils, *HLQ*, special issue, 72 (2009), 133–46 (141).

high-ranking prisoners, they could expect to maintain a standard of living that was in keeping with their status.

For example, Anne Boleyn – following her arrest for alleged affairs with Mark Smeaton, Henry Norris, Francis Weston, William Brereton, and her brother George – was imprisoned in her own royal apartments in the Tower, which contained a presence chamber and canopied chair of state. She retained free range of these apartments even after the warrant for her execution was signed. Importantly, these were the very rooms in which she had stayed the night before her coronation. This mark of respect for Anne's status, however, also contained a profound irony, for while it allowed her to be kept in the kind of surroundings to which she had become accustomed, these rooms also served to remind her of what she had lost. Henry Howard, the Earl of Surrey, was keenly aware of the pain that could be inflicted by incarceration in a too familiar place:

> So crewell prison howe could betide, alas,
> As proude Wyndsor, where I in lust and joye
> With a kinges soon my childishe yeres did passe,
> In greater feast than Priams sonnes of Troye.[21]

Surrey wrote this poem while he was imprisoned at Windsor Castle in 1537 for striking a courtier. As he intimates in the lines above, his place of imprisonment held memories of his teen years, when he had spent time in Windsor Castle with the 'kinges soon', Henry Fitzroy, the Duke of Richmond, who had died in 1536. In the lines that follow, Surrey describes this time as a kind of golden age now lost. By making this the site of his imprisonment, a place that held happy memories for the poet 'retourne[d] a tast full sowre'.

Because high-status prisoners could expect a certain level of respect from their keepers, any deviations were presumably a way of adding a punitive measure to detainment. Stephen Gardiner, the Bishop of Winchester, complained during his incarceration in the Fleet in 1547 that he was only permitted a cook and two servants to wait on him, and that he was denied a chaplain, a barber, a tailor, or a physician.[22] It is notable that he was complaining not about particular hardship, but that he was not being treated according to his ecclesiastical station. Another example of this kind of subtle punishment is the diet given to Hugh Latimer and Thomas

---

[21] Henry Howard, Earl of Surrey, *Poems*, ed. Emrys Jones (Oxford, 1964), 25.
[22] Example cited by Freeman, 'Rise of Prison Literature', 142. See also J. A. Muller, *Stephen Gardiner and the Tudor Reaction* (New York, 1926), 169, 183.

Cranmer while they were imprisoned at Oxford. Because of a reimburse-
ment dispute, the Oxford bailiffs' accounts for Latimer and Cranmer
survive for the relevant part of the municipal year 1555/6.[23] The accounts
record the composition and costs of the prisoners' individual daily diets by
item and dish for 245 meals. Carl Hammer has shown that while the
prisoners' diets conformed to the general conventions of the period, both
Cranmer and Latimer were maintained at a dietary level significantly below
that authorised for persons of their status, and Cranmer's precedence as
archbishop was not recognised; he interprets this as a 'subtly coded
message of humiliation'.[24]

For the government, there were clear advantages to be afforded by this
decentralised, privatised prison system. Importantly, it allowed the government to maintain a vast number of prisons with minimal cost. But the
drawback was that it had very little control over how they were run. Some
of the benefits that money and social stature could buy in these fee-paying
institutions posed a serious threat to the prisons' security. The presence of
free men and women in the prison, such as servants and spouses, was
probably only tolerated because it provided an additional revenue stream
for the prison governors and keepers. Because these inhabitants could not,
usually, be prevented from leaving the prison, they provided an important
opportunity to smuggle writings and other goods in and out of cells.
Visitors served a similar function.[25] In most cases, the smuggling of
writings was done on an ad hoc basis, but Protestants imprisoned during
the reign of Mary I established an organised network of carriers
who enabled communications to continue between prisoners and their
co-religionists in various locations across England and the Continent. The
authorities were not unaware that this was going on. Indeed, Edward
Stanley, the Earl of Derby, complained to Parliament that John Bradford
'hath done more hurt by letters, and exhortyng those that haue come to
him in religion, then euer he did when he was abroad by preaching'.[26]
But the hands of the government were tied. It was down to governors to
search cells and confiscate writing materials; and while there are records
that such policing occurred, it is also clear that administrative inefficiency

---

[23] Parker Library, Corpus Christi College, Cambridge, MS 128, 367–401.

[24] Carl I. Hammer, 'A Hearty Meal? The Prison Diets of Cranmer and Latimer', *Sixteenth Century Journal*, 30:3 (1999), 653–80 (680).

[25] On the provision of financial support for Protestant prisoners in the reign of Mary I, see Thomas S. Freeman, '"The good ministrye of godlye and vertuouse women": The Elizabethan Martyrologists and the Female Supporters of the Marian Martyrs', *Journal of British Studies*, 49 (2000), 8–33.

[26] *TAMO* (1563), 1255–6.

and the corruption of keepers, who could be paid to turn a blind eye, meant that such measures were only piecemeal.

Even more troubling for the authorities was the fact that it remained extremely difficult to oust those who held office within a prison once they had bought their way in. This meant that governors who were incompetent, corrupt, or (worse still) sympathetic to their prisoners' causes could easily undermine the wishes of the government. Thomas Freeman has traced one particularly striking example of how jailers' religious beliefs and political leanings might be in direct tension with that of the government. Thomas Philips was a pointmaker arrested on suspicion of heresy in 1529 and sent to the Tower, where he remained for a number of years without being charged. Eventually he was made a kind of underkeeper, a position somewhat analogous to a trustee, in charge of other prisoners. It was in this capacity that Philips let the early Reformer John Frith, who was in the Tower on a charge of heresy, out of the Tower on day release. It is also reported that he allowed other prisoners to visit Thomas Bilney, another known Reformer. But he did not stop at going easy on evangelicals; he also actively sought to convert prisoners to the reformed faith. In 1539 he persuaded Nicholas Carew, who had been imprisoned for his alleged part in the Exeter conspiracy (a supposed attempt to depose Henry VIII in favour of Henry Courtenay, the father of Edward), to convert to the evangelical faith and denounce in his scaffold speech the superstitious faith by which he had previously lived.[27]

Inability to control the sympathies of governors became more pronounced in Mary I's reign because many of those working in prisons had been appointed during Edward VI's reign, including some known Protestant sympathisers such as the governors of the King's Bench and the Marshalsea, Sir William Fitzwilliam and Sir Thomas Holcroft respectively.[28] The foundation of Bridewell also posed a problem for the Catholic authorities in Mary I's reign. The campaign for the establishment of an institution designed to amend the character of petty criminals through labour, which led eventually to the founding of Bridewell shortly

---

[27] Freeman, 'Rise of Prison Literature', 142–3. He cites the following sources on Philips: British Library, Additional MS 421, fol. 113r; *CW*, vol. IX, 126–7; *Narratives of the Days of the Reformation*, ed. J. G. Nichols, Camden Society, OS, 77 (London, 1859), 27; Edward Hall, *Chronicle*, ed. Henry Ellis (London, 1809), 827; and *Original Letters Relative to the English Reformation*, ed. Hastings Robinson, Parker Society, 2 vols. (Cambridge, 1846–7), vol. II, 625.

[28] For further details see Thomas S. Freeman, 'Publish and Perish: The Scribal Culture of the Marian Martyrs', in *The Uses of Script and Print 1300–1700*, ed. Julia Crick and Alexandra Walsham (Cambridge, 2004), 235–54 (237–8).

before Edward VI's death, was led by Protestant clerics and a group of London elites with evangelical leanings. In 1552 Bishop Nicholas Ridley preached a sermon before Edward VI entreating the king to have a care for the relief of the poor, which he followed up with a letter to William Cecil, couched in Christo-centric language, appealing for the grant of the king's royal palace, Bridewell.[29] Similar rhetoric and arguments appeared in the city's 1552 supplication, signed by twelve influential Londoners – John Ayliffe, George Barne, Thomas Berthelet, John Blundell, Martin Bowes, William Chester, Richard Grafton, John Gresham, Rowland Hill, Andrew Judde, Thomas Lodge, and John Marshe – each of whom had demonstrable Reformist leanings.[30] Grafton appears to have served as a governor at Bridewell during the reign of Mary I, since he is mentioned thus in Foxe's 'Book of Martyrs' in a case regarding William Gye and Richard Waterson, who were arrested for buying and selling a vernacular New Testament and sent to Bridewell for a beating: 'they made a warrant to M. Grafton, and sent Waterson and Gye to Bridewell to bee beaten vppon the crosse. And because the matter should not be slyghtly handeled, Story was sent wyth them to see it done'.[31] What is notable about the punishment is that Edmund Bonner, the bishop of London at this time, sent his own official to preside over the beating, which implies he feared Grafton would treat these men too 'slyghtly'. Importantly, Grafton was an influential printer and it was he who was behind the 'Great Bible', the first officially sanctioned English-language Bible (discussed at the beginning of this chapter), as well as a number of publications, which found him imprisoned three times in the early 1540s because the texts were deemed to be hostile to the religiously conservative new regime. As Bonner no doubt suspected, Grafton would therefore have been unlikely to view the possession of the Scriptures in English as a transgression requiring punishment.

What this example shows once again is a decentralised prison system that was disconnected from central government and lacking a standardised model – either architecturally or ideologically. Prisons were regulated by their own agendas and penal theories, and run for profit, making them

[29] *John Howes' MS, 1582: Being a brief note of the order and manner of the proceedings in the first erection of the three royal hospitals of Christ, Bridewell & St. Thomas the Apostle*, ed. William Lempriere (London, 1904).
[30] Lee Beier, 'Foucault Redux?: The Roles of Humanism, Protestantism, and an Urban Elite in Creating the London Bridewell, 1500–1560', in *Crime, Gender, and Sexuality in Criminal Prosecutions*, ed. Louis A. Knafla (Westport, CN and London, 2002), 33–60 (47–8). See also Laurie Throness, *A Protestant Purgatory: Theological Origins of the Penitentiary Act, 1779* (Aldershot, 2008), 170–3.
[31] *TAMO* (1563), 1815.

insecure and prone to inefficiency or, worse still, corruption. The lack of adequate surveillance or social separation in these antipanopticons allowed multiple blind spots and openings for counter-public behaviours: they were secret places where people could put ink or charcoal to paper, or exchange ideas, proscribed goods, and writings, which could be dissemin-ated beyond the prison by free men and women who lived within these institutions, by frequent visitors who brought money and goods in order to sustain prisoners, and even by prisoners themselves, when permitted to leave the prison walls under the eye of a keeper. These characteristics invite us to imagine the prison, not as something that contained the prisoner and sealed him or her off from society, but rather an institution that was riddled, both literally and figuratively, with cracks and hidden spaces. This chimes with the vocabulary of porosity and permeability that is repeatedly used by scholars working on the early modern prison to describe the ease with which people, objects, and writings moved in and out.[32] It is the very fragmentariness of the system that provided openings for a counter-public literary sphere.

Writing from the inside

Writings produced by prisoners in the early modern period reflected the inefficiency, disorder, and corruption of the system in which they were detained. There were two ways in which this happened and they correspond, roughly, with two separate waves of prison writing. In the last years of the sixteenth century, and at the beginning of the seventeenth century, prisoners increasingly wrote satires representing prisoners, their keepers, and the conditions in which they were kept. Such texts repre-sented the system as cruel and corrupt, and contained both implicit and explicit appeals for reform.[33] The rise of such appeals seems to correspond with the changing prison demographic in these years: debt litigation increased markedly in London in the period 1580–1640 as market activity increased, and new laws were enacted mandating the incarceration of

---

[32] See, for example, Brad Gregory, *Salvation at Stake: Christian Martyrdom in Early Modern Europe* (Cambridge, MA, 1999), 25; Guy Geltner, *The Medieval Prison: A Social History* (Oxford, 2008), 74; Throness, *Protestant Purgatory*, 111; Murray, 'Measured Sentences', 152–3; Freeman, 'Publish and Perish', 236.

[33] For examples of such texts, see Luke Hutton, *The blacke dogge of Newgate both pithie and profitable for all readers* (London, 1596); William Fennor, *The compters common-wealth, or A voiage made to an infernall iland* (London, 1617); [Geoffrey Mynshal], *Certaine characters and essayes of prison and prisoners. Compiled by Nouus Homo a prisoner in the kings bench* (London, 1618). On other kinds of petitions and complaints, see Murray, 'Measured Sentences', 158–60.

vagrants.[34] The result was a rising prison population that did not have the means to buy the kinds of amelioration available to the high-ranking political and religious prisoners, who were behind the majority of prison writings produced in the middle years of the sixteenth century. By contrast, in the writings of these earlier prisoners – which are the concern of this study – there is a marked absence of commentary upon the prisons in which they were kept, either in terms of the prisons' physical conditions or their administration. They reflected the fragmentariness of the prison system in a less obvious way.

Even when we might more reasonably expect to see complaints about prison life in these earlier writings, such as in the many letters addressed to Thomas Cromwell by prisoners seeking his mercy, examples are surprisingly rare. We can occasionally find specific details: for example, a letter from John Field tells Cromwell that he is kept 'both day and nyght in cold yrons'; and John Rudd's letter says that he is kept in a narrow cell cut off from all communication with the other prisoners.[35] Nevertheless, the majority of prisoners limit their complaint to the fact that they are held in 'a strayte prysonne'.[36] The ambiguity of this phrase is clearly illustrated by the petition of Richard Conquest, in which he uses the phrase 'strayte prysonne' at the beginning of his letter, only to say later that 'your seide subgiet is not straytely inprysoned. But is fayne for lacke of helpe to begge . . . for the almesse of peopill'.[37] From our background knowledge about prisons – that it was only those without financial support who were forced to beg – we might deduce that the conditions in which Conquest lived were likely to have been squalid, and his diet meagre. However, the lack of specificity demonstrates that the formulation 'strayte prysonne' is a conventional one and tells us nothing about the actual conditions of the prison.

The relative absence of calls for the reformation of jails in mid-Tudor prison literature might be something of a surprise. However, there is a reason for this. Early prisoners did not use their writings to fight against the system or to try and change the nature of prisons; instead, their approach was more subtle. These writers sought to take advantage of the

---

[34] See A. L. Beier, 'Vagrants and the Social Order,' *Past & Present*, 64 (1974), 3–29; Craig Muldrew, *The Economy of Obligation: The Culture of Credit and Social Relations in Early Modern England* (Basingstoke, 1998), 3, 199–271.

[35] TNA, SP 1/111, 231r; SP 1/82, fols. 236r–v. See also John Fisher's letter to Cromwell, in which he complains that his diet is slender and he has neither shirt nor sheet (BL, Cotton MSS Cleopatra E vi, fol. 161r), and various letters by John Philpot describing the 'Bishops cole house', for example ECL, MS 260, fol. 148r, and ECL, MS 260, fols. 164r–v.

[36] See, for example, TNA, SP 1/71, fol. 2r; and SP 1/81, fol. 126r.

[37] TNA SP 1/88, 62r.

institutional inefficiency and the blind spots it opened up. The types of methods, or 'tactics', that people have at their disposal to reassert their authority against institutional powers is the concern of Michel de Certeau's social study, *The Practice of Everyday Life*. His definition of 'tactics' is a useful one for thinking about the ways in which prisoners, and especially incarcerated writers, responded to early modern jails. A 'tactic' is

> a calculus which cannot count on a 'proper' (a spatial or institutional location), nor thus on a borderline distinguishing the other as a visible totality. The place of a tactic belongs to the other. A tactic insinuates itself into the other's place, fragmentarily, without taking it over in its entirety, without being able to keep it at a distance.[38]

To illustrate precisely what he means by this, de Certeau suggests how, for example, a North African living in Paris or Roubaix (France) might insinuate into the system imposed on him by the construction of a low-income housing development the ways of 'dwelling' peculiar to his native Kabylia. 'Without leaving the place where he has no choice but to live and which lays down its laws for him, he establishes within it a degree of *plurality* and creativity'. Both the concept and language are useful for us: the following chapters will suggest that individual prisoners and groups of inmates found ways to practise proscribed ideas and behaviours within the prison, which opened up opportunities for acts of resistance and the emergence of dissident literature. These small rebellions – activities that de Certeau might describe as 'hunter's tricks, manoeuvrable polymorph mobilities, jubilant, poetic, and warlike discoveries' – result in small victories on the enemy's turf.[39] The assertion that a tactic cannot count on a 'borderline distinguishing the other as a visible totality' corresponds with the blurred boundaries between the inside and outside, and the lack of distinction between constraint and liberty in the early modern prison. And, de Certeau's descriptions of how a 'tactic insinuates itself into the other's place, fragmentarily' conjures the language of fissures and openings that has consistently been employed by scholars to describe the decentralisation and disorganisation of the early modern penal system. Perhaps most importantly, the idea of a tactic implies finding the opponent's weak point, and this is precisely what prison writers did. In this way, de Certau's theory of tactics shows what a prisoner can achieve when he is not under complete surveillance and control.

---

[38] Michel de Certeau, *The Practice of Everyday Life*, tr. Steven Rendall (Berkeley, CA, 1984), xix. See also 29–30, 36–7.

[39] Ibid., 30, 40.

The leaky boundaries of the prison served Tudor prisoners' concerns, which were to write to friends, family, and co-religionists beyond the prison's walls. This is demonstrated by the forms their writings took, such as religious polemic, letters and treatises of pastoral guidance, treatises and tracts seeking patronage, and poetry designed for a courtly audience. These were the products of writers who had their eyes very much trained beyond the walls of the prison, and who were alert to the opportunities and avenues by which their works could be smuggled out. Such texts are testaments to the importance many prisoners placed upon living a life of *negotium*: of active participation in public or dissident counter-public realms, as opposed to a life of *otium* or contemplative withdrawal. A key tactic for prisoners was to write as if they were still part of a social group beyond the prison walls and thereby to insinuate themselves back into the public realm. For those involved with larger political or religious struggles – which had a bearing on the lives of the whole nation, or on the salvation of peoples' souls – to focus on one's own hardship would have seemed self-absorbed and petty, but it would also have been to admit defeat. The fissures and interstices in the prison system allowed prisoners to actively participate in discourses continuing outside the prison. Thanks to their free-moving servants and visitors, they could stay abreast of the latest news, receive books and letters, and write in response to them. Thus we see individuals like the early Reformer John Frith entering into polemical exchanges with conservative writers such as Thomas More and John Rastell outside the prison, continuing to fight for the Reformist cause in England. What is notable about a great number of these writings is how little affected they are by incarceration. The fact that we know certain texts were produced in prison is often only because of information supplied by later editors, printers, biographers, and scholars.

One of the genres which most effectively illustrates the prisoner's keen sense of how to insinuate himself into 'the other's place' is the trial narrative. The emergence of trial narratives can be seen as a direct response to the custodial and coercive functions of the prison in the early modern period. As a genre, it found particular popularity with evangelical and Protestant prisoners following the publication of the early fifteenth-century accounts of John Oldcastle and William Thorpe's heresy trials in 1530.[40] In fact, aside from letters, this was the main literary output of Protestant prisoners in the reign of Mary I. Importantly, we can see this as

---

[40] *The examinacion of Master William Thorpe preste accused of heresye before Thomas Arundell, Archebishop of Ca[n]terbury, the yere of ower Lord.MCCCC. and seuen. The examinacion of the*

a genre which takes particular advantage of the weaknesses and fissures in the early modern penal system. The heresy trial, and the various formal and informal examinations that led up to it, were an integral part of a legal process designed to subdue the Reformist elements in English society. However, the question–answer structure of examinations crucially left openings for the prison writer to insinuate their own agendas into the discourse of heresy trials.

Trial narratives are a textual response both to the speech-conscious culture of trial and the documents produced in the final judicial stage of the trial process. Official trial records in episcopal registers are usually comprised of a list of the articles put to the accused, with their answers – often in a much condensed form – either added in the margin or as a long list afterwards. The idea that answers were a separate body of text, which could be inserted or not as the reader saw fit, allows us to see how prisoners too might view the charges and questions with which they were faced as prompts for the insertion of their own text. In contrast to the overly schematised and truncated records produced by the courts, prisoners' own accounts of their examination were vividly written first-person accounts (usually set out as a dialogue), which filled out the gaps in the official version of events with circumstantial detail and reported speech. Two of the most famous trial narratives were written by Anne Askew following her examinations in 1545 and 1546. Towards the end of her *lattre examinacyon*, Askew uses the question–answer structure as an opportunity to proclaim and defend her beliefs:

> Then wolde they nedes knowe, whether the breade in the boxe were God or no? I sayd. God is a sprete, and wyll be worshypped in sprete and truthe, Joan. 4. Then they demaunded. Wyll you planelye denye Christ to be in the sacrament. I answered that I beleved faythfullye the eternall sonne of God not to dwell there. In witnes wherof I recyted agayne the hystorye of Bel, and the ix. chaptre of Daniel, the vii. and xvii. of the Actes, and the xxiiii. of Mathew, concludynge thus. I neyther wyshe deathe, nor yet feare hys might, God have the prayse therof with thankes.[41]

Askew's account sketches what must have been a lengthy response to her examiners' question about the real presence of God's body in the Communion wafer, for she recites the 'hystorye of Bel' as well as various other biblical passages supporting her non-belief in transubstantiation. Such a long reply, and its careful and accurate reference to the Bible, suggests that some level of textual enlargement taking place within the aperture opened up by the question. Effectively this is a criminal's confession – the very thing that sealed her death, as the final sentence expresses. However, its biblical underpinning provides Askew's speech with an authority that transforms it into a positive declaration of faith. In so doing, this passage demonstrates the ease with which prisoners could appropriate the trial process to authorise their own theological positions.

But the trial narrative is more than just a statement of belief. Importantly, it turns a form of discourse that was designed to bring about either the defendant's recantation or their condemnation into an opportunity for instruction. In the process of turning an examination into a trial narrative, the writer also transformed inquisitorial procedure into theological debate, through which the author could demonstrate both their wisdom and faith, while simultaneously undermining the authority of their interrogators.[42] As a result of this process, prisoners' extended answers often read like short lectures or sermons: they teach correct theological doctrine to their readers, supporting their case with biblical evidence. And their responses, littered with rhetorical techniques and quick wit, also provide a model of how to act during interrogation, showing ways in which to avoid self-incrimination without actually swearing against one's beliefs. In this way, successfully forged trial narratives could hope to strengthen their co-religionists in their beliefs, to instruct those who might have to undergo inquisition in the future, and even to convert new members to the cause. Prisoners' rewritings of their trials did not overthrow the process of the heresy trial; the legal structure still remained oppressive, condemning many to death or forcing others to recant. But this small victory, this 'hunter's trick', allowed prisoners the opportunity to create a text for the edification and instruction of their co-religionists outside the jail.

The next chapter will examine other examples of prisoners' tactics – 'jubilant, poetic, and warlike discoveries'.[43] Some seem much less warlike: the examples of prisoners' graffiti and marginalia offer very small victories indeed. Others, like Thomas More's much discussed Tower works, subsequently came to be regarded with great reverence. What the case of More's Tower works highlights is that the true impact of a prisoner's textual

---

[42] For a more thorough discussion of the genre of the trial narrative, see Genelle Gertz, *Heresy Trials and English Women Writers* (Cambridge, 2012); and Ruth Ahnert, 'Imitating Inquisition: Dialectical Bias in Protestant Prison Writings', in *The Culture of Inquisition in Medieval England*, ed. Mary C. Flannery and Katie L. Walter (Woodbridge, 2013), 146–163.

[43] De Certeau, *Practice of Everyday Life*, 40.

strategies are not always immediately apparent. For instance, most trial narratives were originally written with the immediate aim of ministering to an underground community. However, as Chapter 5 will demonstrate in further detail, many of these narratives were subsequently collected into the various editions of John Foxe's 'Book of Martyrs'. Through the process of being compiled and published, these writings – which had been produced in and for a Protestant counter-public sphere – became part of an authorised history of persecution, read and celebrated within the public realm. And although modern scholars recognise that these trial narratives represent an alternative reality, tactically rewritten to serve a particular agenda, they have continued to be read as an important piece of documentary evidence for how the authorities prosecuted suspected heretics in the sixteenth century. One of the main reasons for this is the relative scarcity of accounts from the other side. As already mentioned, official records were characteristically terse and schematised; but, more importantly, few survive, and those that do are not always complete.[44] Because of this, even Eamon Duffy, in his recent revisionist history of Mary I's programme of persecution, was forced to defer to Protestant trial narratives: 'we have no choice but to rely on these accounts in trying to trace the Marian campaign against heresy, but we need to bear constantly in mind that we see that campaign and its personnel almost entirely through the eyes of its victims and opponents'.[45] These archival gaps left by the Tudor authorities mean that, quite beyond the prisoner's hopes, these prison writings have insinuated themselves into the history books as the nearest thing we have to an official version of events.

---

[44] For example, Bonner's register survives but contains only select documents from trials, such as abjurations. Cranmer's register contains several heresy commissions under Henry VIII and Edward VI, and provides details on the trials of Anabaptists but without including a transcript. See John F. Davis, *Heresy and Reformation in the South-East of England, 1520–1559* (London, 1983), 14; and Paul Ayris and David Selwyn (eds.), *Thomas Cranmer, Churchman and Scholar* (Woodbridge, 1999), 306.

[45] See Eamon Duffy, *Fires of Faith: Catholic England Under Mary Tudor* (New Haven, CT and London, 2009), 103.

CHAPTER TWO

Writing the prison

[S]pace is like the word when it is spoken, that is, when it is caught in the ambiguity of an actualization, transformed into a term dependent upon many different conventions, situated as the act of a present (or a time), and modified by the transformations caused by successive contexts ... In short, space is a practiced place.[1]

Michel de Certeau's pithy definition, 'space is a practiced place', builds upon generations of philosophical, sociological, and anthropological studies. The distinction he draws between space and place – which he suggests derives from the act of inhabiting, and from the activities the 'user' undertakes or practises within, a given place – extends the phenomenological work of Edmund Husserl. Husserl stresses the privileged position of the human body: for him, the experienced 'here' is wherever and whenever I move. As a result, he writes that space is realised 'through kinaesthesia, in which the character (*das Was*) of the place is optimally experienced'.[2] What distinguishes de Certau's theory, that space is produced by its users, from that of his predecessor is the way in which he contextualises it within a larger theoretical framework outlining the ways in which individuals and groups can reclaim autonomy from the all-pervasive forces of commerce, politics, and culture. Thus, the street – geometrically defined by urban planners – is transformed into a space by its walkers. More specifically (returning to the example quoted in the previous chapter), a North African living in Paris or Roubaix can, by practising the life of his native Kabylia, establish within that place 'a degree of *plurality* and creativity'.

De Certeau's work has been hugely influential in the move, in cultural studies, away from a focus on producers and their products, and on to the consumer. But in other disciplines this focus on consumers is by no means

---

[1] Michel de Certeau, *The Practice of Everyday Life*, tr. Steven Rendall (Berkeley, CA, 1984), 117.
[2] Edward S. Casey, *The Fate of Place: A Philosophical History* (Berkeley, CA, 1997), 217–19.

new. Although they may not have considered the larger philosophical implications, writers of history and literature have long recognised the importance of describing specific places, structures, or institutions through the individuals and groups who live and function within them – particularly when that place or structure is remote from their readers, either geographically, culturally, or chronologically. Readers enjoy anecdotes; it breathes life and complexity into a narrative, while simultaneously making it more accessible and immediate. The disciplinary structures of the sixteenth-century prison – its architecture, ideology, and administration – can only tell us so much about the function of this institution. Similarly, thinking about how these structures affect and shape the lives of the prisons' inmates creates a producer-focused history. The only way to gain a full sense of the prison as a space is to examine how prisoners operate within it, or in other words, how the prison is 'practised' by its inmates.

This chapter will bring to light some of the clandestine tactics that prisoners used to express their autonomy from within disciplinary structures. The discovery that prisoners have such modes of resistance at their disposal challenges the thesis of victimology that has dominated scholarship on the Reformation until now. Although historians are increasingly aware of the weaknesses of the penitential system in the early modern period, it is still customary to see Reformation prisoners as passive victims of a repressive legal institution. Brad Gregory, for example, has affirmed that 'prison experience entailed not calculating agency and self-interest, but passivity in a double sense – both suffering and "being done unto"'.[3] This is true to some extent, for the lifestyles and writings of prisoners were dependent upon the possibilities offered by their circumstances. But, even within the most restrictive systems there are tactics for maintaining a sense of autonomy. De Certeau cites dwelling, moving about, speaking, reading, shopping, and cooking as the activities that seem to correspond to the characteristics of tactical ruses and surprises: 'clever tricks of the "weak" within the order established by the "strong", an art of putting one over on the adversary on his own turf, hunter's tricks, manoeuvrable polymorph mobilities, jubilant, poetic, and warlike discoveries'.[4]

Activities practised in the prison cell such as reading, meditating, and praying might be described as examples of de Certeau's 'clever tricks

---

[3] Brad Gregory, *Salvation at Stake: Christian Martyrdom in Early Modern Europe* (Cambridge, MA, 1999), 133.
[4] De Certeau, *Practice of Everyday Life*, 30, 40.

of the "weak"'. They may seem to be innocuous compared with the power that the penal system had over the prisoner. However, when individuals write about their occupation in these activities (either explicitly or implicitly) they become part of an active, creative process. The authorities were clearly aware of the power that certain sorts of writing could have, and sometimes went as far as confiscating reading and writing materials.[5] The types of writing that particularly concerned the authorities were the polemics and treatises on doctrinal issues, which explicitly constructed counter-public spheres of discourse, both inside and outside the prisons. But the authorities may have underestimated the power of apparently neutral writings to change exactly what the prison signified in the popular consciousness. One such example is the body of letters addressed to Thomas Cromwell in the 1530s by prisoners seeking mercy. What is notable about these epistles is the frequency with which the authors describe themselves, not as supplicants or petitioners, but rather as Cromwell's devout 'bedesmen'. Richard Jones writes: 'I wold I were able to do your maistershippe more pleasure than to pray for you'.[6] The other notable thing about this group of letters (as already mentioned in Chapter 1) is the fact that very rarely do these letters describe the physical hardship from which their writers' seek relief. This has a strange effect. Ostensibly, by seeking Cromwell's mercy, these letters are reasserting the fact of Cromwell's authority, and the author's subjection. However, by underplaying the physical conditions from which they wish to escape, and characterising the cell rather by the activities practised therein – prayer, and specifically prayer for Cromwell – the letter changes the author's position from one of subjection to one of humble devotion. This change functions to redistribute power: while the author is at Cromwell's mercy, Cromwell is simultaneously indebted to the prisoner for the devotions that the prisoner has undertaken on his behalf. In so doing, it shows just how easily prisoners might redefine the prison. In this case, the place of the prison is rewritten as a space characterised by prayer and intercession – more like an abbey or monastery than a jail.

---

[5] For example, Thomas More's reading and writing materials were confiscated on 12 June 1535. Nicholas Ridley also seems to have had his books removed: at the end of his prison writing *A Conference between Nicholas Ridley ... and Secretary Bourn with others, at the Lieutenant's Table in the Tower* he complains to the Secretary about their removal (*TAMO* (1563), 999). It is also reputed that, due to lack of ink, some prisoners wrote in blood. For example, See *TAMO* (1563), 1708, which says that letters written in their blood were produced at the trials of Richard Roth and Ralph Allerton.

[6] TNA, SP 1/78, fol. 21r. See also SP 1/81, fols. 98r, 115r; SP 1/88, fol. 71r; and SP 1/111, fol. 231r.

Thus, this chapter is not concerned with explicit narratives of opposition and the rallying of dissident communities against the dominant powers, but, rather, with the 'clever tricks' by which prisoners might appropriate the prison for their own purposes or insinuate incarcerated texts into the public realm of discourse: 'putting one over on the adversary on his own turf'. It explores 'texts' in the broadest sense of the word; the chapter begins by examining the graffiti left behind in the Tower of London before turning to inscriptions made by Edward Seymour and Lady Jane Grey in the margins and blank pages of manuscripts and printed books that they had in prison with them. To modern viewers, graffiti might appear to be the ultimate act of dispossession: along with the marginal annotations in books, graffiti resists publication or reproduction by other means and thus poses no ostensible threat to the authorities. What it does, however, in its most basic form, is provide the prisoner with a defence against obscurity (complete suppression), and more involved examples can provide records of the prisoner's piety.

By direct contrast to these 'marginal' works, the third and fourth sections of this chapter examine some more canonical works, which also happen to be prison writings: Thomas More's Tower works and the significant corpus of metrical Psalms produced behind bars, including those of Thomas Wyatt, Henry Howard, Earl of Surrey, Anne Askew, Thomas Smith, and John and Robert Dudley. Despite being produced in the confines of a prison cell, the subsequent reputation of these works seems to defy the label 'tricks of the "weak"'. This is testament to the success of the ruse: 'tactics do not obey the law of the place, for they are not defined or identified by it'.[7] While the writings made by the graffitists, by Seymour and Grey, work within the system prescribed by their penitential location – practising their cells as spaces for piety and sites of writing – More produces writings that transcend the system by eschewing the particularity of prison production. Similarly, the writers of metrical Psalms may have chosen texts that spoke on behalf of their personal tribulation, but their interest appears to have been as much in the innovation of new verse forms as in finding a conduit for their complaint. Both More and these poets simultaneously appropriate the prison as the site of writing, and produce writings that break down the dichotomy implicit in the term *counter-public*.

---

[7] De Certeau, *Practice of Everyday Life*, 29.

Graffiti

The Tower of London houses an extensive collection of early modern graffiti. In his recent catalogue of these inscriptions, Brian Harrison records well over three hundred entries.[8] But even from this figure it is difficult to comprehend the real extent of the graffiti because some monograms have been left unnumbered, while others have been grouped together under one entry. Many do not bear dates, but by counting those examples that do, and those made by identifiable figures, we can tell that at least seventy-four of the entries date from the sixteenth century.

The most common graffiti dating from the reigns of Henry VIII, Edward VI, and Mary I are inscriptions of prisoners' names and initials. These inscriptions tend to cluster in individual locations rather than being evenly distributed throughout the prison, just as modern graffiti tends to proliferate in certain areas of the city. The walls of the Beauchamp Tower contain the majority of examples from the mid sixteenth century, which might suggest either that it was one of the main holding places for prisoners at this time, or else that Tudor prisoners who were held there were given the idea to inscribe their names by the existence of earlier examples, such as that of 'THOMAS TALBOT, 1462'. As Figure 3 shows, the inscriptions in this tower are not isolated marks, but rather crowd the walls, in some places interlocking. On the right-hand side of this image are a number of Henrician examples, starting with 'SARO FIDELL [I will be loyal], INGGRAM PERCY, 1537', which appears about halfway down. The next but one below reads, 'FRANCES OWDALL, 1541' alongside a shield featuring the arms of the Uvedale family, which is followed by 'RAVLEF BVLMER, 1537', and, right at the bottom (and only partially visible), 'GEORGE ARDERN, 1538'. Also, near the top of the left-hand side we can read the slightly longer inscription: 'REPREN[D]: LE / SAGE ET IL TE AVMERA [rebuke a wise man and he will love you], IC, 1538' probably made by John Collins.[9]

But it is not just the pre-existence of graffiti that inspires people to add their names to walls; individuals may have added their mark because they saw their companions making inscriptions. Of those mentioned above, Ralph Bulmer, Ingram Percy, and Father John Collins were imprisoned for their involvement in the 1536 uprising, the Pilgrimage

---

[8] Brian A. Harrison, *The Tower of London Prisoner Book: A Complete Chronology of the Persons Known to have been Detained at Their Majesties Pleasure, 1100–1941* (Leeds, 2004), appendix 2.
[9] It is unclear why this biblical inscription should be in French. It may be a family motto, but I have been unable to find any records confirming this.

Figure 3 Graffiti in the Beauchamp Tower, Tower of London.

of Grace, and therefore must have shared a cell. And they were not alone. Others imprisoned for their participation in this rebellion include the makers of the following inscriptions: 'ADAM SEDBAR, ABBAS IOREVALL, 1537', Adam Sedbergh, the last abbot of Jervaulx, executed at Tyburn, 26 May 1537; 'DOCTOR COOK, 1540', Lawrence Cook, Prior of Doncaster, executed at Tyburn, 4 August 1540; 'WILLIAM BELMALAR', Sir William Bulmer, brother to Ralph, pardoned; and 'MARMADUKE NEVILE', probably pardoned, perhaps as a direct result of the letter he sent to Cromwell.[10] The inscription 'LANCASTER HERALD', accompanied by an

---

[10] Marmaduke Neville's inscription bears the date 1569. However, from the letter that he wrote to Cromwell from prison, dated 1537, we know that his incarceration was much earlier than this (TNA, SP 1/114, fols. 30–1). Harrison hypothesises that the date was altered or added to by

armorial shield bearing *milrinds* (irons on which a millstone turns), suggests it was written by Thomas Miller/Milner, the Lancaster herald accused of betraying the king's plans to the pilgrims. Similarly, the graffito of 'IOHN SEYMOR' – the son of Lord Protector Somerset who was committed, with his mother, on 17 October 1552, and is believed to have died in prison – is accompanied by the inscription 'C.C. HOWT. 1553', the name of Seymour's servant. The whole body of inscriptions, then, represents both a real community of people who occupied the cell together and a textual community – a roll call of the people who occupied that cell at different times.

A more creative example of this self-naming graffiti is that made by Thomas Abell, a chaplain to the queen, who was imprisoned first in 1532 for writing in favour of the validity of Katherine of Aragon's marriage, and again from 1534 until 30 July 1540, on a charge of misprision of treason in connection with the prophecies of Elizabeth Barton, which resulted in his execution. He signed himself by writing the name 'Thomas' above a picture of a bell with the letter *A* in it (Figure 4). However, the use of a rebus is taken to another level altogether by John Dudley's ornate graffito (Figure 5), which comprises a large coat of arms of the Dudley family, the name 'Iohn Dudle', a floral border, and four lines of verse, which read:

> Yow that these beasts do wel behold and se
> may deme withe ease wherefore here made they be
> with borders eke wherin a[re to be found]
> 4 brothers names who list to serche the ground.

The incomplete inscription is a little riddle that points to the significance of the image above it. The 'beasts' refer to the animals of the Dudley family crest (a lion and a bear holding a staff), and the '4 brothers names' can be found in the symbolic flowers of the 'borders': roses for Ambrose, gillyflowers for Guildford, oak-leaves for Robert (*robur* is Latin for oak), and honeysuckle for Henry. John Dudley had been imprisoned along with these four brothers and his father following the succession crisis concerning Lady Jane Grey.

Finally, there is a small category of graffiti comprising short sentences of wisdom or devotion. Two such inscriptions were made by Father

---

nineteenth-century renovators, because when the prisoner and poet John Augustus Bonney recorded the graffiti in 1794, he saw two inscriptions by Neville, both dated 1537 (Harrison, *Tower of London Prisoner Book*, 139).

Figure 4 Thomas Abell's rebus, the Beauchamp Tower.

Figure 5 Ornate graffito by John Dudley, the Beauchamp Tower.

John Collins, who was implicated in the Pilgrimage of Grace and executed at Tyburn on 9 January 1539. His monogram appears a number of times alone, and twice more appended to biblical verses. The first of these (as mentioned above) is Proverbs 9.8, 'REPREN[D] LE SAGE ET IL TE AVMERA'. The other inscription reads 'LERNE TO FEARE GOD. I.C. 1538', which probably derives from either Deuteronomy 6.3, Leviticus 25.7, or Proverbs, where the phrase 'fear the lord' recurs many times. Two figures imprisoned for their reputed involvement in the Wyatt Rebellion, Robert Rudstone and Thomas Fane (both of whom were subsequently pardoned), inscribed similar sentences in the walls of White Tower. Rudstone wrote: 'HE THAT ENDURETH TO THE ENDE SHAL BE SAVID. M[ATTHEW]. 10. R RVDSTON, DAR[TORD]. KENT, ANO 1553'. Fane inscribed the following passage from the Book of Revelation: 'BE FAITHFUL UNTO DEATH AND I WILL GIVE THE A CROWNE OF LIFE. T. FANE, 1554.' Added to this is the name 'D. T. L. CULPEPER OF AILSFORD, KENT'. Thomas Culpeper was the uncle of Sir Thomas Wyatt, and was probably hanged at Dartford in 1554.

Compared to the major writings that emerged from the Tower of London, such inscriptions seem to be of no consequence in terms of either their literary value or their impact outside the prison. Writing a text like John Frith's *Boke . . . answeringe vnto M. mores lettur* – which was a restatement of his belief in the non-presence of Christ's body in the sacrament of the altar – was a bold challenge to orthodox belief, and demonstrated that his incarceration would not silence him. Of course, this explicit defiance came at a cost. Frith himself acknowledged that writing such an inflammatory piece from his prison cell was likely to 'purchese [his] moste cruell deth', because it both formed a black-and-white statement of his heretical beliefs and because it furthered the Reformist cause that the state was trying so hard to suppress.[11] Writing one's name on the wall, by contrast, held no such danger for the graffitists, because it could not be perceived as a challenge to the authorities. Such graffiti contained no heresies or other inflammatory material. Moreover, the name of a prisoner admitted on religious grounds was indistinguishable from that gouged into the walls by a common-or-garden criminal, like that of James Rogers (accused of highway robbery and theft from churches) and Thomas Stevens (accused of robbery from Stoke Church). And, most importantly, it would not be seen by anyone but prisoners and possibly

---

[11] John Frith, *A christen sentence and true iudgement of the moste honourable Sacrament of Christes body [and] bloude* (London, [1548?]), sigs. A.3v–4r.

prison guards. But this does not mean that the graffiti had no significance for those who made it and saw it daily.

Juliet Fleming has attempted to elevate the status of early modern graffiti. She argues that the modern perception of graffiti as 'the mark of a human subjectivity that survives and protests its own radical dispossession' is at odds with the attitude to this writing art in the sixteenth and seventeenth centuries, when graffiti was commonplace and practised by people from all walks of life, and in a wide variety of locations – including homes, churches, and educational institutions. By making a useful connection between household graffiti, which usually comprised sentences of wisdom, and commonplace books, Fleming suggests that the early modern intellectual economy was predicated on 'a socially constituted subject and on notions of authorship that were collective, aphoristic and inscriptive, rather than individualistic, lyric and voice-centred'.[12] This argument has some relevance for the graffiti by Collins, Rudstone, and Fane, for the sentences that they employ are not their own compositions but truths that are already extant in the Bible. The verses chosen also defy subjectivity: the imperatives 'Lerne to feare God' and 'Be faithful unto death and I will give the a crowne of life' leave it ambiguous as to whether the command is directed at the inscriber, to subsequent readers, or both. In this context, then, the sentence does more than speak for itself; it speaks for every prisoner who chooses to suffer death for his faith. Rudstone's chosen verse further evades positive identification with its inscriber because the identity of the man who 'shal be saved' is entirely contingent upon whether he 'endureth'. Finally, the sense of a socially constituted subject is emphasised in the similarity between the sentiment of the sentences 'Be faithful unto death and I will give the a crowne of life' and 'He that endureth to the ende shal be savid'. It suggests a shared or generalised response to incarceration and the threat of impending death.

Yet these aphoristic inscriptions are not typical of prison graffiti in the reigns of Henry VIII through Mary I.[13] As mentioned above, the majority of the examples constitute names and monograms – a trend that essentially runs counter to Fleming's thesis. For, in its impetus towards naming, it seems clear that that Reformation prison graffiti should be viewed in the terms that she eschews: as 'the mark of a human subjectivity that survives and protests its own radical dispossession'.

[12] Juliet Fleming, *Graffiti and the Writing Arts of Early Modern England* (London, 2001), 41.
[13] This form of graffiti is much more typical of the Elizabethan period.

Firstly, the inscription of the name, whether it is a simple monogram, a complex rebus, or attached to a sentence of wisdom, is intrinsically an assertion of human subjectivity. Secondly, all the extant Tower graffiti was clearly made to survive because, in contrast to domestic graffiti – which was made in ephemeral materials such as chalk, charcoal, marking stone, smoke, or blood, and scratched rather than chiselled – the names were carved.[14] Thirdly, and most importantly, prison graffitists *are* dispossessed, for they have been ousted both from their homes and from positions of power. This does not devalue the status of the graffiti described above; rather, it demonstrates that self-naming graffiti shared the qualities of de Certeau's 'tactics'. We can therefore understand that the significance of this graffiti does not inhere in its content alone, but in the relationship between the name inscribed and the context in which it is recorded.

The majority of the names that we see in the Tower of London dating from the middle years of the sixteenth century share one main feature: the individuals they memorialise fell from a position of social or political power. During this period the Tower tended to house political and religious prisoners as opposed to common criminals, meaning that many of its inhabitants had once been members of the very power structures that had subsequently overcome them. John Seymour, for instance, was the son of Edward Seymour, Protector Somerset; members of the nobility such as Sir Ingram Percy,[15] Sir Ralph Bulmer, and Sir William Bulmer would have also been accustomed to a certain degree of sway within society; and abbots and priests such as Thomas Abell, Adam Sedbergh, and Lawrence Cook would have had great influence as the spiritual leaders of the established church. It is logical that prior experiences of power might give individuals confidence that their names meant something, and would be recognised by subsequent prisoners. John Dudley certainly seems to have been of this mind. In the poem accompanying his rebus he writes: 'Yow that these beasts do wel behold and se / may deme withe ease wherefore here made they be'. The beasts he speaks of are the lion and bear in the family crest, thereby implying that those who look at the crest properly will be able to identify it 'with ease'. Dudley's apparent belief in the importance of recording his family's names is underlined by the time

---

[14] See, by contrast, the verses of Jane Grey reputedly scratched with a pin on the walls of the Tower, recorded in *TAMO* (1563), 990; and the 'lost' verses written by Elizabeth during her imprisonment at Woodstock upon a door-frame and a windowpane, recorded in *Elizabeth I: Collected Works*, ed. Leah S. Marcus, Janel Mueller, and Mary Beth Rose (Chicago, IL, 2000), 45–6.

[15] See Geoffrey Elton, *Studies in Tudor and Stuart Politics and Government* (New York, 1974–92), vol. III, 183–215.

and effort expended on conceiving this riddle, designing and laying it out, and finally executing it in stone for posterity. In any other context – in a book, on a building built or owned by the family, for instance – this ornate work might be seen as a mark of ownership or an expression of power and authority. However, by sheer dint of its location, the graffiti adds the family name to the history of the prison, and writes the prison into their family history. This act of record could be seen to serve two potentially contradictory functions. On the one hand, the immortalisation of the graffitist's name on the prison wall functions as evidence of his suppression. But on the other hand, this record acts as a defence against anonymity – that most complete form of suppression. Located broadly within the prison, a name asserts the writer's existence, even as it was (potentially) about to end.

While the prisoners did not have a choice about where they recorded their names after entering the prison, they could determine other, more localised contexts within which their names were written and read by subsequent viewers. The sentences of wisdom recorded by Collins, Rudstone, and Fane could be interpreted as one such context. While copying out a Bible verse on to a wall by itself is, as Fleming rightly notes, an inclusive action, the moment that a name is added individuation occurs. Even though the sentence still offers wisdom to each subsequent viewer, it has become irrevocably associated with the name or monogram inscribed beside it, thereby ensuring that the given individual is remembered in relation to that particular, pious phrase. On a functional level, the addition of a religious sentence might mark writers out for remembrance, but it also makes an implicit assertion about their faith. In implies that the sentence has particular relevance to them, that they have meditated upon it, and that the prison is therefore a space in which they practised their faith.

The other context in which a prisoner might consciously place his name is that of other graffiti. As mentioned above, C. C. Howt chose to sign his name beside that of his master, John Seymour; and Thomas Culpeper, the uncle of Sir Thomas Wyatt, inscribed his directly next to Fane's inscription.[16] The act of signing one's name beside somebody else's has a clear associative power that implies a personal bond of loyalty.

[16] A larger corpus of more loosely related graffiti can be found in Beauchamp Tower, including: the rebus by John Dudley; the inscription 'ROBART DVDLEY'; a carving of a branch bearing oak leaves and acorns above a frame showing the initials 'R. D.' (again, for Robert Dudley); and several inscriptions of the name 'IANE', including one accompanied by the Grey coat of arms, which have traditionally been ascribed to Guildford Dudley, the husband of Jane Grey (although there is no conclusive proof of his authorship).

In the case of Culpeper and Fane, it is possible that these men made their graffiti in one another's presence, for Fane dated his graffito 1554, which is the same year that Culpeper was executed; but community is also something that can be constituted posthumously, as in the case of Howt, who dates his inscription 1553 – the year following Seymour's death. The latter example illustrates how the pre-existence of graffiti might provide the motivation for a prisoner to inscribe his name in the wall. Even though the corpus that exists now in the Tower of London would only have been partially constituted in the mid sixteenth century, prisoners admitted to cells in this period would, increasingly, have been faced by multiple examples of graffiti. In adding their name, then, they were not only creating a personal record, but also integrating themselves into and extending the corpus of names already there. There is clear tactical benefit to this. Because the majority of examples are names, the body viewed together implies a community – albeit temporally dispersed – and therefore solidarity.

These localised contexts for the name inscriptions, chosen or constructed by the graffitists, illustrate de Certeau's point that a tactic can only ever insinuate itself into a place fragmentarily. However, the failure of these inscriptions to empower the graffitist in any meaningful way is, ironically, that which speaks to the subsequent viewer most powerfully. It is only because these men were subjected that we are struck by the stark out-of-placeness of their illustrious names on the walls of a prison, telling us that they do not belong there.

Graffiti on the page

The addition of names and other ownership marks are also a common feature of marginalia. In his study of marginalia and the other ways in which books are consumed, William Sherman has asserted that marginal annotations might be considered 'graffiti' too. Just as meaningful phrases or entire short texts might be inscribed in walls, so analogous writings were composed in margins and blank spaces within the covers of books.[17] One example of this phenomenon, now held in the British Library, is by Edward Seymour, the Duke of Somerset, and is an annotation he inscribed on the flyleaf of an almanac while he was being held in the Tower of London (Figure 6). It reads:

[17] William H. Sherman, *Used Books: Marking Readers in Renaissance England* (Philadelphia, 2007), 23.

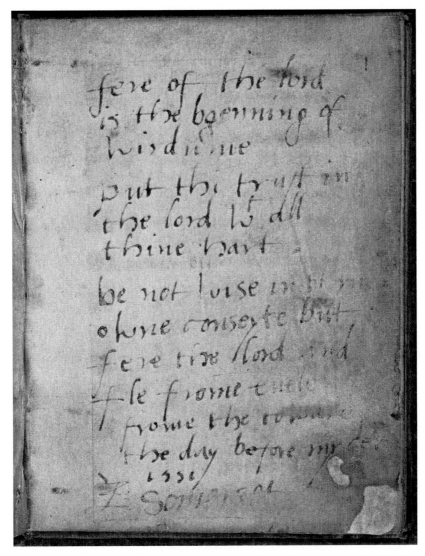

Figure 6 Sentences copied from Proverbs 9.10 by Edward Seymour on to the flyleaf of his almanac.

fere of the lord
is the b[e]genning of
wisdume

put thi trust in
the lord with all
thine hart

be not wise in thyne
owne conseyte but
fere the lord and
fle frome euele
frome the toware
the day before my det[h]
1551
E. Somerset.[18]

The similarity that this annotation bears to the graffiti produced by
Collins, Rudstone, and Fane is striking. Like those graffitists, Seymour
adds his name to some pious sentences, on this occasion Proverbs 1.7, 3.5,
and 3.7; and his choice of verses is notably close to Collins's 'Lerne to feare
God'. The main difference, of course, is the location of the inscription.
While the graffitists' inscriptions are lent their significance by their location, a book is a moveable object and can only tell us the places in which it
has been if its owner chooses to record that fact. In his inscription,
Seymour fixes the moment of its writing both in place and time: 'frome
the toware / the day before my det[h]', which, if true, means that this
annotation was made on 21 January 1552 (1551 by contemporary dating).

This precision suggests a certain degree of care on Seymour's part to
record what could have been one of his last acts of writing. This, in turn,
implies that he may have imagined a posthumous function for the inscription, one not dissimilar to that of the prisoners' graffiti discussed above.
The inscription was clearly not written as a mnemonic device. If Seymour
had wished to have a written prompt to meditate on these Proverbs,
presumably he would have written them down earlier in the two-month
period of his second imprisonment. But written when they were, it is clear
that the inscription does not function as a prompt *to* meditate, but rather
as an assertion that Seymour *has* meditated on these verses. The fact,
furthermore, that he chose to sign and specifically date the inscriptions
implies he did not imagine or intend that the book – and implicitly the

---

[18] BL, Stowe MS 1066, flyleaf.

record of his piety in the face of death – should be lost to obscurity.[19] We might compare Seymour's forethought to preserve his act of devotion on paper with an unsigned and undated inscription on the back cover of an early fifteenth-century book containing a Psalter and some Wycliffite materials now held in the Huntington Library (Huntington MS HM501). An early sixteenth-century hand has written '[p]resoner a pesoner [sic], [cry]st hellpe every presoner' (fol. 152v).[20] But despite the suggestion that the writer was incarcerated, there is no way to prove this, and so it becomes merely a reminder to subsequent readers to pray thus. Seymour's addition of his name to these verses, like the graffitists, makes it clear that although they may have general application, in this context they express something personal about their scribe. The choice of an almanac as the book in which he wrote this annotation also appears to be significant. Of course it may have been the only blank piece of paper he had available to him at the time; but, like Bibles, almanacs were often where individuals recorded significant events.[21] Almanacs are books of history, a place for working out days and dates. In adding himself to such a volume, Seymour, whether he intended to or not, wrote himself into history.[22]

Seymour was clearly aware of the currency that written records had. This is apparent from the preface that he wrote to Miles Coverdale's translation of a text by Otto Wermüller (known as *A spyrytuall and moost precyouse pearle*) during the period between his two imprisonments. Ostensibly the preface is a testimony to the text's great value and the importance of making it available in a printed edition for the edification of all. Within this testimony, however, is embedded a short passage concerning the personal fruit that Seymour had gained when reading this book:

---

[19] The book in fact remained in the family, apparently passing to his son Edward Seymour, Duke of Hertford, whose wife wrote her name on the back pastedown ('Katerine Hartford, Caterine Seamoar').

[20] See C. W. Dutschke et al., *Guide to Medieval and Renaissance Manuscripts in the Huntington Library* (San Marino, CA, 1989), HM 501. I would like to thank Daniel Wakelin for this reference.

[21] For instance, see Bernard M. Rosenthal, *The Rosenthal Collection of Printed Books with Manuscript Annotations: A Catalog of 242 Editions Mostly Before 1600, Annotated by Contemporary or Near-contemporary Readers* (New Haven, CT, 1997), which contains three examples of annotated almanacs: items 1, 18, and 44.

[22] Historians of the book have long been alert to the public acts of record in marginalia. See, for example, Daniel Wakelin, 'William Worcester Writes a History of his Reading', in *New Medieval Literatures*, ed. Wendy Scase, Rita Copeland, and David Lawton (Oxford, 2005), vol. VII, 53–72 (62–4).

> In oure greate trouble, whyche of late dyd happen vnto vs (as all the worlde
> doth knowe) when it please God for a tyme to attempte vs wyth hys
> scourge, and to proue if we loued hym, In reading thys boke we dyd fynde
> greate comforte and an inwarde and godlye workynge power much releuyng
> the gryefe of oure mynde.[23]

This passage makes a public record of the fact that Seymour read *A spyrytuall and moost precyouse pearle* during his first imprisonment along with his fellow prisoners. What is notable about this account, however, is Seymour's studied avoidance of the word 'prison', and use instead of the euphemistic phrase 'owre greate trouble'. The effect of this ellipsis is entirely in keeping with the trend in prison writing noted at the beginning of this chapter: it forces attention away from the space of the prison itself and on to the activities practised therein – Seymour and his cell mates reading the text, and drawing comfort from it.

This preface was published along with Coverdale's translation in 1550, and on several further occasions in the sixteenth and seventeenth centuries.[24] It is important that, before he came to write his annotation in his almanac, Seymour had already recorded in print the effects of reading in a prison cell. This suggests that he already understood the importance of the written record, not only as a defence against obscurity, but also for shaping exactly how one is remembered. The preface was a shrewd way of externalising his inward and personal acts of devotion without explicitly issuing an account of his imprisonment; by attaching it to a text which he was keen should be published ('we haue requyred hym of whom we had the copye of thys boke the rather at our request and commendacyon, to set forth thys boke in prynte'),[25] Seymour ensured both that the account was immortalised in print and that those reading it would be clear as to just what pious thoughts he had been reflecting on during his incarceration. The annotation in the almanac executes the same 'trick' for a smaller audience.

Seymour was not the only prisoner to leave such important marginalia in the books he had in prison. During her incarceration, Lady Jane Grey used blank spaces in her New Testament and prayer book to write to members of her family and to Sir John Bridges, then lieutenant of the Tower. The New Testament contained a letter written to her sister Katherine Seymour the night before her execution; the prayer book, now

---

[23] *A spyrytuall and moost precyouse pearle* (London, 1550), sig. A.7r.
[24] See *STC* numbers 25256, 25258, 25258.3, 25258.5, 25259, 25259.5, and 25259.7.
[25] *Precyouse pearle*, sig. A.7r.

held in the British Library, contains two letters written to Grey's father (one from Grey herself, and one from Guildford Dudley) and the one to Bridges.[26] While the use of flyleaves and margins for correspondence may seem to be less suggestive of a desire to create a text for posterity than Seymour's inscription or the examples of graffiti – mainly because the letters imply a single reader – the location of these inscriptions suggests otherwise. The white spaces in Bibles were the traditional location for recording the important moments in a family's history such as births, marriages, or – as in the case of Grey's letter to her sister – deaths because they were valuable books, both monetarily and spiritually, handed down from generation to generation.[27] In being added to such a book, the letter stood a greater chance of survival than it would have done if it had been written on a loose piece of paper.

Unlike Seymour's inscription, which had no relation to the volume in which it was made, Grey's letter to her sister does have an oblique relation to the text, commending as it does the value of this holy book:

> I haue here sent you (good sister Katherine) a boke, which although it be not outwardly trimmed with gold, yet inwardly it is more worth then precious stones. It is the booke (deare Sister) of the law of the Lord. It is his Testament and last wil which he bequethed vnto vs wretches: which shal lead you to the path of eternall ioy: and if you with a good mind read it, and with an earnest minde do purpose to folow it, it shall bryng you to an immortall and euerlasting life. It shall teach you to liue, and learne you to dye.[28]

By sending the New Testament out of the Tower with this inscription, Grey draws attention to the reading matter she had therein, but which she now no longer needs as she faces death.[29] By telling her sister that reading the Bible has the power to bring Katherine to 'an immortall and euerlasting life' and, later in the letter, that that she is 'assured that [she] shall for

---

[26] BL, Harley MS 2370. From the content of his letter, written in the lower margins of fols. 74r–80r, we know that Grey wrote to Bridges at his request ('as you have desired so simple a woman to wrighte in so worthye a booke'), and that he also solicited from her the promise that she would leave him the book after her death. See also *Rerum*, 238.

[27] Stephen Orgel, 'Margins of Truth', in *The Renaissance Text*, ed. Andrew Murphy (Manchester, 2000), 91–107 (95).

[28] *TAMO* (1563), 986.

[29] For a description of a seventeenth-century prison library, see T. P. Connor, 'Malignant Reading: John Squier's Newgate Prison Library, 1642–46', *Library*, 7 (2006), 154–84. We can also ascertain some of the reading material prisoners had in jail from their correspondence. For example, we know that John Bradford had some of Saint Jerome's works with him in prison because in a letter to Dr Hill he offers to lend him the 'laste part' (ECL, MS 260, fol. 203v).

losing of a mortall life, winne an immortal life', Grey makes it clear that she has been making use of her reading material.

Thomas More's Tower works

Of all the marginalia written within prison walls, maybe the most famous are those written by Thomas More in his prayer book, a volume made up of a Book of Hours and a liturgical Latin Psalter. The marginalia are not spread evenly throughout the volume. Amongst the pages of the Book of Hours, the only marginalia are the thirty-seven lines of the 'Godly Medi-tation', which are written in English, two verses per page, in the top and bottom margins of eighteen consecutive pages, with the last line occupying a page of its own (see Figure 7).[30] The majority of the marginalia can be found in the Psalter, which contains one hundred and forty-three Latin annotations between Psalms 3 and 105, as well as numerous lines and flags, and a series of lettered lines (a–p) which have been collected to form the cento prayer in the *The Workes of Syr Thomas More Knyght . . . wrytten by him in the Englysh tonge*, printed by William Rastell in 1557. In addition, pasted inside the back cover, there is single leaf that gives the opening verses for a sequence of five psalms (21, 19, 73, 97, 110).[31]

More's annotations differ from the marginalia and graffiti discussed above in a number of ways. Firstly, while Seymour and Grey's marginalia do not relate directly to the content of the volume in which they are written, the majority of More's annotations are direct commentaries on the text beside which they are located (the exception being his meditation and the sequence of five Psalms). Secondly, compared to Seymour's inscription and the examples of graffiti discussed above, which engage in the selection and copying of biblical passages, More's commentaries on the Psalms and his meditation both constitute original compositions and responses to the text. Thirdly, due to variations in the handwriting – not only between the meditation (which is copied out in a neat hand) and the Psalm annotations (which are often executed in a more hurried or casual hand), but also within the annotations – we can see that More's marginalia were not all written on one occasion. From this we can deduce that More's annotations

---

[30] *Thomas More's Prayer Book: A Facsimile Reproduction of the Annotated Pages* (New Haven, CT, 1969), sigs. C.1r–D.1v. Subsequent references to this edition will be made by signature number in the text.

[31] The significance of this sequence remains obscure. In his valuable work of reference, *The Bible in the Works of Thomas More*, 5 vols. (Nieuwkoop, 1969–72), Germain Marc'hadour shows that these particular Psalms occur nowhere else in the Tower works (vol. 1, 101–80).

Figure 7 The closing lines of Thomas More's 'Godly Meditation', inscribed
in his prayer book.

sprang from reading and meditation that was practised over a period of
time and therefore that the content of the annotations could have served as
mnemonic devices when he returned to the text. Finally, unlike most of
the preceding examples, More did not append his name to these
marginalia.

Despite these differences, however, the annotations share some significant features with the content of Seymour's marginalia and broader trends
in early modern graffiti. As is the case for the passages copied out by
Seymour and Rudstone, for example, it is clear that many of the verses
annotated by More, and the annotations themselves, potentially have a
very personal application. However, we should not ignore the highly
aphoristic quality of the marginalia. For example, while the annotation
beside Psalm 87.5–10, 'in tribulatione uehemente et in carcere' (in great
tribulation and in prison, sig. I.4v), draws out the specific application the
verse 'posuerunt me in lacu inferiori: in tenebrosis et in vmbra mortis'
(they have laid me in the lower pit: in the dark places, and in the shadow of
death) might have for imprisoned individuals, More resists any gesture of
personal identification. This withdrawal from the truly personal is also true

of the 'Godly Meditation' written in the margins of the Books of Hours. While subjectivity is implied in this meditation by More's use of the personal pronoun – 'Gyve *me* thy grace good lord / To sett the world at nought / To sett my mind faste vppon the / And not to hange vppon the blaste of mennys mowthis' (sig. C.1r–v, my emphasis) – its devotions are highly conventional, and thus essentially impersonal. As Eamon Duffy rightly notes, the meditation 'contains nothing that any devout early Tudor Christian, reflecting in their closet on their own mortality, might not have uttered'.[32] Rather than an explicitly personal identification with his reading material, then, More's annotations show a keen awareness that these verses are apt for any person in tribulation. This is nowhere more visible than in the seven annotations making reference to the Turkish invasion of Hungary, which of course is the context for *A dialoge of comfort against tribulacion* (sigs. B.2v, G.4r, H.7v, H.8r, K.1v). In looking to this near contemporary event, these annotations create an implicit sense of communality in tribulation.

The significance of More's marginalia within his Tower works as a whole has been much discussed. The flagged Psalms and annotations chart a clear set of concerns that are mirrored elsewhere in the writings, which has led scholars to interpret the marginalia almost as a set of preparatory notes for the other works that More wrote from the Tower: the *Dialogue, De Tristitia Christi, The Treatise on the Blessed Body*, his instructions, meditations, and prayers, and the catena of biblical verses in More's holograph that are collected at the end of the Valencia manuscript. For example, Psalm 15.4, which is annotated with the words 'tribulationis utilitas' (the advantage of tribulation), also appears in the *Dialogue*.[33] Similarly an annotation to Psalm 12.1 – 'Qui scrupulum habet in confessione et animo suo non satisfacit precetur hunc psalmum' (He who has scruples in confession and is not satisfied in his own soul should pray this Psalm, sig. A.7ᵛ) – reflects More's discussion of the topic, using the fable of the over-scrupulous ass, in Book II of the *Dialogue*.[34] But the marginalia is also characteristic of a more significant and

---

[32] Eamon Duffy, *Marking the Hours: English People and their Prayers, 1240–1570* (New Haven, CT, 2006), 110–11, 116–17.

[33] *CW*, vol. XII, 48. Subsequent references to More's *Complete Works* will be given by volume and page number in the text.

[34] Other annotated or marked Psalms that appear elsewhere in the Tower works are: 6:2 (*Dialogue*), 10:5 (*De Tristitia*), 13.5 (*De Tristitia*), 21.17 (*Catena, De Tristitia*), 32.9 (*Dialogue*), 41.2 (*Catena*), 54.23 (*Catena*), 63.2 (*De Tristitia*), 67.2 (*Dialogue*), 68.7 (*Catena*), 72.1 (*Catena*), 72.24 (*De Tristitia, Devout Prayer*), 75.6 (*De Tristitia*), 75.13 (*De Tristitia*), 83.7 (*Dialogue, De Tristitia*), 90.1 (*Dialogue*), 90.4 (*Dialogue*), 90.5 (*Dialogue*), 90.6 (*Dialogue, De Tristitia*), 102.3 (*Dialogue*), 102.14 (*Dialogue*).

overarching trend in the Tower works towards what we might describe as the ecumenical perspective – that is, More's desire to extend the relevance of his observations to the whole Christian world, or the universal church.[35] This impetus has all too often been ignored by those scholars who wish to stress the specific autobiographical significance of the themes that More discussed in his *Dialogue* and *De Tristitia*.[36] This generalising trend is the basis of More's 'trick': that is, his disassociation from the institutional system, and the space, in which he is imprisoned.

More's ecumenical drive manifests itself variously in the Tower works, but is most obvious in the four following aspects: the establishment of a general definition of tribulation and method of comfort; his explicit address to a readership in the *Dialogue* and *De Tristitia*; the lack of personal identification, or even assertion of authorship in any texts except his correspondence; and the absence of reference to imprisonment apart from the relatively brief treatment of the *fear* of incarceration in the *Dialogue*. In the *Dialogue*, through the person of Anthony, More gives the following definition of tribulation: 'tribulacion semeth generally to signifie nothyng els, but some kynd of grefe, eyther payne of the body or hevynes of /the\ mynd' (*CW*, vol. xII, 10). More's use of the word 'generally' immediately prior to his definition of tribulation emphasises that he has consciously avoided specifics, seeking rather to abstract any personal insight he has into tribulation. Later in the dialogue Anthony does address more specific examples of tribulation, including incarceration. We should note, however, three things about the treatment of this potentially personal detail. Firstly, the discussion does not really deal with the lived experience of imprisonment, but rather with the fear of entering prison. Secondly, More overturns the notion of prison as a specific architectural enclosure, and argues instead that every man is in the metaphorical prison of the world. Both these features make the discussion relevant to a much wider readership than if it were merely aimed at those in prison. Finally, this treatment of imprisonment occupies only one portion of book three of the *Dialogue*, amounting to just 9 per cent of the treatise as a whole, thereby demonstrating that the vast majority of this text is not about imprisonment at all.

---

[35] See *OED, ecumenical, adj.* 1.
[36] See for example Richard Marius, *Thomas More: A Biography* (New York, 1985); and G. R. Elton, 'The Real Thomas More', in *Reformation Principle and Practice: Essays in Honour of Arthur Geoffrey Dickens*, ed. Peter Newman Brooks (London, 1980), 21–31.

More deals with personal concerns and details in much the same way in *De Tristitia*. When pointing out the autobiographical nature of this text, scholars usually home in on More's somewhat lengthy defence of timid martyrs. But even within this discussion, where there is a clear risk of veering into personal identification, we can observe More's keen desire to keep his discussion as inclusive as possible. For example, he makes a correction to his own text changing a sentence from 'ergo ad manus uentum est ubi cominus cum principe huius mundi diabolo / et diris eius satellitibus / cominus certandum est' (Therefore it has come to the point of a hand-to-hand conflict with the prince of this world, the devil and his cruel minions) to 'Ergo ubi sic ad manus uentum est ut cum principe huius mundi diabolo / et diris eius satellitibus / cominus certandum sit' (When it has come to the point where it is necessary to struggle hand-to-hand with etc.); the amended phrase is followed by the statement that a man cannot then back away (*CW*, vol. xiv, 71).[37] The deleted phrase forms a statement that may only chime with a small minority of potential readers. Those not currently facing persecution, or those who do not perceive of their faith being challenged, probably will not think it has come to the point of hand-to-hand combat. However, the amended passage forms a conditional phrase, which merely alerts the reader that such a time will come. This is a warning that is relevant to and edifying for all.

The ecumenical impetus in the two major treatises is emphasised by their implied readerships. In *De Tristitia* this readership is explicitly invoked through the use of the second person ('An non audis hic ex ipsius ore pauli timorem suum'; In these words do you not hear from Paul's own mouth his fear (*CW*, vol. xiv, 81)) and direct addresses to the reader ('Hoc in loco lector paululum sistamus gradum et imperatorem nostrum / iacentem in terra supplicem / pia mente contemplemur'; Reader, let us pause for a little at this point and contemplate with a devout mind our commander lying on the ground in humble supplication (*CW*, vol. xiv, 113–15)). In the *Dialogue*, the readership is implied by the fictional narrative of dissemination that frames the treatise. At the very end of their conversation, Vincent says to Anthony: 'I purpose vncle as my pore witt and lernyng will serve me, to put your good counsayle in remembrauns, not in our own language onely, but in the Almayne tong to' (*CW*, vol. xii, 320). And at the beginning of the *Dialogue* we are informed of a fictional process of dissemination that is meant to have occurred after Vincent had recorded

---

[37] Other instances where we can observe More's revisions demonstrating a change from a personal to a more objective stance can be found in the notes to *CW*, vol. xiv, 55, 129, 133, 281, 407, 415.

the dialogue: 'made by an hungaryen in laten / and translatyd out of laten into french, and out of french into Englysh' (*CW*, vol. xii, 3). While the information that the text has been recorded in three languages is false, it nevertheless suggests that More may have imagined a broad circulation for the *Dialogue* across Europe.

In this latter case of implied readership we can see that the fictional authorship and process of dissemination erase More from his text. It is, supposedly, a Hungarian's record of a real conversation, and not a text produced by Thomas More from his prison cell. This act of self-effacement is not restricted to the *Dialogue*. More also leaves his name off the holograph manuscript of *De Tristitia* (known as the Valencia manuscript) and the prayer book. However, potentially more important than his failure to sign his name to these manuscripts is More's decision not to identify himself as an *incarcerated* author (except, once again, in his correspondence). Not only does this appear to be a significant departure from the trend of writing for posterity that we observed in the scribblings of Seymour, Grey, and the graffitists – who stress they write 'frome the Tower', or who leave their mark *in* the Tower – but also from one of the most important models for prison writing that these early modern prisoners had: Boethius. In his decision to use the mode of dialogue to chart an individual's mental journey from fear and despair to a place of strength and faith, More is probably as much indebted to Boethius as he is to Plato. In his *Consolation of Philosophy*, Boethius represents this journey through a fictionalised version of himself, which also allows him to create an image of himself, and an account of his hardships, for posterity. More, by contrast, avoids this use of faux-autobiography, using instead a young Hungarian called Vincent to chart the transition from fear to faith. More's departure here from the Boethian model might not be quite so striking if it were not for his earlier forays into the dialogic form. The fact that in both of More's previous uses of explicit dialogue – *Utopia* and *A Dialogue Concerning Heresies* – he did make one of the participants a fictionalised version of himself suggests that More very intentionally and pointedly chose to write himself out of his *Dialogue of Comfort*.

Critics normally account for the lack of any identifying features in the Tower works as stemming from More's prudent avoidance of self-incrimination. From the surviving accounts of the interrogations of Thomas More, John Fisher, and their servants concerning the correspondence reported to have passed between More and Fisher, it is clear that Cromwell was keen to find treasonous opinions expressed

in writing.[38] However, the fact of the authorities' interest in no way proves
More's fear of interception; and for this reason we should not allow the
possibility that this shaped his literary output to cheapen our perception of
the texts. Are we really to believe that the entire trend towards the
ecumenical perspective in More's prison works can be accounted for by
his desire to protect himself from incrimination? For if so, the implication
is that these texts are not enough in themselves; that the process of
encoding through generalisation must be somehow reversed in order to
understand the true significance of these texts. However, I would argue
that More's attention to detail – as shown, for example, by the example of
self-editing discussed above – suggests something more than just a practical
aim of hiding authorial identity. It demonstrates a much more nuanced
concern for style, and a concern that these texts might adequately edify a
readership who, potentially, has no knowledge of the prison-context of
their composition.

Clarence H. Miller, in his Yale edition of *De Tristitia*, takes to task this
apparently overwhelming urge to unpick More's creations in search of the
personal. He acknowledges there is no doubt that More had quite personal
reasons for undertaking the writing that he did. But he argues that for
More it was not enough merely to channel his tribulations in 'ordered
literary composition'; he must also impart comfort to his friends, family,
and all 'the suffering members of Christ's body' (*CW*, vol. XIV, 748).
More's process of generalisation was part of a grander design. One part of
it, as Miller states, was to serve a readership. The other was to make an
assertion about the power of prison writing itself: that writing has more
power than merely to record that 'I' was in prison on this date, or that 'I'
read and meditated upon these particular Bible verses (which, essentially, is
the limit of what the graffiti and Seymour's marginalia achieves). These
reader-focused texts implicitly have the power to transcend the particularity of prison composition. It *is* possible that More eliminated his identity as
incarcerated author from these texts because of stresses and pressures from
the state; but the elimination simultaneously functions as a challenge to
these authorities, implicitly boasting that the prison cannot define either
his activities or the shape of his writings. The ultimate dismissal of the
state's power comes, not by explicitly asserting that the prison has not
subdued him (for the minute he does so he demonstrates that it *has*
influenced him), but by sidestepping the topic altogether.

---

[38] See TNA, SP 6/7 fols. 6r–9v (More and Fisher); BL, Cotton MSS Cleopatra E. vi, fols. 169r–171v
(Fisher); and TNA, SP 1/93, fols. 51r–60v (their servants).

More comes close to making an explicit assertion to this effect in two conversations that are reported in his correspondence. The first, in a letter to Alice Allington (explicitly from Margaret Roper, but bearing all the hallmarks of More's composition),[39] reports a conversation between More and his daughter in which he says:

> [The King] hath taken fro me nothinge but my libertie (wherewith (as help me God), his grace hath done me so great good by the spirituall profytt that I trust I take therby, that amonge all his great benefites heaped vpon me so thicke, I reken vpon my faith my prisonment euen the very chief).[40]

This passage contains a bold claim that More believes that the prison, which is intended as a place of punishment, will be a space in which he takes 'spirituall profytt'. This, however, is merely a verbal assertion and does not detail the means by which he intends to appropriate the cell as a space of edification. These are more clearly implied in a second letter, this time from More to Margaret, dated 2 or 3 May 1535, where he gives an account of an interview before the Council:

> I answerd in effect as byfore, shewyng that I had fully determyned with my selfe, neyther to study no medle with eny mater of thys world, but that my hole study shulde be, vppon the passyon of Chryst and myne owne passage owt of thys worlde.[41]

In this second passage More represents himself as having two distinct choices, either to live in 'the worlde', or to adopt a life of spiritual study. The choice in reality is between life in the world, and imprisonment and death. However, we can see here that the activities of such study comes to stand for and to replace imprisonment. Thus More makes the boast, first to the Council and then to his family and circle of friends through the letter, that this life of study has surpassed the significance of his incarceration. Thus the practices that bring about 'spirituall profytt' define his incarceration; his incarceration does not define his activities.

The major prison works execute a similar 'trick', writing the prison out of the Tower works. Even though the *Dialogue* and *De Tristitia* might be called products of the prison in a very real sense – since they result not only from the empty time facing More in his cell, but also from the reading

---

[39] William Rastell, More's nephew and editor of his *Works*, appears to have thought it possible that More wrote the letter because in his preface to it he wrote: 'But whether thys aunswer were wryten by syr Thomas More in hys daughter Ropers name, or by her selfe, it is not certaynelye knowen.' *The Workes of Syr Thomas More Knyght* (London, 1557), 1434.

[40] *The Correspondence of Sir Thomas More*, ed. Elizabeth Frances Rogers (Princeton, 1947), 531.

[41] Ibid., 552.

and meditation upon his prayer book that occupied him there – this is
not immediately apparent from the texts themselves. It is true that if we were
to sit down and read the prayer book side by side with the treatises, then we
could observe how these texts represent the fruits of More's imprisonment.
However, it is significant that this information would have been unavailable
to the general Christian reader, at whom these two treatises were aimed. It
seems similarly unlikely that readers of the first printed edition of the
Dialogue, published by Richard Tottel in 1553, would have recognised the
story of a female jail visitor who pities a prisoner for having the door shut
upon him every night (despite herself being unable to sleep with the
windows or door to her chamber open) as a disguised account of a visit
from More's wife, Dame Alice.[42] This does not mean to say that there are
not additional layers to the narrative waiting to be uncovered. We cannot
deny that there certainly appear to be a number of in-jokes embedded in the
text, for the enjoyment of More's closest family and friends.[43] And, as many
scholars have pointed out, the *Dialogue* alsos works as an allegory concerning the threat of violence at the hands of Henry (in the guise of the Great
Turk), for those who do not accept an essentially foreign, reformed faith (in
the guise of Islam). More certainly seems to have enjoyed crafting a text that
artfully encompassed all these layered readings, suggesting his hope that they
would be successfully smuggled out of the prison. However, what we should
realise is that, by disguising these autobiographical features, More is not so
much writing into the *Dialogue* an account of his imprisonment to be found
by a small minority of potential readers, as he is erasing it for the majority of
readers. On the most general level, we must acknowledge that More is not
writing about his prison cell but about Anthony's house in Hungary and, in
the case of *De Tristitia*, the garden of Gethsemane.

The modes of writing that More chose to pen from his cell also belie
the constraints of prison. His choice to write a dialogue clearly recalls
Boethius' scribal activities in his sixth-century prison, but it is important to
remember that the form is not usually the preserve of the incarcerated
author. Rather, the dialogue is a high art form associated with humanists,
from the great fifteenth-century Italian writers Lorenzo Valla, Poggio
Bracciolini, and Leonardo Bruni,[44] down to More and his contemporaries.

---

[42] See Nicholas Harpsfield, *The Life and Death of Sr Thomas Moore, Knight*, ed. E. V. Hitchcock,
    EETS OS 186 (Oxford, 1932), 97–8.
[43] See *CW*, vol. XII, cxxxv–cxlvii.
[44] See David Marsh, *The Quattrocento Dialogue: Classical Tradition and Humanist Innovation*
    (Cambridge, MA, 1980); and Virginia Cox, *The Renaissance Dialogue: Literary Dialogue in its
    Social and Political Contexts, Castiglione to Galileo* (Cambridge, 1992).

As discussed above, More had made use of the dialogic form long before his imprisonment, not only in *Utopia* and the *Dialogue of Heresies*, but also as part of the polemical technique he employed in texts such as *The Confutation of Tyndale's Answer*. It is clear that he did not view it as an expressly incarcerated mode of writing, or as an expression of the dispossessed. Quite the reverse: from his use of the form in the *Dialogue Concerning Heresies* and the *Confutation*, which were part of a state-sponsored attack on heresy, we can see that like the Catholic controversialists, who had long used the form to defend orthodox views,[45] More perceived the dialogue to be an expression of authority. Even though he does not attach his name thereto, his decision to write a dialogue is a bold and ambitious gesture. By writing in this high art form, he is being self-consciously learned. It implies that the author is part of an international elite, a cosmopolitan man who has an in-depth insight into the religious and political turmoil that has been going on in Hungary in recent years, and that this text could have been written anywhere.

De Tristitia also has its gaze trained beyond the prison walls. This is most obvious in the meditative sense: the author and the reader are both watching Christ in the garden of Gethsemane, imagining and empathising with his mental anguish. But it is precisely this empathy that has persuaded so many scholars of the prison-specific context of its composition. There is, of course, a clear parallel between More contemplating his death in his prison cell and Christ contemplating *his* death in the garden.[46] But not only is it prosaic to bother pointing out this parallel, it also entirely misrepresents the significance of this devotional piece. Just as the dialogue is not a form of writing peculiar to the incarcerated writer, neither is meditation on Christ. Meditation on the life and death of Christ, and very specifically on his human torment, had been the mainstay of medieval faith, and it continued to be an important aspect of Catholic devotion in the sixteenth century.[47] More had, in fact, recommended two of the most influential texts in this tradition, Thomas á Kempis's *Imitatio Christi* and Pseudo-Bonaventure's *Meditationes Vitae Christi*, in his *Confutation of Tyndale's Answer*.[48] It is unsurprising,

---

[45] See Rainer Pineas, 'Thomas More's use of the Dialogue Form as a Weapon of Religious Controversy', *Studies in the Renaissance*, 7 (1960), 193–206.

[46] See for example Louis A. S. M. Schuster, 'The Tower of London: More's Gethsemane', *Moreana*, 74 (1982), 39–45.

[47] For discussion of this tradition, see Sarah Beckwith, *Christ's Body: Identity, Culture, and Society in Late Medieval Writings* (London, 1993).

[48] *CW*, vol. VIII, 37. Peter Ackroyd conjectures that More may have read the Hilton and Kempis while he was in residence at the Charterhouse, because the London Carthusians had these two volumes in their library. See *The Life of Thomas More* (London, 1998), 97.

then, that there are a number of parallels to be found between these two texts and *De Tristitia*: the focus on Christ (present in both); emphasis on the example of Christ in pursuing a spiritual life, known as *devotio moderna* (Kempis); the dramatic imagination of oneself present at the events of Christ's life (Pseudo-Bonaventure); and the generalisation of one's own private meditations to create a meditative guide suitable for a wide-ranging readership. By imitating such works, More also makes an implicit claim about location. Although these books were both monastic productions (Kempis was a member of the Brethren of the Common Life, and Pseudo-Bonaventure is believed to have been a Franciscan), and originally intended for an enclosed audience, they subsequently became available to a broad lay readership: the *Meditationes* was translated by the Carthusian Nicholas Love, and the *Imitatio* by Lady Margaret Beaufort (book IV) and William Atkinson (books I–III).[49] Thus, More implicitly associates himself with a tradition that had escaped the confines of the monastic cell.

In addition to the contribution that the *Dialogue* and *De Tristitia* make as texts, More's decision to write a dialogue and a devotional guide contains an implicit boast. The graffitists Seymour and Grey might in some ways be seen to adhere to James Simpson's formulation, that 'the institutional simplifications and centralizations of the sixteenth century provoked correlative simplifications and narrowings in literature':[50] although they do demonstrate that the products of the 'weak' man could both recast the significance of the prison and outlast the repressive system under which they were made, they clearly work within the narrow confines (the margins of pages, the walls of a cell) with which they are faced. By contrast, More's 'trick' was that he practised writerly activities that associated him with spaces and modes of writing outside the prison confines. But the content of these writings is in some ways incidental. Merely by dint of existing, these texts say something about More and his response to imprisonment. By writing, and not writing about prison, More suggests that his identity as an author transcends his identity as a prisoner; although the prison has given him the chance to write, it is writing that defines his incarceration, not incarceration that defines his writing. As de Certeau writes: 'tactics do not obey the law of the place, for they are not defined or identified by it'. By then imagining a readership

---

[49] William Atkinson and Lady Margaret Beaufort, *A ful deuout and gostely treatyse of the imitacyon and folowynge the blessed lyfe of our moste mercyful sauyour cryste* (London, 1504).

[50] James Simpson, *Oxford English Literary History*, vol. II, *Reform and Cultural Revolution: 1350–1547* (Oxford, 2002), I.

for these works, More demonstrates his desire that he might continue to be acknowledged as a writer. Most of all, though, by writing More is asserting that he is not daunted. His reading and writing materials may have subsequently been taken away, but it does not matter; it matters only that More wrote.

Prison Psalms

Another prisoner who sought to produce a work of general edification during his incarceration was the Marian prisoner John Hooper. His *Certeine comfortable expositions* derive generalised lessons from selected Psalms (22, 62, 71, and 76). For example, from his reading of Psalm 22.4 – 'Although I walke thorough the vallie and shadowe of death, I will feare no euill, for thou art with me, thy rodde and thy staffe comfort me' – Hooper extrapolates, 'And whatsoeuer the dangers bee, and howe horrible soeuer they seeme, Christe being with vs, we neede not to feare'.[51] This is a generalised definition of tribulation, which is reminiscent of More's in *A dialoge of comfort*: 'tribulacion semeth generally to signifie nothing els, but some kind of grefe, eyther payne of the body or hevynes of the mynd'. It would have been easy for Hooper to identify the 'vallie of the shadowe of death' with his prison cell, or the certainty that, unless he recanted, he was bound for the stake. But instead he asserts that the comfort provided by this verse has relevance for all people, 'whatsoeuer' the dangers they face.

However, Hooper did not as studiously avoid any reference to recent English history as did More, and it is through such references that one can detect an implied Protestant readership for his generalised lessons. For instance, glossing Psalm 23.2 – 'He shall feede me in pleasant pastures, and he shall leade me by the riuers side' – he writes:

> Let euery man and woman therefore examine their owne conscience, without flattering of them selues, and they shal find that the most part of this realme of England in the time of our holy and blessed king Edward the sixt, were fed with this holy foode of Gods worde, or else might haue bene fed with it. For it was offered and sent vnto them, as well by most godly statutes and lawes of Parleament, as by many Noble men, and vertuous learned Preachers.[52]

---

[51] John Hooper, *Certeine comfortable expositions* (London, 1580), sig. D.2r.
[52] Ibid., sig. C.iv.

In this passage he elevates the Edwardian regime as one that provided spiritual food, thereby making the realm at this time synonymous with the Psalmist's 'pleasant pastures'. Such praise of the previous reign – a time when the 'Parleament, ... many Noble men, and vertuous learned Preachers', promoted Protestantism as the orthodox expression of faith – contains an implicit condemnation of the current Catholic monarch. Even though it is never explicitly stated, the fact that the Edwardian regime is aligned with the 'pleasant pastures', means that Mary's reign can be nothing other than the 'vallie of the shadowe of death'. Such an interpretation, however, would only be accepted by the reader if he were a supporter of Protestantism. Thus, while Hooper never identifies the need for such comfort and edification with the persecution being undergone by Protestants at this time, we see that he is using the Psalms as a means of maintaining pre-existing Reformist communities.[53]

John Bradford, another Marian martyr, also invoked the Psalms to speak for a community. But while Hooper's exposition had subtly alluded to a Protestant readership, Bradford's prose paraphrase explicitly presented this community as a counter-public by making a direct analogy between the persecuted Jewish nation and Reformation martyrs. Quoting the passage, for instance, on how the heathens polluted the Temple in Jerusalem, Bradford writes of contemporary England:

> even so now verie manye heathen and lymmes of Antichrist though out-
> wardlie they profess Christ are come in to thyne enheritance and church
> which thow hast with us in this Realme of England: and have defyled thy
> hoolie temple that is the soules and bodies of manye which have professed
> the in whom as in thy temple thow shuldest dwell.[54]

In order that his meaning should be understood, Bradford goes on to explain that the method by which the bodies and souls ('temple[s]') have been polluted is the nation's resort to 'idolatrical and antichristian service': the delivery of religious services in Latin, the invocation of saints, and the idolatrous worship of the Eucharist. And rather than leave the parallel between the persecuted Jews and contemporary martyrs implicit, he tallies up the deaths of 'Fryth, Barnes, Garritt, Jerome, Lambert, Lascelles, &c., and ... ladie Jane'.[55] The purpose behind Bradford's clarity is

---

[53] Elsewhere in his prison writings, Hooper more actively and practically shapes the Protestant counter-public. See for example his letters encouraging the formation of Protestant cells in London (BL, Additional MS 19400, fol. 27r (holograph); LM, 114–17), or his praise and support of the congregation of Protestants in the Counter, who had been arrested in Bow churchyard during their time of prayer (ECL, MS 261, fols. 11r–14r).

[54] ECL, MS 261, fol. 174r.   [55] Ibid.

entirely functional: to instruct. As a former leader, it was vital that he, like Hooper, continued to provide pastoral guidance and clear teaching to his co-religionists to resist Catholicism. To identify with the persecution of God's chosen race was to illustrate just how their current tribulation was precisely the mark of their election: to self-define as a counter-public was vital to the impetus of the cause.

However, the majority of prisoners who produced Psalm paraphrases in the mid sixteenth century were not concerned with producing explicit narratives of opposition or rallying dissident communities against the dominant powers. It was much more common during the reigns of Henry, Edward, and Mary for prisoners to write metrical paraphrases of the Psalms. Metrical Psalms were written from prison by Anne Askew, Henry Howard, the Earl of Surrey, Thomas Smith, and Robert and John Dudley; Thomas Wyatt also wrote versifications of the Penitential Psalms, following Aretino, although it is unclear whether these were written in prison.[56] Whereas Hooper and Bradford used the Psalms as a vehicle for constructing and maintaining a counter-public – ministering to a perse-cuted community, and constructing that group's narrative in opposition to the repressive regime – the metrical Psalms are personal, individualised laments which do not present themselves in opposition to the public realm but rather seek to insinuate themselves into it. Whereas Bradford and Hooper sought clarity for the purposes of edification, the poems are both self-serving and equivocal: they employ 'tricks of the "weak"'.

Wyatt and Surrey's Psalms in particular have gained considerable critical attention, most of which has tended to see them as 'occasional poems', reflecting directly on their authors' incarcerated state and the events that brought them there.[57] The fittingness of the Psalms selected by Wyatt, Surrey, Askew, Smith, and the Dudleys as vehicles for these prisoners' personal supplications to God is undeniable: they are filled with laments over persecution, false friends, and fears that God has turned his back on

---

[56] There is disagreement about whether Wyatt's *Paraphrase of the Penitential Psalms* was written during his 1536 imprisonment or his 1541 incarceration, or whether they might not have been written in prison at all. H. A. Mason, for example, argues for a 1536 dating (*Humanism and Poetry in the Early Tudor Period: An Essay* (London, 1959), 180, 186, 198, 217–20); Alastair Fox, for 1541 (*Politics and Literature in the Reigns of Henry VII and Henry VIII* (Oxford, 1989), 280–1); while Greg Walker argues that the *Paraphrase* was written during his period at Allington Castle after the 1541 incarceration (*Writing under Tyranny: English Literature and the Henrician Reformation* (Oxford, 2005), 351n.).

[57] Beth Quitslund, *The Reformation in Rhyme: Sternhold, Hopkins and the English Metrical Psalter, 1547–1603* (Aldershot, 2008), 16. See also Elizabeth Heale, *Wyatt, Surrey and Early Tudor Poetry* (London, 1998), 173.

the Psalmist. As with the sentences chosen from Proverbs by Seymour, or the biblical verses inscribed in the walls of the Tower by Collins, Rudstone, and Fane, the choice of certain Psalms indicates that these poets recognised their power to speak on behalf of their author's situation, and to give them suitable comfort. For example, four of the individuals translating the Psalms – Askew, Surrey, Smith, and John Dudley – chose Psalm 54, in which the Psalmist appeals to God for his mercy, and for vengeance upon the false friends who have turned against him. Thus when Surrey writes that 'It was a frendly foo, by shadow of good will, / Myne old fere and dere frende, my guyde, that trapped me',[58] we think of the former friends and family members – including Richard Southwell, George Blage, Edmund Knyvet (cousin), and Surrey's sister – who gave witness against him.[59] And John Bale, by printing Askew's paraphrase alongside her examinations, adds a reading context for the verses that provides clear identities for the 'faythlesse men' who 'agaynst [her] ryse': her examiners.[60]

Other writers appear to have chosen their Psalms because they contain a reference to incarceration. For example, in his translation of Psalm 141, Thomas Smith writes 'Of prison, o Lord, bring my bodie out, that I may give prais to thi name, / And iust men will without any doubt resort to my company again',[61] which follows Coverdale's translation in his 1535 Bible, 'Brynge my soule out of preson, that I maye geue thakes vnto thy name: which thinge yf thou wilt graunte me, then shal the rightuous resorte vnto my company'.[62] In a similar case, Wyatt follows his source for the framing narrative to his Penitential Psalms by representing the cave as a prison-like space: 'Withdrawyng hym into a dark Cave / Within the grownd wherein he might hym hyde, / Fleing the light, as in prison or grave'.[63] We can

---

[58] Henry Howard, Earl of Surrey, *Poems*, ed. Emrys Jones (Oxford, 1964), 102 (lines 22–3). Subsequent references are to this edition and will be made by page and line number within the text.
[59] Susan Brigden, 'Henry Howard, Earl of Surrey and the "Conjured League"', *Historical Journal*, 37 (1994), 507–37 (536).
[60] *The Examinations of Anne Askew*, ed. Elaine V. Beilin (Oxford, 1996), 72. Compare Bale's packaging of Askew's Psalm with the effect of Surrey's prefatory verse epistles to Psalms 72 (addressed to Sir George Blage) and 87 (to Sir Anthony Denny). These epistles appear in both BL, Additional MS 36529, and the Arundel Harington Manuscript (Arundel Castle Harington MS, no. II). See Surrey's *Poems*, ed. Jones, 32–3, 130.
[61] Thomas Smith, *Literary and Linguistic Work: Part 1, Certaigne psalmes or songes of David (1549)*, ed. Bror Danielsson (Stockholm, 1963), 17. See also Smith's translation of Psalm 145 (at page 30). Subsequent references are to this edition and given by page number within the text.
[62] Miles Coverdale, *Biblia the Bible* (Cologne?, 1535).
[63] Thomas Wyatt, *Collected Poems*, ed. Kenneth Muir and Patricia Thompson (Liverpool, 1969), CVIII, lines 60–2. Subsequent references are to this edition and will be made by poem and line number within the text. Although the words 'wherein ... light' and 'grave' were added by Wyatt, the reference to the prison ('carcere') appears in Aretino.

assume that this was not merely coincidence, for references to prison also find their way into Smith's paraphrases even when his source does not contain the word. For example, in his source text – Coverdale's translation of Psalm 119.5 – the verse is rendered: 'Wo is me that my banishment endureth so longe: I dwell in the tabernacles of the soroufull. My soule hath longe dwelt amonge them, that be enemies vnto peace'. Smith, however, turns it into a lament about imprisonment, 'Alas for me this is my chaunce, my banishment still to endure, / In prison strong so long to daunce, in a cabon of sorowes ure' (*Literary and Linguistic Work*, 20).

Such evidence suggests that we should interpret the Psalms as a conduit for the prisoner's voice, as Bale encourages his reader to with his title: 'The voice of Anne Askewe out of the 54. Psalme of David'. However, it is important to avoid the temptation to read these works merely as straightforward biographies of the poets. As with More's choice of writings, the metrical Psalms in fact hide more than they reveal. In their expressions of tribulation, these writers are remarkably conventional. Surrey stays pedantically close to his source;[64] and even Smith's addition of the 'prison strong' to Psalm 119 does not appear out of place due to the fact that there are plenty of other references to incarceration, metaphorical or otherwise, elsewhere in the Psalms.

It has been argued by Stephen Greenblatt and Brian Cummings that the posture of being a translator, and, moreover, a slave to convention, provided these poets with 'prophylactics' against suspicion.[65] As Andrew Taylor has noted, paraphrase presents 'a method of interpreting Scripture without venturing into fully-exposed commentary or theological exegesis'.[66] The poets' reliance on a biblical source provided them with a means of both biographical and doctrinal equivocation. However, while a wealth of commentary has elucidated these equivocations – beginning with Surrey's reading of Wyatt's paraphrase of the Penitential Psalms as an attack on the concupiscence of Henry VIII[67] – the resulting poems were more than just covert forms of biography and of social and religious commentary. It is not accidental that the writers of metrical Psalms

---

[64] James Simpson, *Burning to Read: English Fundamentalism and its Reformation Opponents* (Cambridge, MA, 2007), 155, 167. Simpson also demonstrates that many passages that seem to be most personal in fact follow John Campensis's paraphrase, 164–5.

[65] Stephen Greenblatt, *Renaissance Self-Fashioning: From More to Shakespeare* (Chicago, IL, 1980; reprinted 2005), 121; Brian Cummings, *The Literary Culture of the Reformation: Grammar and Grace* (Oxford, 2002), 224.

[66] Andrew William Taylor, 'Psalms and Early Tudor Humanism', unpublished PhD thesis (University of Cambridge, 2002), 227.

[67] Surrey, *Poems*, 29.

eschewed an explicitly counter-public stance in favour of crowd-pleasing
literary endeavour. With the exception of Askew, the other writers of
metrical Psalms might be more accurately described as political, rather
than religious, prisoners: while religious in content, the equivocation in
these works implies a politic awareness of the importance of not explicitly
subscribing to one, potentially damning, position.[68]

The relationship between literature and concealment is, in many ways, a
given. In reference to this period, Greg Walker has written perceptively on
the relationship between covert expression and the emergence of new
literary forms, as poets 'sought ways of writing of and for "this realm of
England" that did not necessitate and presuppose a sympathetic royal
reader'.[69] It is important to acknowledge that these imprisoned poets'
works did have currency within the public realm ('this realm of England'),
and that this currency owes itself to Wyatt and Surrey's poetic mastery.
However, while Walker is right in suggesting that, by inventing new or
rediscovering old ways of writing, poets found the means to covertly
express their dissidence, the implication that the encoding of personal
grievances and broader political commentary was the *main aim* of such
writings might be stretching the point. Rather (again, with the exception
of Askew), it is likely that this aim was secondary to a more fundamental
one: to retain both a public presence and a credible voice. The choice of
Psalms would be an ideal vehicle for such a purpose, for not only are the
Psalms a biblical source full of persecution but also one of the most literary
books of the Bible. In a very long tradition, accepted by both pre- and
post-Reformation scholars of the Bible, the Psalms were thought to have
been composed by King David. Early modern poets were interested in the
Psalms for several obvious reasons: 'they were the oldest poetry known at
the time; and they were written under direct inspiration from God, which
indicated his approval of writing poetry'.[70] Therefore, while explicitly the
work of a supplicant, the Psalms have a powerful ability to authorise a poet
for, like David, they are claiming to have the power to put God on record.
Wyatt, Surrey, and Smith in particular were alert to this: they selected and
edited their material in such a way as to emphasise the *activities* of the
Psalmist – meditating, praying, singing, and recording.[71]

---

[68] On Askew's equivocation, see Chapter 1 above.
[69] Walker, *Writing under Tyranny*, 424.
[70] Hannibal Hamlin, *Psalm Culture and Early Modern English Literature* (Cambridge, 2004), 85
[71] The relative absence of these themes in the paraphrases by Robert and John Dudley is in keeping
with what Zim has described as their 'perfunctory attitude' to meditation (Rivkah Zim, *English
Metrical Psalms: Poetry as Praise and Prayer, 1535–1601* (Cambridge, 1987), 107).

This emphasis on activity comes primarily from the nature of the Psalms selected. With the exception of Psalm 102, translated by Smith, all of the Psalms selected for paraphrase might be described as 'mediated' accounts of prayer. 'Unmediated' Psalms are those which comprise only the *content* of the prayer, such as praise of God or a lament concerning personal misfortune; a mediated account, by contrast, embeds this content within a narrative, or contains self-reflexive statements, which asserts that 'I am praying', or 'I am singing'.[72] Psalm 145, for instance, opens with this assertion: 'Alleluia. Lauda, anima mea, Dominum; laudabo Dominum in vita mea, psallam Deo meo, quamdiu fuero' ('Prayse the Lorde (o my soule:) whyle I lyue wil I prayse the Lorde, yee as longe as I haue eny beynge, I wil synge prayses vnto my God'). Only the first four words can really be described as the content of the prayer; the self-reflexive statement that 'psallam Deo meo' draws the reader's attention to the fact that these words are a song, and are thus brought into being by the Psalmist. The most common phrase to serve this function is 'oratio mea', which occurs in six of the thirteen selected 'mediated' Psalms (6, 54, 85, 87, 101, and 142). Wyatt's choice of material emphasises this mediation even further, for Aretino's *I Sette Salmi* frames the seven Penitential Psalms within a narrative describing the penitent David as singing with his harp in the cave.

These poets' interest in poetic utterance, however, is not only expressed in their selections but also in their expansions and adaptations of this material. The paraphrases of Smith, Surrey, and Wyatt reflect a particular concern with recording the Psalmist's labour. For example, Smith's additions to his source for Psalm 142 emphasise the act of meditation:

> Yet do I remember the tyme that is past
> And muse upon thi woorke bothe first and last.
> Thus hither and thither thoughtdriven in a dolefull wise,
> In the worke of thi handes I do my self exercise. (18–19)

(Yet do I remember the tymes past. I muse vpon all thi workes, yee I exercise my self in the workes of thy hondes.) (Coverdale)

In this passage we can see Smith's significant reliance on Coverdale, and also his departures: the first, second, and fourth lines almost exactly

---

[72] I exclude from this definition any additional introductions external to the Psalmist's narrative, such as the introduction to Psalm 3: 'Psalmus. David, cum fugit a filio Absalom' (This is not translated in Coverdale's Bible, but the Great Bible translates it as 'A psalme of Dauid when he fledd from the face of Absalon hys sonne').

reproduce his source, but the third is an entirely new addition. While 'dolefull' suggests that these poets were using the Psalms to record their sad, persecuted state, its coupling with the adjective 'thoughtdriven' (which expands upon the words 'remember' and 'muse' in the previous two lines) reflects on the activity of the poet *in response to* his state of subjection. Similarly, the phrase 'hither and thither' suggests the Psalmist's persistence in his meditation on God's works. Smith is keen to emphasise mental activity (with God as its focus) as the correct response to persecution.

But Smith is not only concerned to draw attention to how the Psalmist thinks upon God's works, but also with how he leaves a record of them in the world – spoken in prayer and praise, and (implicitly) written down for future generations. Although the idea of public record is invoked throughout Smith's eleven paraphrases, the most thorough treatment can be found in Psalm 144, which might be considered an unusual choice for a prisoner to paraphrase because it is one of thanksgiving; Smith translates two such Psalms, but none of the other poets discussed here – Wyatt, Surrey, or the Dudleys – do. Rivkah Zim accounts for this peculiarity by arguing that they reflect an improvement in Smith's situation, as reported by William Cecil (who was imprisoned with Smith) in a letter.[73] However, given the emphasis on the role of the Psalmist as reporter in the original Psalm, and Smith's significant expansion of this theme, it seems equally possible that he selected the Psalm because it emphasises the power and influence of the Psalmist's words:

> For my part my tongue shall ay still walk;
> Of thi glorie, I will not lyn.
> I will of thi wurship, and praise talk,
> And of thi wounderfull workes begyn   (28)

(As for me I wil be talkinge of thy worshipe, thy glory, thy prayse and wonderous workes)   (Coverdale)

The content of this passage is similar to the excerpt from Smith's paraphrase of Psalm 142, given above; but whereas that passage spoke only of meditation, here the Psalmist asserts that he will not keep these thoughts to himself ('I will of thi wurship, and praise *talk*'). The source contains only one reference to speech. By contrast, Smith's version contains two, or three if we include the assertion that 'I will not lyn' (cease), which implies

---

[73] Zim, *English Metrical Psalms*, 101.

the act of speech mentioned in the previous line.[74] This addition and repetition stresses the Psalmist's desire to be God's orator. He also adds the line 'For my part my tongue shall ay still walk', which, given Smith's incarcerated position, is highly suggestive: it seems to assert that although his body might be restrained and unable to walk free, his tongue is not. Elsewhere in this Psalm he writes:

> Eche day will I give thankes to thee,
> To that me will I endeuer;
> To laude thi name my worke shalbe,
> For that I will studie for ever. (28)

(Euery daye wil I geue thankes vnto the, and prayse thi name for euer and euer.)   (Coverdale)

Comparison with Coverdale demonstrates that each alternate line of Smith's paraphrase is an expansion, which, as in the previous excerpt, emphasises the active role of the Psalmist in recording God's glory. However, whereas in the previous passage he merely reiterated the idea of speech that is in the original, here he introduces a new idea of labour, through the words 'endeuer' and 'studie'. Smith's emphasis on 'studie' is reminiscent of More's statement that 'my hole study shuld be, vppon the passion of Chryst and myne owne passage owt of thys worlde'. As demonstrated above, More's study was not only exerted through reading, meditation, and thought, but also through the active process of writing. When Smith writes of 'studie', we might reasonably assume then that he is thinking of the whole gamut of studious endeavours, for the eleven paraphrases really do seem to be a series of literary 'studies'.

Smith's editor, Bror Danielsson, calls the paraphrases 'schoolboy exercises', and argues that 'metrically Smith is very much at the learner stage', citing as evidence the fact that, very often, Smith seems to start with a firm metrical pattern in mind but usually fails to retain it to the end of the poem. Although this is true of many of Smith's paraphrases, Danielsson fails to acknowledge the extent of Smith's endeavour, noting merely that the Psalms are a 'manifestation of Smith's academic many-sidedness';[75] for him, Smith is redeemed by his other, more 'successful' works. However, even if the execution of Smith's metrical 'studies' is not impressive, his breadth is. He writes Psalms, which begin at least, in the following verse forms: iambic heptameter (Psalm 152), iambic tetrameter (30, 40, 85, and

---

[74] *OED*, lin, v., 1.   [75] Smith, *Literary and Linguistic Work*, ed. Danielsson, 9, 11.

142 in heroic couplets; 144 and 145 in an *abab* rhyme scheme), trochaic hexameter (102),[76] Poulter's measure (119), and variations on the tail-rhyme (70 and 54).[77] Therefore, although the language is sometimes laboured under the pressure of making it fit to metrical rules, and, conversely, the rules are relaxed to make room for his poetry, this is all evidence of the 'endeuers' which Smith undertook during his imprisonment, both spiritually and poetically.

That Smith's 'studies' were to be seen (i.e. not remain as private devotions) is demonstrated by the appearance of the holograph manuscript in which they survive. This manuscript is a presentation document executed in remarkably neat and well-spaced writing (in comparison to Smith's habitually cramped hand), with a title page laying out the circumstances of the poem's production – in 'the Tower of London ... 1549' – a situating tactic that is reminiscent of Seymour's addition of the phrase 'frome the toware' in his marginalia. While Cathy Shrank argues that this self-memorialisation is typical of Smith,[78] it is important to stress that he is also following closely in the footsteps of his forebears in this genre, namely Wyatt and Surrey, whose Psalm paraphrases had been printed some years prior to Smith's incarceration (although Surrey's were falsely attributed to Sternhold, along with his paraphrases of Ecclesiastes).[79] Wyatt and Surrey's likely influence on Smith's prison writings is supported by their interest in innovative verse forms; Smith's experimentations in verse may have lacked dexterity, but they share the spirit of Surrey and Wyatt's earlier forays into Psalm paraphrase.

The poetic form of Wyatt's Penitential Psalms, for instance, was a new import to England from Italy: its prologues were rendered in *ottava rima*, and the Psalms themselves in *terza rima*. As has frequently been noted, *terza rima* requires a significant technical mastery over form and metre: Greenblatt has argued that in adopting this new poetic technique, Wyatt finds a language sufficient to express the unifying theme in the paraphrase,

---

[76] Psalm 102 is particularly problematic. Although it begins with trochees, it quickly deteriorates into iambs, with some whole stanzas taking this inverted form. The first line of stanza 5, for example, is in iambic heptameter: 'So far as is the rising from the setting of the sone' (17).

[77] In both paraphrases the first two lines are in iambic dimeter, followed by a single line in iambic tetrameter, which three-line pattern is repeated to make a six-line stanza. Unlike the traditional form, the two pairs of lines (1 and 2, 4, and 5) are not rhymed couplets: in Psalm 70 they remain unrhymed; and in Psalm 54 the rhyme scheme is *abcdbc*.

[78] Cathy Shrank, *Writing the Nation in Reformation England, 1530–1580* (Oxford, 2006), 179.

[79] Thomas Wyatt, *Certayne psalmes chosen out of the psalter of Dauid* (London 1549); Henry Howard, Earl of Surrey, *Certayne chapters of the prouerbes of Salomon drawen into metre by Thomas sterneholde* (London, 1549 or 1550).

'which we may describe in religious terms as penitence or in psychological terms as a loving submission to domination'.[80] This submission is to meter, rhythm, verse form, but also to God and, implicitly, Henry. Similarly, Surrey's metrical Psalms were also rendered in an innovative verse form: an early example of unrhymed English hexameters, a metrical experiment that was rarely used before the 1580s.[81] Like Wyatt's *terza rima*, one could interpret this verse form as a structure that asserts mastery over language. Crucially, with its strong pauses at the end of the twelve-syllable lines, the form causes Surrey to write in this phrasing. In so doing, he subjects his readers to a particular discipline: he controls their very breathing. In subjecting their verse to this 'domination', then, one might also infer a poetic reflection of the control exerted over language by Henrician legislation – particularly the Treason Act of 1534. Wyatt's guardedness, his utter control both over what he writes and how he writes it, suggests his willingness to play by the rules imposed by the state and an understanding of how to participate in the public realm of discourse even from a position of incarceration.

Yet within these strictures there is room for the kind of creativity and plurality that interests de Certeau so much. Indeed, de Certeau equates the clandestine tactics undertaken by individuals caught in the nets of discipline with the rules of meter and rhyme: 'a body of constraints stimulating new discoveries, a set of rules within which improvisation plays'.[82] There is some evidence that Wyatt and Surrey were asserting this kind of autonomy. Wyatt, of course, is famous for his uneven meter, which, as I will discuss in Chapter 5, the Tudor editor Richard Tottel sought to regularise. In fact, it has been commented that Wyatt's versification in his paraphrase of the Psalms is 'more crabbed and inharmonious than, perhaps, in any other part of his works'.[83] However, de Certau's observation suggests that this crabbed quality may not simply be a mark of Wyatt poetic failings (as Tottel clearly believed). Rather, those moments where Wyatt's feet are out of step can be interpreted as demonstrations of his freedom from metrical structures. Deviations from metrical regularity provide the

---

[80] Greenblatt, *Renaissance Self-Fashioning*, 126.

[81] W. A. Sessions, *Henry Howard, The Poet Earl of Surrey: A Life* (Oxford, 1999), 54. For a rare fifteenth-century example of this verse form, see Daniel Wakelin, *Humanism, Reading, and English Literature, 1430–1530* (Oxford, 2007), 70–2, 77–80.

[82] De Certeau, *Practice of Everyday Life*, xxii. Compare this with Greg Walker's argument in the final chapter of *Writing under Tyranny*, 422–32.

[83] Patricia Thomson, *Thomas Wyatt: The Critical Heritage* (London, 1995), 60. She also comments on the distortions that Wyatt introduces to pronunciation through his rhyme schemes, 61.

opportunity to add emphasis, and to inject a sense of personal emotion
into the verse. As George T. Wright has observed, Wyatt's paraphrase of
the Penitential Psalms 'joins a steadier iambic meter to emphatic and
expressive phrasing'.[84]

> I lord ame stayd: I, sek withowt recure,
> Fele al my lyms, that have rebelld for fere,
> Shake in dispayre, onles thou me assure.
> Mye flesshe is troubled, my hart doth feare the speare;
> That dread of death, of death that ever lastes,
> Threateth of right and drawethe neare and neare.
> Moche more my sowle is trowbled by the blastes
> Of theise assawltes, that come as thick as hayle,
> Of worldlye vanytie, that temptacion castes
> Agaynst the weyke bulwarke of the fleshe frayle.
>   (Wyatt, *Collected* Poems, CVIII, lines 97–106)

Wright draws attention to how the use of repeated words and phrases,
internal rhymes, expressive trochees and spondees, an epic caesura, alliteration, assonance, and consonance divert the expected iambic pentameter.
He equates these techniques with the creation of intense feeling in the
verse (which may account in part for why Wyatt's verse is frequently read
as biographical). But what is perhaps more interesting is the effect of these
techniques on the meaning of the verse. Significantly, a stress is frequently
placed on the personal pronoun: '*I* lord ame *s*tayd: *I*, *s*ek withowt recure';
'*Mye flessh*e is *tr*oubled, *my* ha*r*t *d*oth *feare* the *speare*' (stresses italicised).[85]
Similarly, by opening lines two and three of the passage above with
trochees, Wyatt places unexpected emphasis on words indicating the
Psalmist's actions ('*Fele al* my *l*yms'; '*Shake* in di*spa*yre'). By acting outside
the constraints of meter, then, Wyatt draws attention to the speaker,
particularly to the Psalmist's response to his subjection. As a result, we
can see that these metrical experiments provide a subtle message, asserting
the autonomy of a figure brought low by sin and persecution. Most
crucially, it shows how poetry provides the means of assertion.

By extension, the declaration of poetic identity through the Psalms also
provides a crucial means of asserting autonomy. Surrey is perhaps the most
explicit user of this device. As Zim has obsersed, 'Surrey also intended his
Psalms to stand as literary memorials to himself: by sending them to
friends accompanied by explanatory epistles Surrey, in effect, set up these

---

[84] George T. Wright, *Shakespeare's Metrical Art* (Berkeley, CA, 1988), 36.
[85] See ibid.

poems as monuments to his own reputation as a poet.'[86] This forging of
poetic identity is also brought out in the translations themselves.
For example, in Psalm 87 Surrey expands his source material ('Ut quid,
Domine, repellis animam meam, abscondis faciem tuam a me?';
'Lorde, why puttest thou awaye my soule? Wherfore hydest thou thy face
fro me', Psalm 87.15) to stress the necessity of the Psalmist to record God's
glory for others:

> Wherefore dost thow forbeare, in the defence of thyne,
> To shewe such tokens of thy power, in sight of Adams lyne
> Whereby eche feble hart with fayth might so be fedd
> That in the mouthe of the elect thy mercyes might be spredd?
> The fleshe that fedeth wormes can not thy love declare,
> Nor suche sett forth thy faith as dwell in the land of dispaire.
> In blind endured herts light of thy lively name
> Can not appeare, as can not judge the brightnes of the same.
> Nor blasted may thy name be by the mouth of those
> Whome death hath shutt in silence, so they may not disclose.
> The livelye voice of them that in thy word delight
> Must be the trumppe that must resound the glorye of thy might.
> (cviii, lines 19–20)

While the original verse merely complains that God has cast off the
Psalmist's prayer, Surrey turns the complaint into a point of departure
for arguments as to why God should respond to the prayer. He argues
that God's intervention will not only act as a statement of his glory,
but will also inspire oral accounts and praise of his works ('in the
mouthe of the elect thy mercyes might be spredd'); conversely, death
stops up the mouth ('Nor blasted may thy name be by the mouth
of those / Whome death hath shutt in silence'). Having previously
lamented that his own 'death approacheth fast' (line 6), it is clear he is
saying that if he dies he cannot 'be the trumppe that must resound the
glorye of thy might'. Surrey thus expands the short verse into an
extended act of bargaining, where the Psalmist offers his 'voice' in
return for God's favour.

Similarly, Wyatt's concern, both with his ability as a poet to memorialise and with his ability to be memorialised *as* a poet, is evident in his
adaptation of Aretino's *I Sette Salmi*. In this work, Wyatt on two occasions
introduces passages containing the word 'record', for which there is no
equivalent in his source material:

[86] Zim, *English Metrical Psalms*, 97–8.

> Pausid his plaint, and laid adown his harp,
> Fayfull record of all his sorows sharp.[87]   (CVIII, lines 191–2)

> But that so close the Cave was and vnkowth
> That none but god was record of his payne:
> Elles had the wynd blowne in all Israells erys
> The wofull plaint and off theire kyng the terys.[88]   (CVIII, lines 415–18)

The extracts are from Prologues 2 and 4. The mediating frame narrative to the actual Psalms, as suggested above, provides an extended opportunity for the poet to reflect on the activities that brought the Psalms into being. The first extract uses 'record' in the sense of 'witness, evidence, proof', a usage which implies another of the word's meanings: 'the fact or condition of being preserved as knowledge, especially by being put into writing'.[89] Just as the pencil acts as a witness to an event and simultaneously produces the written document that preserves this information, equally David's harp acts both as a channel for his sorrows and as the embodiment of them. The second extract uses 'record' in the sense 'to summon or appeal to one to bear witness'.[90] The statement that God was the only one able to bear witness to the Psalmist's pain is knowingly disingenuous, for this written account memorialises the Psalmist's emotions and his actions for all to mark.

Just as the harp turns from a witness into a hard record, we see the very body of the Psalmist transformed from something active and working in time, into a monument, fixed for eternity:

> Ryght so David that semid in that place
> Marble ymage off singuler reuerence
> Carffd in the rokk with Iyes and handes on high,
> Made as by craft to plaine, to sobbe, to syghe.   (CVIII, lines 305–8)

In turning the Psalmist into a piece of art himself, the distinction between creator and created breaks down. David is *the creator* of the Psalms; he is a poet. But he is also simultaneously *the created*, fashioned by the hands of another artist – ambiguously both God and Wyatt – in order 'to plaine, to sobbe, to syghe'. This is an example of Renaissance self-fashioning at its best.

---

[87] The corresponding passage in Aretino reads, 'quasi consolato fa punto a le querele sue; e deposta alquanto la cetera' (Wyatt, *Collected Poems*, 364). Line 192 of Wyatt's paraphrase, then, is an addition to his source material.

[88] The corresponding passage reads, 'e certamente se i uenti ui fussero potuti entrar dentro gli haurieno inuolate le querele de gli occhi, de la lingua, e del petto, & portandole e le orecchie di tutto il popolo di Israel, ciascuno saria corso a confortare il suo Rè' (Wyatt, *Collected Poems*, 374). Again we can see that the line containing the word 'record' (line 416) is Wyatt's addition.

[89] *OED, record, n'* and *adj.*, 3.a, 2.   [90] *OED, call, v.*, 20.c.

Significantly, though, this self-reflexive memorialisation does not happen in a vacuum but rather 'in that place'; in David's cave. The description of this cave as prison-like makes it easy to see why critics have been so keen to identify the paraphrase as a prison work. While I do not wish to assert without documentary evidence that Wyatt composed these verses in the Tower, his adaptation of Aretino clearly provides his poetic followers with a model of how places can be appropriated and changed by the activities that occur within them – something particularly valuable to the later imprisoned Psalm paraphrasers. In the second prologue, Wyatt writes:

> Semyth horrible no more the dark Cave
> That erst did make his fault for to tremble,
> A place devout or refuge for to save
> The socourles it rather doth resemble:
> For who had sene so knele within the grave
> The chieff pastor of thebrews assemble
> Wold juge it made by terys of penitence
> A sacrid place worthi off reuerence.   (cviii, lines 201–8)

Centuries before Michel de Certeau wrote *The Practice of Everyday Life*, Wyatt explored how the activities practised in a place could change its significance. This passage shares with Fane and Rudstone's graffiti, with Seymour's marginalia, and More's 'hole study ... vppon the passion of Chryst' an understanding of how the practising of pious activities or devotions within a 'horrible' place could make it 'resemble ... A sacrid place worthi off reuerence'. This was not merely an experiential perception of the person occupying that space. As Wyatt's change to line 205 makes clear – which makes the onlooker a third party, and not David, as it had been in Aretino – these activities could also change the space in the perceptions of those outside the prison too.[91] As demonstrated in several of the examples above, prisoners successfully rewrote the Tower of London as a space of religious devotion. But, perhaps more importantly, they practised the prison as a site of literary production.

---

[91] 'e mirandolo il Pastor de i popoli Hebrei con gliocchi bagnati dal pianto lo faceua degno di reuerentia' (Wyatt, *Collected Poems*, 364).

CHAPTER THREE

Prison communities

John Foxe's 'Book of Martyrs' contains a woodcut entitled 'A picture describing the maner and place of them which were in bondes for the testimony of the truth, conferring together among themselves' (Figure 8). It depicts seven men sitting together in a prison cell, which the preceding text tells us is 'an outwarde house wythin Newgate'. Four of the men are identified in the woodcut, although their names are printed in reverse, as 'R. Smith' (Robert Smith), 'Tankerf' (George Tankerfield), 'Simpson' (John Simpson), and 'I. Newman' (John Newman). Some of the men hold open books and appear to be engaged in 'publyke readynge' and discussion; Smith is clearly leading the session with direct reference to the text in front of him.[1] We might reasonably describe this as a 'community'. The label applies in a number of separate but intersecting ways, reflecting the complexity and polyvalence of the word's meaning: these men constitute a body of people who live in the same place (defining them as a *prison* community); they are distinguished from society at large by shared circumstances of religion (defining them as *Protestant* community); and they practise their religious fellowship though shared activities and discussion.[2]

The different attributes of this prison community – of shared place, of common interest, and of communion or fellowship – highlight the two distinct approaches that scholars take to the examination of communities in general. The first is the qualitative approach, which aims to gather an understanding of the human behaviours and emotions that govern community membership. One such example is the work of the anthropologist Anthony Cohen, who has defined 'community' as a resource and a

---

[1] *TAMO* (1563), 1329.

[2] See *OED*, community, *n*, I. 2.b, I. 5.a, II.12 and 9. On the problems of defining the word 'community' – both in its modern sense and in its application to social organisation in early modrn England, see Alexandra Shepard and Phil Withington, 'Introduction', in their *Communities in Early Modern England* (Manchester, 2000), 1–16.

Figure 8 'A picture describing the maner and place of them which were in bondes for the testimony of the truth, conferring together among themselves', from John Foxe's *Actes and monuments of these latter and perillous dayes* (London, 1563), p. 1260.

repository of symbolic meaning that its members construct. He argues that community is built upon two related assumptions: that the members of a group have something in common with each other; and the thing held in common distinguishes them in a significant way from the members of other possible groups. As such, the symbolism of the community 'speaks simultaneously for the collectivity to those on the other side of its boundaries, and to each of its members who refract it through their own sense of belonging'.[3] The second approach to the examination of communities is quantitative. It seeks to measure the formal properties and structures of a given community through statistical, mathematical, or computational techniques. In recent years the idea of applying quantitative network analysis to the study of communties has gained increasing traction. This is partly due to the ubiquity of 'network' thinking in the modern world,

---

[3] Anthony Cohen, 'Of Symbols and Boundaries, or, Does Ertie's Greatcoat Hold the Key?', in his *Symbolising Boundaries: Identity and Diversity in British Cultures* (Manchester, 1986), 1–19 (17). See also, Anthony P. Cohen, *The Symbolic Construction of Community* (London, 1985).

but also, more importantly, to the publications by Albert-László Barabási, Réka Albert, Duncan Watts, and Steven Strogatz in the late 1990s, which showed that real-world networks (such as, for example, neural networks, transport networks, biological regulatory networks, and social networks) share similar organizational characteristics and can be analysed using the same mathematical tools and models.[4]

This chapter will take a predominantly qualitative approach to the study of prison communities by examining the way in which prisoners established common ground and distinguished themselves from other groups, both inside and outside the prison, through their writings. In other words, it will be concerned with the way in which texts created bonds on the one hand, and how they created boundaries on the other. At the same time, while I will not be taking a quantitative approach, I will be utilising some of the basic ideas from the field of network analysis. At a structural level, a community is, necessarily, a network: it is made up of a group of 'nodes', and every encounter creates a social 'link' or 'tie' between them.[5] What the network perspective on community allows us to see, which an emphasis on place does not, is that prison communities were not bound by prison walls. Prisoners sharing a cell were more likely to form links with prisoners with whom they shared a cell rather than with those residing in other prisons. However, one should not forget the likelihood that prisoners would seek to maintain preformed ties with those they knew before their incarcerations, and with prisoners with whom they might have previously shared a cell. Furthermore, it is through these spatially removed ties that broader networks of association can occur, and news and ideas can be more effectively spread. In an important study called 'The strength of weak ties', Mark Granovetter proposed that when it comes to spreading news or finding a job, our weak social ties (those people who are acquaintances rather than friends, or friends who live at a geographical remove) are more important than our closest friends.[6] Most of us have a densely knit structure of friends that we surround ourselves and socialise with most of the time. But we also have acquaintances who are not part of this group; and they are also probably part of another close-knit group of friends. It is through these long-range links that news can travel to remote locations, or take hold with great speed

---

[4] For an overview of the field, see Albert-László Barabási, *Linked* (New York, 2003).
[5] Ibid., 16.
[6] Mark Granovetter, 'The Strength of Weak Ties: A Network Theory Revisited', *Sociological Theory*, 1 (1983), 201–33.

within the public realm. This was certainly the case with sixteenth-century prison communities: while those sharing a particular locus were more likely to experience a form of fellowship, some of the most important alliances were those built across prison walls.

But how can you tell that individual nodes form a community if they are not in one place? And how can you show that people sharing a space share any more than that? The problem is that the concept of ties is an abstract one. However, this chapter will demonstrate that prison writings provide three key ways of conceptualising these abstract connective links. Firstly, prisoners describe their relationship with fellow prisoners in terms of communal activities, events, common property, and the sharing or exchange of goods. Links, then, are imagined as acts and objects. For example, in the preface to *A spyrytuall and moost precyouse pearle*, Edward Seymour describes himself and a number of other nameless prisoners reading this book (Miles Coverdale's translation of a text by Otto Wermüller) together as a group. Prisoners also entered into religious worship together. John Foxe reports that John Bradford, during his incarcerations in the King's Bench and the Counter,

> preached twise a day continually, onles sicknes hindered hym, where also the sacrament was often ministred, and through hys meanes the kepers (so well he was beloued) such accesse of good folkes was there dayly to hys lecture, and to the ministration, of the sacrament that commenly his chamber oft time was welny filled.[7]

According to Foxe's account, those Protestant prisoners that were imprisoned along with Bradford would meet together in services, with sermons delivered by Bradford, and partake in Communion. The veracity of this astonishing statement is supported by a letter that Bradford sent to Joyce Hales, in which he writes: 'I break vp this abbruptlie [i.e. his writing of the letter] because our common prayer tyme calleth me'.[8] Not only is it the shared nature of these activities that emphasises community, it is also the activities they undertake. Sharing Communion, in particular, has a great symbolic resonance, implicating each of the partakers together in the body of Christ. Moreover, the representation of these co-religionists as participating in corporate worship with relative ease provides a striking contrast to the covert measures employed by those Protestants worshipping outside prison.

---

[7] *TAMO* (1563), 1242.   [8] ECL, MS 260, fol. 81v. Cf. ECL, MS 260, fol. 37r (transcript).

The second way that prison writings allow us to conceptualise social ties is through their passage: some texts literally traced the links between prisoners when they were exchanged, carried, and transferred between individuals and groups. The most frequently exchanged writings, of course, were letters; but prisoners also sent one another treatises that they had written, with the aim either of instructing the recipient or else of obtaining their comments and collaboration. Other goods, such as books, money, food, and drink, sometimes accompanied correspondence between prisoners. For example, in the interrogation of Thomas More's servant, John à Wood, he told the council that More sent John Fisher apples, oranges, two images – one of St John and one of the Epiphany – and '2,000*l* in gold'.[9] The ease with which goods passed between prison cells was due to the idiosyncratic administration of sixteenth-century prisons, as was discussed above in Chapter 1. More specifically, the presence of free men and women within the prison, and the access given to visitors, provided a steady stream of potential carriers for these writings and other goods.

The anticipated passage of such writings can tell us much about how these prison communities functioned. Even though there is no way of knowing whether all the surviving prison epistles, for example, reached their intended recipients, the implied reader itself tells us about the extent of prisoners' social networks. For example, Nicholas Ridley's letter to Bradford shows how the author hoped that his letter would reach a number of recipients:

> This letter must bee common to you and M. Hoper, in whome and in hys prison fellowe good father Crome, I blesse god euen from the bottome of my harte: for I doubte not but they both do to our mayster Christe, true, acceptable and honorable seruice and profitable to his flocke, the one with hys penne, and the other wyth hys fatherlye example of patience and constancye and all manner of true godlynes. But what shall I nede to say to you, let this be common amonge your brethren: among whome (I dare say) it is with you as it is with vs, to whome all thinges here are common: meate, money, and whatsoeuer one of vs hath that can or may do an other good.[10]

Ridley appears confident that the letter he has written to Bradford will be read not only by those with whom Bradford was associated in the King's

<hr>

[9] TNA, SP 1/93, fols. 51r–60v. E. E. Reynolds, *The Field is Won: The Life and Death of St Thomas More* (London, 1974), 323, conjectures that the '2,000*l* in gold' must have 'been one of More's bits of fun', perhaps the sum in figures, or a drawing of money bags on a scrap of paper. It may also, I would suggest, be a pun on George Golde's name, the servant of the Lieutenant of the Tower, who is known to have carried letters and other objects between More and Fisher.
[10] LM, 61.

Bench prison ('let thys be common amonge your brethren'), but also another community in the Fleet prison, comprising John Hooper and Edward Crome. This letter thus implies what we already know from other evidence about Bradford: that he was an important hub within the social network of Marian prisoners. It has been observed in social network analysis that 'sprinkled among every walk of life … are a handful of people with an extraordinary knack of making friends and acquaintances'.[11] Bradford has the largest corpus of extant letters of all the Marian martyrs, addressed to a broad range of recipients, both in terms of number and geographical spread. As with all networks, linking to a hub such as Bradford immediately gives that individual access to a much wider range of people. The use of intermediaries to make contact with co-religionists also allows for the extension of social networks beyond their previous parameters. This is demonstrated by a letter sent by the Protestant John Hooper to Thomas Rose's congregation in the Counter, who had been arrested in the churchyard of St Mary-le-Bow during their time of prayer. Hooper had no previous association with these co-religionists, but had been alerted to their story and prompted to write to them by another (anonymous) prisoner – a 'connector' – in the Counter.[12]

The third method by which the existence of ties can be traced between particular nodes is through the transfer of information and ideas. In some cases communication between two nodes is not marked by an extant text, but this does not mean to say that there is therefore no evidence of a link between them. Whenever two people communicate, ideas are necessarily transferred, and this transferral can also act as a demonstration of community. One such example is the correspondence between Thomas More and John Fisher. We know about it now from the documents recording the interrogations of More, Fisher, their servants John à Wood and Richard Wilson, and George Golde, the servant of the lieutenant of the Tower.[13] However, prior to these interrogations, those involved believed that all evidence of this communication – which might have been perceived by the authorities as conspiracy against the crown – had been destroyed when they burnt the letters. What alerted the authorities to the fact that More and Fisher had been in contact with one another from their separate prison cells was Fisher's use of a particular metaphor in his examination on 3 June 1535 – the image of the double-edged sword.

[11] Barabási, *Linked*, 55. See also 55–64.   [12] See ECL, MS 261, fols. 12v–14r.
[13] See TNA SP 6/7 fols. 6r–9v (More and Fisher); BL, Cotton MSS Cleopatra E. vi, fols. 169r–171v (Fisher); and TNA SP 1/93, fols. 51r–60v (Richard Wilson, John à Wood and George Golde).

The double-edged sword has a long biblical history, and one that Fisher himself had utilised in two sermons as a metaphor for divine authority. But this use of the metaphor was new. It was used to signify the civil power wielded by the Act of Supremacy, and also the 'no-win situation' in which it had put him:[14] 'he sayed it semyd hyme that thes new Lawes were lyke a twoo edged sword: "For if one shuld saye," quoth he, "that they were good, they wold kyll his soule. And if he shuld saye they were nought, they wold kyll his bodye"'.[15]

What was significant is that this innovation was not Fisher's; when examined on the same day, 3 June 1535, More used exactly the same metaphor.[16] It appears from evidence given by their servants that Fisher had written to More asking what answer he had made regarding the oath. More had written an answer in reply mentioning this metaphor, and then soon after sent yet another letter, delivered by Golde, to the effect that he would not counsel Fisher to make the same answer lest the Council should think they were in collusion.[17] Whether Fisher consciously echoed More's words in his examination, or whether it was an accident, is unclear. Nevertheless, the common use of this metaphor demonstrates that one might destroy physical signs of interaction, and suppress certain facts, but that the spread of information through such networks cannot be undone.

Texts, then, are used both to construct networks and to disseminate the values and ideals that implicate their recipients within a community. This chapter will explore three examples of how prison writings were employed to create communities, both in a structural sense, in terms of forming ties, and in an ideological sense, through the transmission of ideas about community. This includes poetic collaboration, demonstrated by the verse epistles of Margaret Douglas and Thomas Howard; the projection of a unified, and evidently idealised, image of a prison community to a general readership, in John Harington's translation of Cicero's *De amicitia*;

---

[14] For a fuller discussion of this symbolism, see Cecilia A. Hatt, 'The Two-edged Sword as Image of Civil Power for Fisher and More', *Moreana*, 175 (2008), 67–86.

[15] Nicholas Harpsfield, *The Life and Death of Sr Thomas Moore, Knight*, ed. E. V. Hitchcock, EETS OS 186 (London, 1932), appendix I: the Rastell Fragments, 232.

[16] When asked whether the King was, as by statute decreed, head of the Church [in England] or not, he answered that 'the [statute made in the Parliament] whereby the Kynges Highnes was made supreme hedd as ys aforsayd [was like unto a sword] with too edges, for yf he seyd that the same lawe werre [not] good then [yt] was daungerous to the soule. And yf he seyd contrary to the seyd estatute [then] yt was deth to the body; wherfor he wold make therto none other aunswer by ca[use] {. . .} old not {. . ..} f {. . .} of the shortyng of his lif' (TNA, SP 2/R, fol. 20r).

[17] See the account of More's trial in *LP*, vol. VIII, 974.

and the provision of religious leadership for an extensive dissident community, examined through the various prison works of Nicholas Ridley.

Margaret Douglas and Thomas Howard's epistolary verse

On 8 July 1536 Margaret Douglas and Thomas Howard were arrested for questioning concerning their contract of marriage. Howard was subsequently sent to the Tower and attainted – condemned by statute without trial – for having traitorously aspired to marry the lady Margaret Douglas, Henry VIII's niece and (with Mary and Elizabeth newly declared bastards by a parliamentary bill) a vital pawn in the English succession.[18] Although not sentenced to death like her lover, Margaret Douglas, too, was initially imprisoned in the Tower, albeit separately from Howard.[19] But after she fell ill with a recurring fever in the autumn, she was removed to Syon Abbey, where she was held under house arrest.[20] Both remained incarcerated for over fifteen months, until Howard's death. Charles Wriothesley reports in his *Chronicle* that: 'This yeare, on All Hallowe Even, the Lord Thomas Howarde ... died in prison in the Tower of London ... Also the Ladie Margarett Duglas, that had lyen in prison in the Tower of London for love betwene him and her, was pardoned by the King and sett agayne at her libertie; howbeit, she tooke his death very heavilie'.[21]

A letter from Douglas to Cromwell, sent on 12 August 1536, seems to suggest that from early on in her incarceration she had resolved to give up her relationship with Howard:

[18] There was clearly a need for haste in the passing of the bill of attainder. The bill was introduced in the Lords on the morning of 18 July, and before the noon recess it had been read thrice, approved, sent to the lower house, and returned with the Commons' approval. See *The Statutes of the Realm ... From Original Records ... (1101–1713)*, ed. A. Luders et al. (London, 1810–1828), vol. III, 680, and *Journals of the House of Lords, Beginning Anno Primo Henrici Octavi* (London, 1808), vol. I (1509–1577), 101. For discussion of how this bill created a new form of treason, see David M. Head, '"Beyng ledde and seduced by the devyll": The Attainder of Lord Thomas Howard and the Tudor Law of Treason', *Sixteenth Century Journal*, 13:4 (1982), 3–16.

[19] Eustace Chapuys, in a letter to Emperor Charles V dated 22 July 1536, reported that the death sentence would not be carried out on Douglas because the marriage had not been consummated, and she had since been pardoned. See *Calendar of Letters, Despatches, and State Papers, Relating to the Negotiations between England and Spain, 1485–[1558]*, ed. Royal Tyler et al. (London, 1862–1964), vol. v.ii, 214.

[20] The King's payments of 1538, BL, Arundel MS 97, fol. 6v, records a payment of 14*l* 4*d* to Margaret for medicines used during and after her stay in the Tower; and TNA SP 1/110, fol. 18r, a letter from Agnes, prioress of Sion, to Cromwell, dated 6 November 1536, acknowledges orders to lodge Margaret at the abbey.

[21] Charles Wriothesley, *A Chronicle of England during the Reigns of the Tudors, from* A.D. 1485 to 1559 *(London, 1875–7), vol.* I, 70. See also *The Lisle Letters*, ed. M. St Clare Byrne (Chicago, 1981), vol. IV, 902.

> And my lord wher as yt ys informyd you that I do charge the house with a
> greter nomber then ys convenyent I asuer you I haue but ij mo then I had in
> the court whych in ded wer my lord Thomas sarvandes and the cavse
> that I tok them was ffor the poverty that I saw them in and ffor no cavse
> else / but seyng my lord that yt ys your plesur that I shall kepe non that ded
> be long vnto my lord Thomas I wyll put them ffro me / And I beseche
> you not to thynk that eny fancy doth remayn in me towchyng hym but
> that all my study and car ys how to plese the kinges grace and to contynv in
> hys faver.[22]

A number of facts, however, suggest that she made this protestation merely
because it was politically expedient, and that, in fact, her relationship with
Howard continued during their incarceration. Firstly, taking two of
Howard's servants as part of her retinue into prison suggests that at this
time she had still intended to marry Howard, although she attempted to
dispel this interpretation with the explanation 'I tok them for . . . the poverty
that I saw them in and *ffor no cavse else*' (my emphasis). Secondly, the fact
that after this letter was penned Douglas spent a further fourteen months in
prison implies that either her words were not trusted, or else she was still
perceived as a threat to the succession. Thirdly, and most importantly for
this discussion, during the fifteen-month period of their incarcerations,
Howard and Douglas sent one another a series of original lyrics, which
reflect on the pain of being separated from one's lover. Sending such letters
necessarily maintained the pre-existing ties between these two individuals.

Seven of the poems survive in the British Library as Additional MS
17492, which is known as the Devonshire manuscript (hereafter D).[23] One
of these was penned by a female author (fol. 29r); but from Howard's
reference to Douglas's 'gentyll letters' (plural) we can be fairly certain that
there were a number of other epistolary verses produced by her pen, now
lost. An eighth poem – a cento, composed of lines from *Troilus and
Criseyde* – may also have been written by one of the lovers as it occurs
directly after these seven poems, and appears to have been copied into
D with the previous seven by the same hand (fols. 26r–30r).[24] These
poems were written in answer to one another, and demonstrate a

---

[22] BL, Cotton MSS Vespasian, F. xiii, fol. 241r.
[23] Folio references will be given in the main body of the text.
[24] This Chaucerian poem is discussed at length by Seth Lerer in his *Courtly Letters in the Age of Henry
VIII* (Cambridge, 1997), 144, 148–57. However, Paul Remley has suggested that this cento could
equally have been composed by Mary Shelton, who showed her fondness for the reorganization of
extracts from medieval texts later in the volume. See Paul G. Remley, 'Mary Shelton and her Tudor
Literary Milieu', in *Rethinking the Henrician Era*, ed. Peter C. Herman (Urbana, IL, 1994), 40–77
(52–3, n. 58).

collaborative development of ideas about community and writing, which seems to disprove Douglas'a claim not to love Howard.

The study of Douglas and Howard's poems has been dominated, by and large, by their manuscript context: how this uniquely haphazard coterie manuscript was compiled; the blocks in which the poems were entered; who entered them; and what this may tell us about the social group with whom D was associated.[25] This social group has been identified as a coterie centred on the Howard family – specifically the figures of Mary Shelton, Mary Fitzroy (née Howard), and the aforementioned lovers, Douglas and Howard – and including Thomas Wyatt (whose poetry comprises almost two-thirds of the total compositions), Richard Hatfield, Anthony Lee, John Harington, Harry Stuart, Lord Darnley (son of Margaret Douglas and her later husband Matthew Stewart, the Earl of Lennox), Thomas Clere, and Henry Fitzroy.[26] Scholarly emphasis on the broad literary community associated with D has essentially subsumed the relationship between Howard and Douglas. For example, Julia Boffey has argued that the existence of the collection dictated how those individuals associated with the group processed and recorded their experiences and relationships: 'once this kind of tone had been established in such a collective compilation . . . it was surely likely to be maintained, even by those who had no pressing reason to send love epistles in such tantalizing semi-secret circumstances'.[27] There is, undoubtedly, some truth in this. It is by no means certain, however, that Douglas and Howard imagined the miscellany as the defining context for their poems at the time at which they were first written, although they may have taken on this significance once transcribed into D. Rather, the language and subject matter of the lyrics suggests that, through writing to one another, Douglas and Howard were a discrete community within the D coterie, in which their respective writing strategies were shaped in response to

---

[25] D preserves about 185 items of verse (although many are fragments, medieval extracts, or the like), as well as other ephemeral jottings. These are entered by a number of different hands: at least a dozen and, according to some estimates, more than twenty contributors have added entries in a variety of hands ranging from fine examples of ornamental Tudor secretarial script to unpractised scribbles. On the debate over the identity of the contributors, see: Raymond Southall, 'The Devonshire Manuscript Collection of Early Tudor Poetry, 1532–41', *Review of English Studies*, 15 (1964), 142–50; Remley, 'Shelton', 47, 49–50, 53–4; and Helen Baron, 'Mary (Howard) Fitzroy's Hand in the Devonshire Manuscript', *Review of English Studies*, 179 (1994), 318–35.

[26] For a list of names copied into the manuscript, see Baron, 'Mary (Howard)', table 2.

[27] Julia Boffey, *Manuscripts of English Courtly Love Lyrics in the Later Middle Ages* (Cambridge, 1985), 8–9.

one another, and ideas of what it means to be in this kind of a relationship were constructed collaboratively.

It is not clear whether the order in which the poems appear in D represents the sequence in which Douglas and Howard composed them. Nevertheless, as they stand, the poems chart a process of development. The first five poems, by Howard, seem to represent the first stage of the lovers' literary activity. In each of these poems Howard is intent on representing himself and Douglas as being unified, in spite of the many interventions the authorities can put in their way. For example, in the first poem:

> Alas that euer pryson stronge
> sholde such too louers seperate
> yet thowgh ower bodys suffereth wronge
> ower hartes shalbe off one estate.   (fol. 26r)

This is a perfect image of the community as network: Howard admits that he and his love may be spatially removed, yet, he asserts, their hearts are united. Thus we see that the lament of the subjected prisoner, expressed in the first two lines, is reversed by the statement of defiance in the third and fourth. In each of the five poems, expressions of unity seem synonymous with defiance. The fourth poem reads:

> I thynke the wold that I shold swere
> your company for to forsake
> but ons ther ys no worldly fere
> shal cawse me such an othe to make.   (fol. 27v)

These lines clearly refer to the authorities' attempts to coerce Howard to give Douglas up. He presents the situation as a conundrum: that the loyal lover must necessarily also be the disobedient subject. What is most notable about Howard's assertions of unity in these poems is that, although primarily speaking of his own immovable devotion, he also often presumes to make a statement of unity on behalf of both lovers: 'Ower hartes shalbe off one estate'. While this strategy is rhetorically effective, it has no greater authority than any other lyric poem of the period; it is still written by a lonely 'I'. But when we reach poems six and seven in the series, this literary trend changes. The sixth poem is Douglas's contribution to the surviving body of poems, and it represents a response to those that have gone before – both in an emotional and a literary sense. Her addition acts to transform the poems that precede it from a collection of lyrics written from a single perspective into an epistolary and intrinsically collaborative project.

Douglas interacts with the poems that preceded hers by borrowing and adapting their language. We can observe this approach from the very beginning of her poem, which opens:

> I may well say with joyfull harte
> as neuer woman myght say beforn
> that I haue takyn to my part
> the faythfullyst louer that ever was born.   (fol. 28v)

Douglas's assertion that she has a 'joyfull harte', because of the faithfulness of her lover, sounds like a response to the opening lines from a poem by Howard: 'What thyng shold cawse me to be sad / as long ye reyoyce wyth hart' (fol. 27r). By opening her poem in answer to his rhetorical question, Douglas transforms a mode of writing that, traditionally, anticipates no response into the opening of a dialogue. In so doing, Douglas confirms that she had taken receipt of Howard's verses, reassuring him that their writings might maintain the relationship between them despite their detainment in separate cells. Her words affirm that the comfort he has given himself – reasoning, 'What thing shold cawse me to be sad / as long ye reyoyce with hart' – is not based on a false presumption. Douglas asserts that she *does* have a joyful heart, and thus that Howard has no cause for sadness. Consequently, her response challenges the expectation that the love lyric is characterised by the speaker's isolation. The very existence of a response alters the function of the preceding poems as a body of works: they are no longer simply love lyrics sent out into the ether, but, in finding their intended audience, they become epistolary verses.[28]

In western literature it has become an axiom that the writer, and especially the writer of love lyrics, is an essentially solitary figure: the subject matter of love lyrics is almost always the speaker's unrequited love, whether that be his physical separation from his lover, or unreciprocated feelings.[29] The preconception that the writer of the love lyric is a solitary figure, which Douglas undermines, is of course a myth. In particular, the stockpile of tropes recycled by poets – love as isolation, love as suffering, love as imprisonment[30] – demonstrates just how communal the language of love was. Nevertheless, the posture of isolation is maintained by the poets, who import these ideas because it is inherent in the tropes themselves. The difference with the Douglas–Howard poems is that Douglas

---

[28] On the medieval tradition of epistolary verse, see A. C. Spearing, *Textual Subjectivity: The Encoding of Subjectivity in Medieval Narratives and Lyrics* (Oxford, 2005), 211–47.

[29] Ibid., 182.

[30] See A.C. Spearing, *Medieval to Renaissance in English Poetry* (Cambridge, 1985), 288.

is consciously borrowing from Howard, and, in so doing, creating a community of personal tropes that unite their works. Furthermore, by replying to and reciprocating Howard's sentiments, Douglas implicitly denies this mental isolation. Her reply ('I haue takyn to my part / The faythfullyst louer that euer was born', fol. 28v) asserts that they are unified in their isolation, and thus isolation becomes something communal and shared.

In another passage from Douglas's poem, she borrows these lines from Howard: 'My loue truly shall not decay / for thretnyng nor for punyshment' (fol. 27r). In her hands they become the following:

> Great paynes he suffereth for my sake
> contynually both nyght and day
> for all the paynes that he doth take
> from me hys loue wyll not decay.
>
> Wyth thretnynges great he hath ben payd
> off payne and yke off punyshment
> yet all fere asyde he hath layed
> to loue me best was hys yntent.   (fol. 28v)

It is in the fourth, fifth, and sixth lines that the phraseology of Howard's poem reappears most explicitly, and notably not just in rhyming words (which obviously invite similar sentiments). However, the same excerpt from his poem is actually the basis for the whole eight lines given here; the other five lines merely expand on the sense. It is also important to note that in the process of borrowing, Douglas does not follow Howard's use of the second person to talk about his lover, but rather employs the third person, which implies a reader other than (or, in addition to) Howard, which in turn implies that their unity is posed, mannered, self-fashioned. The effect of this is to transform Howard's two-line assertion of loyalty into an eight-line boast concerning her lover's devotion to her. The nature of the boast in itself is interesting. Normally boasts are self-serving and prideful modes of expression. However, Douglas's boast is not about her own qualities but her lover's; in detailing them she expresses their shared will. This shared will implicitly excludes others. In the line 'Wyth thretnynges great he hath ben payd' a third person, the one who has 'payd' Howard with threats, is excluded by the use of a passive construction; similarly, her boast 'to loue me best was hys yntent' implies the courtly world of potential loves that he has rejected in her favour. These two subtle acts of delimitation – denying the power of enemies or other potential lovers to come between them – coupled with the idea of a third party reading this poem suggest that Douglas's assertion of unity is dependent upon the exclusion and defiance of those who might wish to come between her and Howard.

The poem that follows Douglas's in D appears to respond to the ideas of emotional and literary exchange that she had introduced. Howard writes:

> To yowr gentyll letters an answere to resyte
> both I and my penne there to wyll aply
> and thowgh that I can not your goodnes aquyte
> in ryme and myter elegantly
> yet do I meane as faythfully
> As euer dyd louer for hys part
> I take god to record which knowyth my hart.   (fol. 29r)

These lines suggest that, in his textual relationship with Douglas, Howard began to see emotional and literary exchange as intrinsically linked. Here he articulates his awareness that the expression of love has become dependent upon skill in versifying. In particular, he expresses a concern that his 'ryme and myter' are too poor to repay Douglas's 'goodness' or too inadequate to show what is in his 'hart', so he asks God to 'record' his inner feelings. This use of the modesty topos is conventional in fifteenth- and sixteenth-century love lyrics.[31] Even if he may in fact be right to apologise for his verses (for they are not the finest examples of Tudor lyric), such conventionality is a sure sign that the poet's concern is more than the mere conveyance of emotion. Howard's use of the word 'aquyte' – a word usually used in its legal sense at this time, meaning to pay a debt or discharge a liability – implies that he wishes not only to repay goodness with goodness, but also skill with skill.[32] This reciprocity suggests a mutual encouragement, providing each other with both emotional support and artistic motivation, spurring one another on to further literary activity.

However, perhaps prompted by Douglas writing about him in the third person, and despite not doing so himself,[33] Howard also imagines their literary activity as eventually constituting a corpus of writings to be read by other people. Howard subtly addresses the notion of a subsequent readership through his use of the verb 'record': 'I take god *to record* which knowyth my hart' (my emphasis).[34] This verb means both to bear witness

---

[31] See, for example, *Secular Lyrics of the XIVth and XVth Centuries*, ed. Rossel Hope Robbins (Oxford, 1952), nos. 130, 163, 177, 188, 192, 196, 207.

[32] *OED, acquit, v.*, I. 1.

[33] In only one of the six poems in this series attributed to Howard does he refer to his lover in the third person. See fol. 28r lines 10 and 14.

[34] See also his use of the word 'report' in the third poem, fol. 27r.

in an oral act of record and to relate in a written account,[35] which implies
that Howard wished these poems to serve as more than ephemeral epistles.
As we saw in Chapter 2, the word 'record' also appears a number of times
in Wyatt's paraphrase of the Penitential Psalm, most commonly in those
cases where Wyatt wished, self-reflexively, to draw attention to the psalmist in the process of composition. Howard's poem bears a similar, although
less sophisticated, self-reflexivity. Twice in this sixth lyric in D, he includes
self-identifying passages that would not have been required by Douglas:
'yowr louyng husband', and 'adwe my none swete wyfe / from T.H.'
Although Howard also uses the phrase 'my none swete wyfe' in another
of the poems (fol. 27v), the repeated use of identifiers in this context makes
it feel somewhat overstated. We might assume, then, that Howard
included these passages so that the original context of the poem's composition might be identified by readers subsequent to Douglas, possibly by the
coterie members who copied this collection of verse into D.

   After all, it is unlikely that either Douglas or Howard added the poems
to the coterie manuscript. It has been claimed that the handwriting in
which the prison poems are copied could be Howard's, which would mean
that at some stage he had D in the Tower with him.[36] However, it is more
commonly argued that the hand is that of Mary Shelton, who, as Remley
has pointed out, would have been in a good position to facilitate the secret
correspondence of Douglas and Howard during their confinement because
her father was in command of one segment of the palace guards, and her
brother was groom porter of the Tower of London.[37] Yet, the manuscript
context in which the poems became embedded need not compromise their
status as a self-contained corpus of writings. It is true that one of the most
common dynamics of coterie literary production was to privilege the
coterie relationship over the authorial claim. As Arthur Marotti has demonstrated, within coterie culture the notion of authorship was fluid:
authorial ascriptions were rare, and, in the system of manuscript transmission, it was normal for lyrics to elicit revisions, corrections, supplements,
and answers, for they were part of an ongoing social discourse.[38] The
Chaucerian cento added to Douglas and Howard's prison poems could
be an example of this ongoing discourse, if it was authored by Shelton.

---

[35] *OED, verb, v.'*, III. 8.a, 9.a.   [36] Baron, 'Mary (Howard)', 326–7.
[37] Remley, 'Shelton', 54. The hand that copied the Tower works into the volume is clearly the same as
    that which copied the various medieval extracts into D at fols. 89v–92r, which Remley, persuasively,
    identifies as the work of Shelton. See also Raymond Southall, *The Courtly Maker: An Essay on the
    Poetry of Wyatt and his Contemporaries* (Oxford, 1964), 172–3.
[38] Arthur F. Marotti, *Manuscript, Print, and the English Renaissance Lyric* (Ithaca, NY, 1995), 2, 136.

However, there are two pieces of evidence to suggest that whoever copied these verses into the miscellany expected the coterie readership to comprehend the exclusivity of the symbolic community constructed in the prison poems, as well as this self-contained corpus that they create.

The first point to consider is the make-up of the manuscript and how the prison poems fit into the volume. The poems form a self-contained block, copied into the manuscript by a single hand, and preceded by a whole blank page.[39] This may be due to the fact that the body of poems was entered randomly, and the gaps on either side of it only partially filled by subsequent copyists; or it could be that the preceding poems, a page of fragments and two Wyatt poems, had already been entered and that the copyist intentionally left the page unoccupied. Either way, the effect is to emphasise the collection's separation from the poems before it, and, by contrast, its internal coherence. Another feature that functions to differentiate this block of poems from others in the manuscript is the identifying marks therein. The first are those embedded by Howard in the sixth of his poems, as discussed above: 'adwe my none swete wyfe / from T.H.' The second is the name penned hastily at the bottom of folio 26v, under the poem beginning 'Wyth sorowful syghes and woundes smart', which appears to read 'margt'.[40] The hand that added this mark demonstrates clear similarities to Shelton's, but, if she is the copyist of the body of poems, this name was probably added subsequently, because it is written in a slightly darker ink and in a much less legible script. The name's addition to this page is slightly curious because the poem is obviously not by Margaret ('to see her dayly whom I loue best / yn great and untollerable sorows strong'), although one might feasibly argue that the annotator was identifying the subject of the poem rather than its author. What this addition does tell us, however, is that the coterie readership recognised

[39] Although, as one might expect, the earliest entries in the volume seem to have been made in its opening pages by Hand 1 (as Baron, designates the hand on fols. 2r–3r and 4r–6r in 'Mary (Howard) table 2), the leaves of D were not used sequentially. Rather several 'collections' of poems were entered by a number of scribes in individual blocks, and separated by blank leaves; neither are these sections manifestly entered in order. The Douglas–Howard corpus constitutes one such block. Although scholars vary over the identification of the hand that entered the seven poems and the Chaucerian cento (occupying fols. 26r–30r), it is unquestionably different from the hands that entered the poems preceding it on fols. 22v, and 23r–25r (Baron, 'Hand 3'), and those following it on fols. 30v–39v (Baron, 'Hand 4').

[40] A definite transcription for this name is difficult due to its careless execution. It is made up of six characters, and the first two letters are clearly an *M* and an *a*; the letter that follows is almost certainly an *r*, and the final letter a *t*. It is the fourth and fifth letters that present a problem. Despite their ambiguity however, I do not find Remley's argument that it reads 'Ma[ry]Sh – lt – ' convincing (Remley, 'Shelton', 54).

the members of the particular and closed community behind these poems, and felt it important to record the name of the lady (for T.H. was already identified) for posterity. Within the norms of coterie manuscript production, these ascriptions are in fact quite unusual. As Marcy L. North has noted, only two-dozen of the poems' authors are actually identified in D; the majority (more than one hundred and fifty) are left unattributed, which illustrates that the trend in this miscellany – as in the majority of coterie manuscripts – is towards anonymity.[41] The fact that the Douglas–Howard poems buck this trend makes them stand out as an atypical subgroup of poems.

That this corpus retains its integrity within the larger body of poems in D is testament to the symbolic power of the community that Douglas and Howard constructed. As Cohen writes, the 'symbolism of community ... speaks simultaneously for the collectivity to those on the other side of its boundaries, and to each of its members who refract it through their own sense of belonging'.[42] The symbolic power of Douglas and Howard's discrete community is clearly apparent to a readership. While the integrity of this show of unity may have been problematised by sources external to D (most notably in Douglas's letter to Cromwell, discussed above), as a body of works they deliver a message of defiant resistance to external powers. The poems almost certainly did not come to the attentions of those against whom they complained ('Alas that men be so ungent / to order me so creuelly', fol. 27v), but they were, nevertheless, read by the coterie readership of D, which comprised prominent figures in Henry's court. In many ways Howard and Douglas were very much at the centre of the literary community surrounding the creation and reception of this miscellany. However, the reader who added the name 'margt' to folio 26v demonstrates the reverence of the coterie readers for the exclusive nature of the community represented in these verses.

John Harington's *Booke of freendeship*

The respect that appears to have been accorded to the prison poems of Douglas and Howard by the coterie surrounding D is not entirely unique, however. Prison poetry in general seems to have had a certain status within sixteenth-century verse miscellanies that made it more likely to be

---

[41] Marcy L. North, *The Anonymous Renaissance* (Chicago, IL, 2003), 161; Marotti, *Manuscript, Print, and the English Renaissance Lyric*, 2–3.
[42] Cohen, 'Symbols and Boundaries', 17.

attributed to an author than poems of more ordinary courtly origins – especially when the compiler had a clear link with the prison poet. This is most apparent in the Arundel Harington manuscript (hereafter AH), a verse miscellany compiled initially by John Harington in the early Elizabethan period, and continued by his son Sir John. AH probably contains the greatest number of poems that have been identified by scholars as prison writings of any sixteenth-century coterie manuscript. A number of these poems are believed to have come into Harington's hands during his two incarcerations, from 18 January 1549 until the spring of 1550 (when he was imprisoned in the Tower and questioned about his master, Thomas Seymour's, relationship with the young Princess Elizabeth, and about his own part in negotiations to marry Edward VI to Lady Jane Grey), and from January 1554 until January 1555 (when he was held on account of his supposed relation to Wyatt's rebellion, during which he spent the first five months waiting on Princess Elizabeth in the Tower, and the remainder in the Fleet).[43]

Prison writings in the manuscript dating from the reigns of Henry VIII, Edward IV, and Mary I include six poems believed to have been written by Harington senior during his two imprisonments;[44] Henry Howard, the Earl of Surrey's 'London hast thow accused me', and his paraphrases of the Psalms and Ecclesiastes;[45] Thomas Wyatt's paraphrase of the Penitential Psalms;[46] John and Robert Dudley's paraphrases of Psalms 54 and 93;[47] Thomas Seymour's 'fforgeatting god / to Love a Kyng';[48] and Thomas Smith's versification of the Ten Commandments.[49] In addition there is a poem with an acrostic reading 'EDWARD SEYMOUr' (the 'r' is not an initial letter on the final line but is supplied by the last letter of the poem), which he may have composed by the Duke Somerset during one of his two incarcerations, and a verse paraphrase of Petrarch's *Trionfo Dell' Eternita* apparently by Princess Elizabeth, which Ruth Hughey has suggested could date from her time in the Tower when Harington waited

---

[43] See *Acts of the Privy Council of England, 1542–1631*, ed. J. R. Dasent, E. G. Atkinson, J. V. Lyle, R. F. Monger, and P. A. Penfold (London, 1890–1964), vol. II, 239; *The chronicle of Queen Jane: and of two years of Queen Mary, and especially of the rebellion of Sir Thomas Wyat; Written by a resident in the Tower of London*, ed. John Gough Nichols (London, 1850), 53. See also Ruth Hughey, *John Harington of Stepney: Tudor Gentleman; His Life and Works* (Columbus, OH, 1971), 30.

[44] *The Arundel Harington Manuscript of Tudor Poetry*, ed. Ruth Hughey (Columbus, OH, 1960), vol. I, nos. 2, 16, 17, 19, 20, and appendix I, no. III. Appendix I constitutes the poems that occupied folios 1r–15r prior to their loss. It is made from G. F. Nott's transcription of the manuscript made in the early nineteenth century, now BL, Additional MS 28635, fols. 2r–v.

[45] Hughey, *Arundel Harington*, nos. 75, 79–90.   [46] Ibid., nos. 154–67.

[47] Ibid., nos. 289–90.   [48] Ibid., no. 291.   [49] Ibid., no. 323.

on her.[50] As in D, the trend in this miscellany is towards anonymity: out of 324 items only 46 have scribal or near contemporary ascriptions; and, of these only 25 were added to poems copied by the scribes associated with John Harington senior (i.e. dating from the period of this study).[51] This anonymity extends to the majority of the prison poems too, but there is an important exception. Ascriptions are provided for four of the prison poems to have been written by individuals whose period in the Tower was coterminous with Harington's own. The Dudleys' paraphrases of Psalms 54 and 93, by John and Robert Dudley, bear the scribal ascriptions 'I. W' (extended by a later hand to read 'Io. Warwick', in reference to John's title, Earl of Warwick), and 'Ro. Dudley'; Thomas Seymour's bears the initials 'T. S.' (later amended to 'T. Seymour'); and Thomas Smith's poem is ascribed to 'Tho. Smithe'.[52] Emphasising this exception to the larger trends in the manuscript, the first three of these poems appear consecutively on folios 209r–210r in the hand of scribe A, followed by the acrostic poem featuring Edward Seymour's name (a possible self-ascription) on folio 210v. All of this seems to support Marcy North's suggestion, that Harington used his few ascriptions intentionally to memorialise the members of his prison coteries.[53]

However, while AH does memorialise some of Harington's fellow prisoners, the idea that through this collection we can gain a sense of the coteries or communities of which Harington was a part in prison is problematic. The romantic assumption made by a number of critics (mostly reliant on Hughey's scholarship) that Harington formed a literary hub to which these disparate nodes connected, and, through him, circulated their poetry, is based on little hard evidence.[54] Firstly, there are no literary acts of collaboration like those demonstrated by Douglas and

---

[50] Ibid., nos. 293 and 320 respectively; Hughey, *Harington of Stepney*, 48. For a discussion of the validity of the ascription to Elizabeth, see *Elizabeth I: Translations, 1544–1589*, ed. Janel Mueller and Joshua Scodel (Chicago, IL, 2009), appendix 1, 459–68.

[51] The remaining twenty-one are attached to poems copied into AH by his son Sir John and his associates.

[52] Elizabeth's poem also bears an ascription, but this is in a subsequent hand.

[53] See North, *Anonymous Renaissance*, 174.

[54] Hughey has been particularly convinced that the coexistence of these figures within the Tower acted as motivation for literary exchange, which in turn formed the basis of AH; she has even gone so far as to suggest that the fact that Harington was in the Tower during the same period as both the Duke of Norfolk (Surrey's father) and Thomas Wyatt the younger might tell us how the Harington family originally came into possession of Egerton MS 2711 and copies of Surrey's poems (for, aside from some occasional transcripts, the manuscript versions of Surrey's poems are to be had only in collections kept by the Haringtons: AH, and BL Additional MS 36529). See Hughey, *Harington of Stepney*, 16–21, Hughey, *Arundel Harington*, vol. 1, 44–6.

Howard except for the Dudley brothers' two Psalms paraphrases (which share both thematic unity in the laments of persecution, prayers for God's revenge, and poetic unity of form, executed as they are in Poulter's measure, and with alliteration). Secondly, aside from the fact we know Harington continued to wait on Seymour and Elizabeth during his two imprisonments, the details of who shared cells is patchy at best. Thirdly, we do not know how much movement was allowed between cells at this time, or whether Harington actively sought to communicate with figures such as Smith, the Dudleys, and Edward Seymour. If Smith and Edward Seymour were not in the same cell as Harington, then it is difficult to believe that they would have *sought* to exchange writings, for it was Edward Seymour who had put his brother Thomas and his associates in prison for their attempts to divert power from his Protectorship; and Smith had been one of the secretaries of state who, only months earlier, had been examining Harington. Fourthly, and finally, it is equally possible that Harington could have come into possession of many of these poems through courtly networks after his imprisonment because, along with Robert Dudley and Smith, he was a prominent figure at Elizabeth's court. The social ties between these poems, then, are merely hypothetical, and cannot indisputably be attributed to the exchanges of a prison community.

What unites these poems, in the absence of verifiable ties, is place. The construction of a community is something that therefore might be imposed by a reader, for whom this locus provides a useful ordering structure. It could also be argued that subsequent readers of the manuscript – both the coterie associated with the Harington family, and scholars studying AH – are encouraged to draw these hypothetical ties by Harington, who, as compiler, both chose to identify these poems' authors and to put them in close proximity to one another. This tantalising illusion of a prison coterie, produced retrospectively by Harington, is sharply contrasted by the rhetorical community that he created in his major prison work, *The booke of freendeship of Marcus Tullie Cicero*, a translation of Cicero's *De amicitia* which he made from a French version of the text by Jean Collin, *Le Livre de Amytié.*[55] Where AH provides a set of nodes whose precise relationship to one another remains obscure, in his

---

[55] *The booke of freendeship of Marcus Tullie Cicero* (London, 1550); Jean Collin, *Le Livre de Amytié de Ciceron* (Paris, 1537). Subsequent references are to this edition and given by signature reference within the main body of the text. On the impact of Cicero on English literature at this time, see Howard Jones, *Master Tully: Cicero in Tudor England* (Nieuwkoop, 1998), and H. B. Lathrop, *Translations from the Classics into English from Caxton to Chapman, 1477–1620* (Madison, WI, 1933), 56–67, 196–202.

translation of Cicero, Harington is concerned almost exclusively with the nature of social ties, which creates a sense of cohesiveness that the former lacks.

Produced during his first imprisonment, and published in the year of his release, this text addresses the idea of community in a number of ways. It has three parts. The first is a dedication, 'To the righte vertuouse, and my singuler good Lady, Katherine duchesse of Suffolke' (Katherine Brandon), a good portion of which praises the profit of prison, especially for the companionship it provided its author. The second is a preface addressed to the reader, which cites biblical sources on friendship to stress the wisdom of this pre-Christian text. The third and most substantial part of the book is the body of the translation itself. This treatise addresses the philosophy of friendship through the personal relationship of Laelius and the deceased Scipio, and the apparently aborted friendship of two public figures, Sulpitius and Quintus Pompeius. What is most striking about Harington's threefold exploration of communities is that, in its emphasis on those things that might be considered to create the ties in a network – the ideology that binds its members, and their shared experiences, aims, and activities – the individual nodes become almost incidental.

The tendency to lose sight of the individual within its social network is demonstrated, firstly, in the historical relationship at the centre of *De amicitia*. Laelius' speech, which comprises the largest part of the treatise, is instigated by the death of his best friend Scipio. But, in fact, this bereavement merely acts as a launch pad for a general discussion of the qualities that make a good friend, and what characteristics expose a bad one. This movement from the specific to the general shows not only that the subject matter of friendship is at once highly personal and universal, but also that it is both a private and a public concern.[56] The reason that the material is so flexible is that, in focusing on the ideology of how friendship is established, it represents an abstract model of how networks form. Confirming what Barabási has observed in his work on complex networks – that all networks, whether they be neural networks, transport networks, biological regulatory networks, or social networks, behave in much the same way – Cicero's text makes plain that different kinds of relationship

---

[56] As Alan Stewart observes, *De amicitia* constitutes a dialogue about the glorious, but personal friendship of Laelius and Scipio, within the context of a public debate concerning the apparently aborted friendship of two public figures, Sulpitius and Quintus Pompeius; and it takes place in the private domestic setting of Scaevola's house, in a text written by Cicero for public reading. See Alan Stewart, *Close Readers: Humanism and Sodomy in Early Modern England* (Princeton, NJ, 1997), 150–8.

also follow the same broad tendencies. Thus it is possible for any subsequent reader of *De amicitia* to apply these rules and tendencies to his own relationships. In this text, then, the nodes are irrelevant; what matters for its readers are the structures that tie them together.

The possibility of mapping other relationships on to this text is undoubtedly why Harington chose it for translation. One aspect of this, as a number of scholars have been keen to emphasise, could be the personal resonance that *De amicitia* – a treatise reflecting on the friendship between Laelius and his dead friend Scipio – must have had for Harington, whose master Seymour was executed early in Harington's first period of incarceration. Harington's loyalty to Seymour, both before and after his death, was commented upon by both friends and opponents: the secretary of state, Sir William Petre, after examining Harington on 25 January 1549, observed that 'He [Harington] labors to have byn in the *Towre* with the Lord Admyrall';[57] and Harington's son testified that until his death, Harington considered himself one of the 'old Admiralitie (so he called them that had bene my Lords men)'.[58] If Harington had wished to express his continued loyalty through *De amicitia*, then the closing pages presented an ideal opportunity:

> Scipio surely although he was taken awaie sodeinly from this life, liueth yet with me, and shall liue euer. For I alwaies loued the vertue of that man, whiche is not deade with me, neither standeth it daiely alone before myne eye, who alwaies haue had it in sight, but also to our childrens children shall it be noble and notable ... Truely of all the thynges whiche fortune or nature gaue me, I haue nothyng to matche with Scipioes freendship. (sigs. H.8v–I.1r)

After this he speaks of things they did together, and things they shared, before observing: 'The remembraunce and onthynkyng of the which thynges, if with hym thei had died, I coulde by no meanes haue borne the lacke of so friendly and louing a man' (sig. I.1v). 'Remembraunce and onthynkyng' translates the French 'la recordation et memoire', which closely follows the Latin 'recordatio et memoria'.[59] What is particularly striking is that Harington does not render 'memoire' as 'memory' but rather as 'onthynkying', a word which appears neither in the *Oxford*

---

[57] *A Collection of State Papers ... Left by William Cecil, Lord Burghley*, ed. Samuel Haynes (London, 1740), 85.

[58] John Harington (the younger), *Orlando Furioso in English heroical verse* (London, 1591), 151.

[59] Collin, fol. 43v; Marcus Tullius Cicero, *De senectute; De amicitia; De divinatione*, tr. William Armistead Falconer (London, 1923), vol. XXVII, 104.

English Dictionary nor in the *Middle English Dictionary*, suggesting that it is Harington's own coinage. If Harington was the first to coin this word, it serves him well. The passages above may *describe* the way in which the bonds of friendship are not eradicated by the death of one of the parties, but the word 'onthynking' provides a word that encapsulates this whole attitude – the ideals, the practices, and the state of mind. The most significant feature of the coinage, I would argue, and the one that seems to have most relevance to Harington's own circumstance, is the distinction he makes between 'onthynkyng' and 'remembraunce'. While both words have a similar formulation – comprising the word 'think' (or the Latin, 'memor'), and an intensifying prefix – the prefix *re* in 'remembraunce' signifies a thought that is inherently bound up with the past. By contrast the prefix *on* implies a thought process that is not only retrospective, but also ongoing. The concept of 'onthynkyng' gets at the continuing and unbreakable nature of true friendship.[60]

However, while much of the circumstantial evidence supports a biographical reading of Harington's translation, this possibly personal resonance is kept private: Seymour's name is mentioned nowhere within its covers. This is at odds with Harington's more public memorialisation of his friend elsewhere. His poem about Seymour, 'Of person Rare, Stronge Lymbes, and manly shapp', is headed in AH: 'A sonnet written vpon my Lord Admirall Seymour'. This poem was also added to a portrait of Seymour which, according to Harington's son, was presented as a gift to Queen Elizabeth.[61] In light of this, the absence of any mention of his master in Harington's translation is striking. His unwillingness to prescribe this exclusive reading of the texts demonstrates his awareness that the ties can serve any number of real or potential relationships. This text, then, serves a function not unlike the Psalms, which provided incarcerated poets with useful material that on the one hand provided a conduit for personal lament, and on the other hand a guise of pedantic translation that allowed these works to be read within the public realm without risk of censure. While Harington may indeed have undertaken this project as a personal act of 'onthynkyng', this remains separate from the public functions to which he put this text, as demonstrated by his paratexts.

---

[60] It is also possible that Harington may have been inspired by John Cheke's attempts to purge English of Latin and French borrowings. See Manfred Görlach, *Introduction to Early Modern English* (Cambridge, 1991), 50–1, 164, 174.

[61] *Arundel Harington*, fol. 16r; Harington (the younger), *Orlando*, 151. This image is now held at Longleat House, Wiltshire.

As Gerard Genette writes, the dedication is 'always a matter of demonstration, ostentation, exhibition: it proclaims a relationship, whether intellectual or personal, actual or symbolic, and this proclamation is always at the service of the work'.[62] The opening lines of Harington's dedication, 'To the righte vertuouse, and my singuler good Lady, Katherine duchesse of Suffolke', suggests that the relationship that he will be demonstrating will be that between Harington and his intended patron. But, interestingly, this is not the only relationship Harington invokes in this paratext. In fact, the first one he gives any focused attention to is the relationship with his fellow prisoners:

> As my prisonment and aduersitee, most honourable lady, was of their owne nature ioigned with great and sundrie miseries, so was the sufferance of the same eased, by the chaunce of diuerse and many commoditees. For thereby founde I great soule profite, a little mind knowlage, some holow hertes, and a few feithfull freendes. Wherby I tried prisonment of the body, to be the libertee of spirite: aduersitee of fortune: the touche stone of freendship, exempcion from the world, to be a contempt of vanities: and in the ende quietnes of mind, the occasion of study. And thus somewhat altered, to auoide my olde idelnesse, to recompense my lost time, and to take profite of my calamitee, I gaue my selfe among other thynges to study and learne the Frenche tonge, hauyng both skilful prisoners to enstruct me, and therto plenty of bookes to learne the language. Among whiche as there were dyuerse notable, and for their sondry mattier woorthy readyng, so none liked me aboue this Tullius booke of freendship. (sig. A 2r)

In this passage, Harington constructs the picture of prison life for Katherine Brandon and his subsequent readers. He uses some of the familiar strategies by which the prison is represented as a place of study and spiritual edification. Part of this refashioning of the prison is achieved by his claim that it is a location that fosters true friendship: the implication being that you find out who your true friends are when you face the shame and hardship of incarceration ('aduersitee of fortune: the touche stone of freendship', a sentiment taken from *De amicitia*).[63] Harington is careful to distinguish between the prison population as a whole and those with whom he actually experiences fellowship ('some holow hertes, and a few feithfull freendes'). But this emphasis on prison friends as the really 'feithfull freendes' is strange material for a dedication because it constructs a community whose membership, while not including all the jail's inmates, is nevertheless

---

[62] Gerard Genette, *Paratexts: Thresholds of Interpretation*, tr. Jane E. Levin (Cambridge, 1997), 134–5.
[63] Cicero, *De amicitia*, XVII, 64; Harington, *Booke of freendeship*, sig. F.3r–v.

circumscribed by the prison walls; relationships with those outside have not undergone the test imposed by 'aduersitee', and so are inherently inferior.

The unity of this incarcerated group is further emphasised by Harington's reference to their shared activities, of which, he reveals, the following translation is a product. The co-operative principles that allowed his translation of *De amicitia* included the sharing of skills and resources. Harington describes receiving instruction in the French language, and being provided with 'plenty of bookes', amongst which was the French translation of *De amicitia* by Collin. Another co-operative service that he tells us he received was proofreading from those who could cross-refer his translation with the original Latin:

> I caused it to be conferred with the latine auctor, and so by the knowen wel lerned to be corrected: after whose handelyng me thought a new spirite and life was geuen it, and many partes semed as it were with a new cote araied, aswell for the orderly placyng and eloquently changeyng of some woordes, as also for the plainly openyng and learnedly amending of the sence, whiche in the Freenche translacion was somewhat darkened, and by me for lacke of knowlage in many places missed. (sigs. A.3v–A.4r)

By detailing all these examples of help received, this dedication reads much like a modern acknowledgments page, with one exception: the actual identities of the individuals who rendered these services remain hidden. This, then, is the second striking absence of verifiable nodes in the texts as a whole, which, unsurprisingly, has led to much speculation. For instance, Hughey has put forward a number of likely candidates for the person (or persons) who provided Harington with their Latin skills in the latter stages of this work.[64] But why are the identities of Harington's prison collaborators omitted from this dedication?

Significantly, the acts of erasure leave behind only two names, aside from the historical characters in the treatise proper: those of the author and his dedicatee Brandon. In so doing, Harington suggests that it is *this* relationship that is of primary importance to him. In discussing his prison community prior to his direct negotiations with Brandon, it might have seemed as if Harington was preferring these relationships over his potential relationship of patronage with Brandon. However, in removing names

---

[64] Hughey puts forward as possible candidates John Cheke and Roger Ascham outside the prison, and Stephen Gardiner, John Feckenham, or Thomas Smith within the prison. Of the prisoners, Hughey argues that the latter would have been the most likely because, despite having been one of the two secretaries of state to question Harington, he was nonetheless a fellow Protestant. See Hughey, *Harington of Stepney*, 33.

which would detail his particular political and social alliances, all he really demonstrates are the social ideologies that he shares with Cicero. Thereby we can see this account as a form of self-recommendation. By asserting that he is a team player, Harington shows that he has the necessary social qualities to enter into an alliance with Brandon:

> Thus whan the thing [Harington's translation] was perfected, and I behelde the fame of the auctor, the nature of the treatise, and the clerenesse of his teachyng, I coulde not iudge to whom I shoulde rather offre it, than vnto your grace, whom the freendelesse dayly find their defence, and the helples repaire to as a refuge. This did I not to teache you, but to let you see in learnyng auncient, that you haue by nature vsed: nor to warne you of ought you lacked, but to sette forth your perfection: the proufe wherof the deade might witnesse, and their ofspring hath iust cause to knowlage it, as mo can record it, then can requite it. (sig. A.4r–v)

Brandon is represented here as the ideal friend, an approach that is consistent with broader trends in early modern dedications. As Heidi Brayman Hackel has observed, 'Patrons are often addressed as extraordinary readers' who 'need not even read the entire book'.[65] In representing Brandon as one who so clearly embodies the ideals represented in the treatise that follows, it is of even greater importance that Harington asserts himself as one deserving of her patronage. But Harington's emphasis on Brandon's qualities as a friend also serves another end: amongst the services he credits her with are kindnesses previously done to him ('[I] haue tasted of your benefites, both in my trouble and also libertee', sig. A5r),[66] which allows Harington to represent Brandon as already his friend, and one who is engaged in analogous acts of communality to those bestowed upon Harington by his fellow prisoners. The dedicated book, following Jason Scott-Warren's thesis of the book as gift, implicitly repays Harington's debts to Brandon, but also invites reciprocity.[67] This has the dual function of placing pressure on Brandon to grant him his wish of patronage, and of directing subsequent readers to map on to the narrative of Laelius and Scipio not the private relationship of Harington and his master (discussed above), but the public one of author and patron.

---

[65] Heidi Brayman Hackel, *Reading Material in Early Modern England: Print, Gender, and Literacy* (Cambridge, 2005), 98.

[66] What kindnesses Brandon showed Harington in particular remains unclear, but we do know that she had done Thomas Seymour the great service of caring for his child after Katherine Parr died. See Cecilie Goff, *A Woman of the Tudor Age* (London, 1930), 150, 167, 174–7.

[67] Jason Scott-Warren, *Sir John Harington and the Book as Gift* (Oxford, 2001), 12, 15–17.

The representation of the prison community provided by Harington in *The booke of freendeship*, then, is far removed from the memorialisation of former prisoners evident in his manuscript miscellany, AH, or in the acts of graffiti and marginalia discussed in the previous chapter. Harington's gaze is not inward to a self-contained body, but outward to networks beyond the prison walls that he hopes to engage in after his release. That this is not just limited to the single dedicatee is emphasised in the second paratext, the preface 'to the reder'. In this preface he writes: 'I thynke there is no man, but that he maie learne out of the saide booke'. Multiple paratexts were common, and served, as Wendy Wall argues, to 'emphasize the compatibility of the privately dedicated manuscript and the publicly sold book', the book could be written in gratitude for (or in hopes of) preferment, but could also be 'addressed to the general reader'.[68] Thereby, in the preface Harington not only asserts that the wisdom contained in his translation is of universal edification; he also, implicitly, demonstrates his desire to be heard within the public realm, beyond the walls of the prison.

Nicholas Ridley and his 'comfortable conferences'

The dearth of hard evidence for inter-prisoner communication and collaboration amongst Harington and contemporary prisoners is starkly contrasted by the extensive paper trail left by the Marian martyrs, documenting their communications both within and between various London and Oxford prisons. Indeed, the sheer volume of this material makes mapping the true extent of the network a huge and complex task. Nevertheless, one can gain a sense of the overall organisation of the network from the interactions centring on just one node.

Nicholas Ridley, the Bishop of London, was initially incarcerated, along with the Grey family, the Dudleys, and their cohort, for his support of the Protestant Jane Grey. After Edward VI's death on 6 July 1553, he had, at the behest of the Privy Council, preached vigorously in favour of Queen Jane, proclaiming that neither Mary nor Elizabeth, who had been declared illegitimate by Parliament during their father's lifetime, was eligible for the throne.[69] However, the company with whom he was then incarcerated is not the same as the prison community with whom he later became associated; those with whom he found fellowship were the various

---

[68] Wendy Wall, *The Imprint of Gender: Authorship and Publication in the English Renaissance* (Ithaca, NY, 1993), 103.
[69] *TAMO* (1563), 903.

Protestant leaders who were arrested during the early stages of the Marian reign. At the end of January 1554 the government – at that time, mistakenly – believed that it had gained the upper hand with Wyatt's rebels and cleared the Tower to make room for the expected crowds of important prisoners. Ridley was placed in a cell along with the archbishop of Canterbury, Thomas Cranmer, the former bishop of Worcester, Hugh Latimer, and John Bradford.[70] From Latimer's account of this time, given in his *Protestation* delivered to Mary's commissioners at the Oxford disputations on 18 April 1554, it appears that these men spent their time studying and meditating upon the New Testament, discussing again the meaning of Christ's sacrifice, and reinforcing their opinions on the spiritual presence in the Lord's Supper.[71]

However, this harmonious cohabitation was not allowed to last for long. On 11 or 12 March, Cranmer, Latimer, and Ridley were transported to the supposedly safe location of Oxford to expedite their trials. During the time they spent in Oxford – over nineteen months for Latimer and Ridley, and almost twenty-four for Cranmer – they were usually confined apart from one another, in a number of locations, by the municipal officials responsible to the crown for their safekeeping. Cranmer, the most important and politically the most sensitive of the prisoners, appears to have spent most of his long confinement in the Bocardo; Latimer and Ridley, on the other hand, spent considerable time privately boarded in the houses of, respectively, the bailiffs and the mayor.[72] From these movements it seems clear that it was government policy to keep the incarcerated Protestant leaders on the move, perhaps, as D. Andrew Penny has suggested, in the hope of disorientating them,[73] but more probably in the hope of breaking up this community of formerly influential church leaders, and thereby preventing them from conspiring.

---

[70] See Diarmaid MacCulloch, *Thomas Cranmer* (New Haven, CT, 1996), 560. Ridley mentions his former cell mates in a letter to Grindal, LM, 52. Cf. ECL, MS 260, fols. 114r–115v (transcript).

[71] See John Strype, *Ecclesiastical memorials; relating chiefly to religion, and the reformation of it, and the emergencies of the Church of England, under King Henry VIII. King Edward VI. and Queen Mary the First* (London, 1721), vol. III.ii, 89–99 (92). Although Strype attributes this detail to Foxe's manuscript, it is unclear from what source this is printed because the passage concerning Latimer's cell mates occurs in none of the following manuscript copies and printed editions of Latimer's *Protestation*: BL, MS Harley 422, fols. 92r–94r, ECL, MS 260, fols. 171r–174r, or *TAMO* (1563), 1046–53.

[72] See MacCulloch, *Cranmer*, 567, 570; and Carl I. Hammer, 'The Oxford Martyrs in Oxford: The Local History of their Confinements and their Keepers', *Journal of Ecclesiastical History*, 50 (1999), 235–50 (238).

[73] D. Andrew Penny, 'Bradford, John (*c.* 1510–1555)', *ODNB* (Oxford, 2004), available from www.oxforddnb.com/view/article/3175 [accessed 18 December 2012].

The government's interest in these men's relative locations signals that, as Anthony Cohen observes, the symbolism of a community 'speaks . . . for the collectivity to those on the other side of its boundaries'.[74] In this case, the prospect of collaboration between these Protestant leaders must have given the authorities cause for concern. However, the physical separation of the men was overcome by the continued exchange of letters and other writings, enabled by an organised and extensive network of copyists, amanuenses, and carriers.[75] It is true that these men's physical separation did grieve them: for example, in a letter written around 20 January 1555, Ridley complains to Bradford, who was then at the King's Bench, that 'on of vs cannot easly nor shortly be of knoleg of anotheres mynd'.[76] But in the absence of a unified *physical* community, these men sought to create a coherent *textual* community.[77] Although they could not 'easly nor shortly' communicate, through the longer and harder means of correspondence Ridley and his some time cell mates (in the periods both before and after they shared a cell) sought to create unity of knowledge, goods, and doctrine amongst themselves and the wider community of co-religionists. This communal ideology in turn served the long-term aim of ensuring that by public declarations of faith, expressed in examinations, trials, disputations, and finally at executions, individuals contributed a coherent representation of the Reformed faith for posterity.

The main vehicles of communication between Ridley and his former cell mates were the letters passed by carriers (whose role will be discussed more in Chapter 4). The most common content of such epistles were words of comfort, greetings to be passed on to other prisoners, and items of news. In a letter written by Ridley during one of his stints in the mayor's house at Oxford to Cranmer in the Bocardo, he passes on news about the planned Cambridge disputations: 'M. Rogers, Doct. Crome, and M. Bradford shall be had to Cambridge, and there bee disputed with as we were here, and that the Doctors of Oxford shall goe likewise thether as Cambridge men came hether'.[78] The sharing of this information serves two important functions in the maintenance of community with Cranmer. Firstly, Ridley ensures that Cranmer is kept up to date with events in the

---

[74] Cohen, 'Symbols and Boundaries', 17.   [75] See Freeman, 'Publish and Perish'.
[76] ECL, MS 260, fol. 272r (holograph).
[77] For use of the term 'textual community', see Brian Stock, *The Implications of Literacy: Written Language and Models of Interpretation in the Eleventh and Twelfth Centuries* (Princeton, 1983), 90. For application to the Reformation, see Brian Cummings, *The Literary Culture of the Reformation: Grammar and Grace* (Oxford, 2002), 15–21.
[78] *TAMO* (1570), 1672.

broader prison community, so that he does not feel isolated. Secondly, he assures Cranmer that whatever he has will be held in common with his former cell mate.

This policy held not only for information, but also for goods. In a letter from Ridley to Bradford, we learn that the latter had sent Ridley a piece of gold, and that he in turn had sent it to the Bocardo, presumably to Cranmer.[79] That we know these goods existed in the first place, and then were passed from prisoner to prisoner, is due to their decision to write about these exchanges. This is telling. While it is likely that mentioning the enclosed item in the letter that it was accompanying could have served a practical end in alerting the recipient if the said object did not arrive, it is also reminiscent of the records of prayer recorded in the letters sent to Cromwell discussed at the beginning of Chapter 2. Just as these bedesmen had wished their private acts to be known, I would suggest that in writing about their physical transactions, Ridley and Bradford demonstrate their concern for record. By writing about the act of sharing, these authors more emphatically communicated and spread their communitarian ideology: for the propagation of such communal values, it was vital that not only were things held in common, but also that the values themselves were held in common.

The ability both to pass goods and to rally the support of co-religionists across various prisons had great benefits for the production and dissemination of texts. It is through such means that prisoners were able to send petitions to Mary and Philip that were signed by prisoners spread across multiple prison sites, such as the *Supplication*, probably written in November or December 1554, asking for a chance to defend, in public debate, the Edwardian religious reforms, which was signed by prisoners in four prisons;[80] and the declaration, dated 8 May 1554, against planned disputation between Protestant and Catholic theologians to be held in Cambridge, which was signed by prisoners in at least three prisons.[81]

[79] ECL, MS 260, fol. 272r (holograph). See also LM, 57, where Ridley thanks Latimer and Cranmer for similar acts of generosity towards his recently imprisoned brother-in-law George Shipside: 'God shall rewarde you both for my brother: You my Lord of Caunt. for your meate and dayly comfort, and you father L. for your mony and comfortable messeges'.

[80] *TAMO* (1570), 1694. This contains the initials of its initiators and supporters: John Hooper (Fleet), Robert Ferrar (King's Bench), Rowland Taylor (KB), Bradford (KB), Philpot (KB), John Rogers (Newgate), and Lawrence Saunders (Marshalsea).

[81] *TAMO* (1563), 1069–71. This is signed by Robert Ferrar (using the alias 'Robert Menauen', referring to his former bishopric in St David's), Rowland Taylor, John Philpot, John Bradford, John Hooper (using the alias 'Ioannes Wigorn *et* Glouc. Episcopus', referring to his former bishopric in Worcester and Gloucester), Lawrence Saunders, Edmund Lawrence, as well as containing the initials I.P. and a T.M (h). I.P might be James Pilkington or John Parkhurst, who severally were in exile at Zurich in

Aside from the main messages contained in these texts, the prison productions sent the authorities the message that Protestant networks were both
extensive and well organised – and that their members were in complete
agreement with one another.

   However, these same networks were also useful for the production of
texts which, in order that they might go under the radar of the authorities,
were designed to be written and circulated scribally. Ridley played an
active part in the collaborative process necessary to produce and disseminate such texts, both as an author receiving the collaboration of proof-
readers, translators, and copyists, and as provider of such editorial services.
Such collaboration shows not only the community ethos of those involved,
but also their shared drive for unity of belief. For example, in a letter to
Bernher, probably written around 18 December 1554, Ridley expresses his
desire that Bradford would translate some of his works, including his
'annotations in priorem librum tonstalli latine plenius', which probably
refers to Cuthbert Tunstall's prison writing *De veritate corporis et sanguinis
domini nostri Jesu Christi in eucharistia* (Paris, 1554), as well as 'many
thinges but as yet confused[ly] put togeder of the <usurpation> abomin-
able vsurpation arrogance and wykkednes of the sea and bishop of rome
and al gather togeder in laten'.[82] This suggests a collaborative writing
process that goes beyond even the level of co-operation demonstrated by
Howard and Douglas's poems, or described by Harington. While it is not
clear whether Bradford ever carried out these translations, for no works
fitting these descriptions survive, the intention Ridley expresses here
illustrates the great level of trust that he must have had, not only in
Bradford's ability to translate Latin fluently but also not to distort his
own authorial intensions. This, I would argue, arises from a sense that their
aims, both religious and textual, were held completely in common – a
sentiment that Ridley expressed to Cranmer in the letter he sent accompanying his account of his disputations at Oxford:

the course of 1554 (See *Original Letters Relative to the English Reformation*, ed. Hastings Robinson
(Cambridge, 1846–7), vol. II, 752); and T.M. could possibly be Tho. Matthew, Tho. Masseye, or
Tho. Moor, who were among the thirty-nine members of Parliament who absented themselves from
the House of Commons from 12 January 1555 because of the measures then being taken against the
Protestant faith (see Strype, *Ecclesiastical memorials*, vol. III.i, 262–3). Hooper and Ferrar's use of
their former bishoprics when they signed is a notably defiant act, implying that the authorities had
no right to strip them of their titles.
[82] ECL, MS 260, fol. 269v (holograph). See also ECL, MS 260, fol. 117r (Latin holograph), a letter
from Ridley to Bradford, which says that it accompanies a treatise, probably Ridley's treatise on
election referred to elsewhere in his letters, but now lost.

I wishe ye might haue sene these myne aunsweres before I had deliuered them, that ye might haue corrected them. But I trust in the substaunce of the matter we do agree fully, both lead by one spirite of truth, and both walkyng after one rule of Gods word ... When ye haue read myne aunsweres, send them agayne to Austen, except ye will put any thyng to them.[83]

In this passage Ridley expresses his belief that the enclosed account of his disputations will demonstrate that he and Cranmer are 'both lead by one spirite of truth'. This is a very powerful sentiment of unity. In relation to the text enclosed, it expresses his belief that Cranmer will be utterly satisfied with the answers that he gave to his opponents, even though Ridley had lacked the opportunity to send his prepared speeches to Cranmer for correction before the disputation took place. This in turn suggests that their beliefs are so consonant that Ridley already knew, to a greater or lesser degree, what Cranmer himself would advise. However, possibly to make sure that Cranmer did not feel excluded by this sentiment (for if Ridley already knows what he will advise, what further need is there of his communication?), and as an expression of willingness to be further married in their thought, Ridley grants permission for Cranmer to add anything to the text, should he see fit ('except ye will put any thyng to them'). Ridley thereby demonstrates that he is less concerned with the notion of personal authorship than he is with ensuring that his theology, and his profession thereof, is consistent with that of his religious community, which thus explains his keenness for Bradford to translate his Latin works.

Ridley was not only the recipient of editorial services, but also carried them out for others, as demonstrated in a letter to Bradford written in early May 1554. In this epistle we learn that Bradford had sent Ridley some writings (probably his *Sermon on the Lord's Supper*) for his perusal and comments, which Ridley was returning with his suggestions marked on them: 'According to your mind I haue run ouer all your papers, and what I haue done (which is but smal) therin may appeare'.[84] The sermon in question appears to have been circulated, because a second manuscript copy survives in addition to the autograph fragment, and it was later printed in 1574.[85] However, while the letter tells us that Ridley did provide comments, we have no evidence as to whether Bradford actually incorporated them: the autograph fragment does have some marginal annotations

---

[83] *TAMO*, (1570), 1671–2. [84] *TAMO* (1563), 1364.
[85] ECL, MS 261, fols. 64r–66r (holograph fragment); ECL, MS 262, fols. 27r–39r (transcript); John Bradford, *Two notable sermons* (London, 1574).

and insertions, but seemingly in the same hand (Bradford's) and ink as the main text, so it remains unclear precisely what changes Ridley suggested and at what stage they were incorporated, if indeed they were. The invisibility of Ridley's role in the making of the final draft of sermon is striking, and invites questions about the other prison writings by the martyrs. In this case we know from external sources that Bradford probably benefited from a co-operative work ethic. But how many other cases are there, where there has been similar collaboration, but no documentation exists to record it? The anonymity of these editors, along with many of the amanuenses and copyists, has something in common with Harington's failure to identify those people who aided him in his project of translating *De amicitia*. It demonstrates that despite the extensive documentation we have for the networks in Marian prisoners, the true extent of the co-operation that occurred can only ever be partial. For the most part, the public declarations provided in writing (as above), or in spoken word at a trial or disputation, were underpinned by dense and complex networks of communications, which at times were rendered almost invisible beneath the carefully choreographed public face of the faith.

This dynamic is probably best illustrated by a text known as *Certein godly, learned, and comfortable conferences, betwene ... D. Nicolas Rydley ... and M. Hughe Latimer*. The conferences mentioned in the title are two separate but related literary exchanges that occurred between Ridley and Latimer during the period of their incarcerations prior to being held in the same cell of the Tower some time between September 1553 and January 1554.[86] The project was clearly conceived by Ridley, who, in the opening passage to the first conference, entreats his intended readership:

> Let me haue (I praye you) your aduyse, in these maters folowing. That is your assent and confirmacion in those thinges, whiche you iudge that God doth allowe, and your best counsel and aduertisement, wher you thinke otherwise, and your reasons for both the same. For the wiseman saieth: One brother which is helped of another, is like a well defensed Citie.[87]

The simile of the 'well defensed Citie' employed by Ridley at the end of the passage encapsulates three key ideas. The first is that collaboration ('One brother which is helped of another') brings strength, which is

---

[86] See Ridley's letter to Grindal, LM, 56; cf. ECL, MS 260, fols. 114r–115v (transcript).

[87] *Certein godly, learned, and comfortable conferences, betwene the two reuerende fathers, and holy martyrs of Christe, D. Nicolas Rydley ... and M. Hughe Latimer* (Emden, 1556), sig. A.5r. Subsequent references to this edition will be made by signature reference within the main body of the text.

emphasised in the passage by the words 'assent', 'confirmacion' (the Latin prefix *con* meaning 'with'), 'counsel' (*con*silium) and 'aduertisement' (*ad* meaning 'to'). The second facet of the simile is that it evokes both the Latin *civitas*, in the original sense of a self-governing city,[88] and the city-states that existed in sixteenth-century Europe: self-contained communities, which we might also call counter-publics because they functioned independently of the officially governed realm. The third is the idea of attack, implicit in the term 'defensed'. Ridley's simile, then, communicates to his intended readership the ideal way that communities should function while under attack: by pulling together. In hostile circumstances, such as those suffered by Ridley and his co-religionists, collaboration does not merely define boundaries but also defends them.

The specific kind of collaboration that Ridley is inviting here is a service similar to the acts of editing described above. He requires advice on the 'maters following', which are the list of eleven 'causes' he has compiled 'that moue me to absteyne frome that Masse' (sig A.5r), inviting his intended readership to 'Write agayne I beseche you fathers and brethren, most dearely beloued in Christe, spare not my paper' (sig. B.2r). He is anxious that the recipients should check that his arguments are sound and add anything felt to be lacking. At this stage he clearly imagined multiple readers; but these wishes were fulfilled by Latimer, who returned the text with a comment added to each of Ridley's causes, and an exhortation not to attend Mass. This pattern was repeated in the second conference. This time, however, Ridley added another component to the conference, a fictional interrogator called Antonian,[89] who faces Ridley with fourteen 'obiections' concerning his non-attendance at Mass, each of which he answers. To nine of these answers, Latimer again adds comments. Through Latimer's collaboration, then, the text can be seen to embody the 'well defensed Citie' that Ridley had invoked.

This significance of the community represented in this text emerges from the tension between its content and its formal structure. In appearance, the *Conferences* are akin to a dialogue: in both the printed versions and the surviving manuscript copy of this text, the transcribers and editors chose to lay out Ridley's 'causes' and Latimer's comments in an alternating structure, with their initials placed in the margins beside their

---

[88] *OED, city,* I. 6.

[89] As Ridley explained (sig. F.1r), the name was taken from that of an Arian bishop who persecuted Trinitarian Christians in the Vandal kingdom of North Africa during the fifth century. Ridley may also have been making a dig at Stephen Gardiner, who had used the pen name 'Marcus Antonius'.

contributions.[90] Despite this format, however, the *Conferences* do not behave like a dialogue. Dialogues almost always represent two conflicting positions. In the case of reported, real conversations, such as the body of 'conferences' that took place between Marian martyrs and prominent members of the authorities, who came into jail to persuade these prisoners of the error of their beliefs, the participants are hardly ever brought to a position of agreement and unity.[91] However, the rhetorical purpose of the fictional dialogue dictates that a process of conversion should take place in one of the participants that, ideally, mirrors the process by which the reader is persuaded of that same truth. The *Conferences* largely defy this convention.

In the first conference, Ridley and Latimer did not attempt to make their *Conferences* feel like a dialogue at all. Doctrinally, Latimer's position is barely distinguishable from Ridley's. For instance, when Ridley voices his first reason for not attending Mass – 'It is done in a straunge tonge, which the people dothe not vnderstande, contrarie to the doctrine of the apostle, 1 Cor. 14.' – Latimer does not add any new material, but only expands on the point already made: 'Wher is no vnderstandyng, ther is neither edyfieng nor conforte' (sig. A.5r). In the second conference the problem that their constant agreement poses for the dialogic form becomes even clearer, since on several occasions Latimer is left at a loss for words: 'Who am I, that I should adde any thing to this' (sig. E.2v). True dialogue between the men is disabled by Latimer's complete agreement with his co-religionist. We start, as it were, from the end point of a traditional dialogue, at the stage where the two contributors have come to unity of opinion and knowledge. It is the assertion of the men's intimacy, the result of which is something more like a sermon delivered in stereo than a dialogue. In their inability even to pose themselves in opposition to one

---

[90] For the manuscript copy of the *Conferences* that survives amongst John Foxe's papers, see BL, MS Lansdowne 389, fols. 147r–170v. One might hypothesise that the layout found in this manuscript and in the printed versions followed that established in the holograph, for Ridley himself describes having placed his and Latimer's initials in the margins: 'where is before my sayings N.R. and before M. Latimer H.L' (LM, 56). Marginal names and initials were also common in Medieval manuscripts and Renaissance printed texts containing commentaries. For an example, and discussion, see Evelyn B. Tribble, *Margins and Marginality: The Printed Page in Early Modern England* (Charlottesville, VA and London, 1993), 49–50.

[91] Examples include Lady Jane Grey's account of her 'communication' with John Feckenham, *TAMO* (1563), 985–6; John Bradford's numerous conferences with the likes of Edmund Bonner, Nicholas Harpsfield, and Hugh Weston, in *All the examinacions of the constante martir of God M. Iohn Bradforde . . . wherevnto are annexed, his priuate talk [and] conflictes in prison after his condemnacion* (London, 1561); and Ridley's communication with Sir John Bourn, John Feckenham and others, *TAMO* (1963), 996–9.

another, and their doctrinal coherence, the reader can observe a literary demonstration of real community as well as the collaborative principals discussed above.

Latimer's additions to Ridley's initial texts also disrupt the possibility of a more literary and rhetorically effective dialogue in the second conference by interrupting the fictional interrogation of Ridley by Antonian. If the reader strips away Latimer's additions, it is possible to see how the exchange that Ridley builds up is self-contained, with questions and answers developing in a logical fashion, with the next question building on the answer that went before. For example, in Antonian's sixth objection, he says: 'That church *which you haue described vnto me*, is inuisible, but Christes is visible and knowen' (sig. C.6v, my emphasis). However, while Latimer's interruptions disable one more conventional kind of reading experience, they introduce another kind that in fact tells the reader something significant about the role of Protestant networks of communication in the preparation for heresy trial.

Latimer's constant disruption of Ridley's interrogation by Antonian has the effect of casting Ridley in two simultaneous, yet discrete, acts of discourse: the interrogation process with Antonian (possibly public), and the private conversation with his friend Latimer. The reason that this second conference does not function like a conversation between three parties is due to the lack of interaction between Antonian and Latimer. It is because the fictional interrogation was written before Latimer's additions, that it appears to the reader that Latimer's additions cannot be heard by Antonian – like a secret voice heard only by Ridley. From the other side, Latimer's emphasis on adding to and further unpacking Ridley's answers means that he never responds directly to Antonian. This latter form of communication clarifies the precise function of this writing, to prepare its makers, and any subsequent readers it was circulated to, for the trials and disputations they were to face; specifically, to ensure that the answers they gave followed the party line. The fact, then, that these two discourses – fictional trial and preparation for interrogation – are spliced together into one text, functions to dramatise how a single martyr's testimony of faith was the product of a whole community's efforts.[92]

However, as well as throwing light on the general trend in the writings of the Marian martyrs – to make sure that knowledge and beliefs were held in common – the *Conferences'* emphasis on community has a very specific

---

[92] For a discussion of how Protestant leaders prepared their less learned co-religionists for examinations and testimonies at the stake, see Freeman, 'Publish and Perish', 246–7.

function. In writing a text that prepares justifications for abstaining from
Mass, one of the objections that Ridley anticipated was that Protestants'
rejection of Mass introduced division into the church: as Antonian puts it,
'yow knowe how great a crime it is, to separate your selfe from the
communion or feloushíp of the church, and to make schisme, or diuision'
(sig. C.2v). The unity of the church represented by the body of Christ is a
powerful and sacred symbol in Christian theology, and so by refusing to
attend Mass, Protestants such as Ridley did themselves out of a ready-made
symbol of community. But Ridley's response to this anticipated attack is
skilful. He argues that the Communion as practised by the Catholic
Church is not a symbol of unity: 'I doo not take the masse as it is at
this daye, for the communion of the churche, but for a popishe deuise,
wherby bothe the commaundement and institution of our saueour Christe
(for the ofte frequenting of the remembraunce of his deathe) is eluded,
and the people of god is miserably deluded' (sig. C.3r). In other words,
Communion promotes unity and cohesiveness within the body; but the
Catholic Mass does not. One of the reasons he gives for this judgment in
the course of the *Conferences* is that in Catholic Mass the 'sacrament is not
communicated to al, vnder bothe kindes, according to the word of the
Lord', which refers to the fact that only bread is given to laypeople taking
Communion (sig. C.2r). Another is that the practice of giving Mass in
Latin prevents true community amongst the congregation, for '[w]her is
no vnderstandyng, ther is neither edyfieng nor conforte' (sig. A.5r).
His choice of the word 'edyfieng' here subtly invokes the simile of the
'well defensed Citie' from the opening of the treatise, thus drawing a
contrast between the ideal of the Protestant community, embodied by
the unifying discourse of Latimer and Ridley, and the Catholic Church,
embodied by the irreconcilable division between Ridley and Antonian.

Unity, as Ridley attests here, is best understood in opposition to the
powers of division and schism. The concept of 'us and them' – whether
that be interrogator and interrogated, Protestant and Catholic – is vital to
the integrity of the prison community. As Cohen maintains, the construction of communities necessarily creates boundaries. But in the case of
prisoners, they not only define themselves as distinct from, but also
persected by those beyond their boundaries. As a result, their unity and
their continued membership of the community is given added significance
and weight. As demonstrated above, Thomas Howard wrote of his relationship with Margaret Douglas as an act of defiance against the authorities, who, not satisfied merely to separate him from Douglas, also sought
to persuade him to give her up; and Douglas boasted of her lover's

continued duty to her even though it came at personal hardship. In so doing, these two lovers asserted one of the assumptions that underpins all of the writings discussed in this chapter: that membership within a community is a virtue, and that this membership is something that provides individuals with a degree of social capital, as Harington clearly hopes. However, while shared ideologies and personal devotion are important factors in the creation of and maintenance of social ties, what ultimately matters is the community's size and organisation: it is this that will determine whether it has any longevity; whether it continues to expand; and what its impact will be within the public realm. As the next chapter will demonstrate, networks only have an impact on the world outside if their ties extend beyond the prison walls.

CHAPTER FOUR

'Frendes abrode'

Memor esto Iesum Christum resuscitatum esse a mortuis, ex semine David, secundum evangelium meum, in quo laboro usque ad vincula quasi male operans, sed verbum Dei non est alligatum! Ideo omnia sustineo propter electos, ut et ipsi salutem consequantur, quae est in Christo Iesu cum gloria aeterna.

Remembre that Iesus Christ, beynge of the sede of Dauid, rose agayne from the dead, acordynge to my Gospell, where in I suffre as an euell doer euen vnto bandes: but the worde of God is not bounde. Therfore suffre I all for the electes sakes, that they also mighte optayne the saluacion in Christ Iesu with eternall glory.[1] (2 Timothy 2.8–10)

St Paul's bold assertion that the word of God cannot be bound sits in direct opposition to the image from the 1539 'Great Bible', which opened Chapter 1. Whereas Henry VIII's piece of visual propaganda sought to promulgate the belief that prison effectively excluded prisoners from the public realm of discourse by representing them without banderoles, St Paul asserts that even though an individual's body might be restricted, writings can reach beyond the prison's boundaries, acting as a 'proxy and prosthesis' for the incarcerated body.[2] The very existence of a study of Reformation prison writings is testament to the fact that writings produced from jail during the reigns of Henry VIII, Edward VI, and Mary I traversed the boundaries of the prison. Furthermore, it has become apparent over the course of this book that many prisoners were writing

---

[1] This letter is traditionally ascribed to St Paul's two-year imprisonment in Rome (see Acts 28.30). Other epistles believed to have been written during this period are Ephesians, Colossians, Philemon, and Philippians, although scholars have also examined the possibility that they might have been written in Ceasarea (where he was also incarcerated), or Ephesus. See Stuart Allen, *Letters from Prison: An Exposition of the Prison Epistles of the Apostle Paul* (London, 1975).

[2] Alexandra Walsham, 'Preaching without Speaking: Script, Print, and Religious Dissent', in *The Uses of Script and Print, 1300–1700*, ed. Julia Crick and Alexandra Walsham (Cambridge, 2004), 211–34 (211).

consciously for a readership beyond the prison walls. This chapter will explore precisely what it means for a prisoner to write a text for someone residing outside, in the public realm, particularly when they believe themselves to be representing 'the worde of God'.

There are three broad motivations to write to a readership outside the prison: the transfer of information; the desire to change something *within* the prison; and the wish to effect a change *outside* the prison. Regarding the first, this function is usually carried out through the genre of letters, which contain news of things happening either within the prison or in a location outside the prison not directly accessible to the recipient. While the intentions behind sharing certain information may shade into the second and third motivations, to effect a change either inside or outside the prison, the authors of such letters do not necessarily express a specific desired outcome. One such example is 'The copy of a letter written and cast out of the Castle of Canterbury', written by anonymous prisoners and printed in Henry Bull's *Certain most godly, fruitful, and comfortable letters of such true saintes and holy martyrs of God*. In their desire to get news of what was occurring within the prison into the public realm – that they were being denied the food brought into prison for their sustenance – they appear to have thrown this letter out of a window. They claim that:

> we write not these our letters to that entent we might not aforde to be famished for the lord Jesus sake: but for this cause and entent, that they hauing no law so to famish vs in prison, should not do it priuely, but that the murtherers harts shuld be openly knowen to all the world, that al men may know of what churche they are, and who is their father.[3]

The prisoners' statement that they do not desire to bring about justice for themselves (i.e. a change within the prison) may be suspect. Nevertheless, their intention to make the details of the cruelty suffered within the prison available to those outside is a powerful statement about censorship of information in the public realm. Other examples of this information-centred correspondence include news about the fate of other prisoners, such as that contained in Robert Smith's letter to his wife Anne: 'There is also gone to death Nicolas Chamberlayne, Thomas Osmond, Wyllyam Bamford. There is also condemned this Monday Diricke Caruer, Thomas Iuison, Iohn Launder, and William Vassy is repriued'.[4] Both examples demonstrate prisoners' recognition that, just as they desired to have news of their friends and family outside the prison, and current

---

[3] *LM*, 682.   [4] *TAMO* (1563), 1336.

events in the public realm, people outside the prison might want to know what was going on within prisons.

The second function, to effect a change within the prison, is, once again, most frequently carried out in correspondence. Some of the innumerable examples of letters addressed to the authorities seeking either freedom, or some other change in the author's circumstances, include: Thomas Cromwell's letters to Henry VIII following his incarceration in 1540, in which he casts himself as a 'prysoner prostrate at the Feate of your most excellent magestye';[5] John Harington's letter to Stephen Gardiner, which promises that if he will 'give earre to myne complaunte, it wyll bynde me to thankfullie repaie this kyndnesse';[6] and Princess Elizabeth's letter to her sister the Queen beseeching her to 'remember your last promise and my last demand: that I be not condemned without answer and due proof.[7] Other prisoners sought benefits through alternative means, such as by petitions to the monarch, as in the case of the *Supplication* to Mary and Phillip signed by John Hooper, Robert Ferrar, Rowland Taylor, John Bradford, John Philpot, John Rogers, and Lawrence Saunders in November or December 1554, which asked for a chance to defend in public debate the Edwardian religious reforms.[8]

Another more subtle means of seeking aid was through the dedication of a book to someone of influence. Edward Courtenay (who had been imprisoned with his parents in 1538 at the age of 12 and remained there in the reign of Edward VI) occupied himself in the Tower with such a project: he translated the *Tratatto utilissimo del beneficio di Giesu Cristo crocifisso verso i Cristiani* and dedicated it to the duchess of Somerset, the wife of Edward Seymour, presumably also sending it to her as a gift. The surviving manuscript demonstrates that, as a gift, it was designed to please: it is a miniature book (80 mm x 60 mm), written out in a precise, miniscule hand (up to eighteen lines per page), and titled and bordered in gold. In the preface he first describes the hardships he has had to suffer because of 'the gilte of myn oune naturall parent', before apologising for the roughness of his translation. He then writes:

---

[5] *Life and Letters of Thomas Cromwell*, ed. Roger Bigelow Merriman (Oxford, 1968), no. 348. See also no. 349.

[6] *John Harington of Stepney: Tudor Gentleman; His Life and Works*, ed. Ruth Hughey (Columbus, OH, 1971), 194.

[7] *Elizabeth I: Collected Works*, ed. Leah S. Marcus, Janel Mueller, and Mary Beth Rose (Chicago, IL, 2000), 41.

[8] *TAMO* (1570), 1694.

Yet i moste humblie beseche your good grace, both taccept well in worthe the good will of my endeuoure, and also for the love of christe (wose glorye this litle boke most playnely declarethe and settithe oute) to haue in your gracis remembraunce (according to your accustomed pittie) the miserable state and dolorous life that it so longe time moste wrethedlie haue sus-teyned, and so to setto your gracious good will and helping hande, that by the same your godlie and pitefull meanes it may pleas my Lordis grace of his manyfolde and habundaunte goodnes, to deliuer me out of this miserable captiuite: and to vouchsafe to take me into his howse as his gracis seruant.[9]

The mercy that Courtenay seeks here is firstly freedom from prison, and secondly to be made Edward Seymour's servant. If this bold request were granted, he would move from a place that housed those whom the authorities considered to be the most untrustworthy figures in England into the household of the most influential man in the kingdom. The posture of humility that he makes in this passage ('i moste humblie beseche'), however, is not quite as straightforward as it initially seems. The choice of text for presentation appears to be a calculated one. It is widely agreed that Courtenay was a dissembling figure when it came to religion, and was willing to swear his allegiance to whichever side would do him the most good.[10] Therefore the text he translated – a work of piety of the Valdes circle in Italy, which drew heavily upon Protestant sources (subsequently declared heretical by Paul IV) – may simply have been chosen to appeal to the fervently Protestant duchess, and to gain him favour with the regime. Furthermore, the posture of humility in this preface is also complicated by the presentation of this text as a gift (as in the case of John Harington's dedication to Katherine Brandon, discussed in Chapter 3). By giving the duchess a gift which is valuable, not because of its material worth but rather because of the time he has spent labouring over it, the power relationship between donor and recipient is problem-atised. For although Courtenay claims to be at the duchess's mercy, she is implicitly indebted to him.[11] It is by making her thus obliged that Courtenay wishes to effect change.

[9] Cambridge, University Library, MS Nn.iv.43, fol. 3r–v (Edward Courtenay, *A Treatice most profitable of the benefit that true christianes receyue by the deathe of Iesus Christe*). Although the gift did not win Courtenay his freedom, it does appear to have reached its intended audience, for there are marginalia in the manuscript that seem to have been added by Edward VI: 'Faith is dede if it be without workes[.] Your louing neueu Edward' (fol. 4v); 'Liue to die and die to liue again. Your neueu Edward' (fol. 92r).
[10] See D. M. Loades, *John Foxe at Home and Abroad* (Aldershot, 2004), 120; R. Bartlett, '"The misfortune that is wished for him": The Life and Death of Edward Courtenay, Earl of Devon', *Canadian Journal of History*, 12 (1979), 1–28.
[11] On the relationship of reciprocity produced by the culture of the gift, see Jason Scott-Warren, *Sir John Harington and the Book as Gift* (Oxford, 2001), 15–16; and Natalie Zemon Davis, 'Beyond

The third function – to effect a change outside the prison – is the focus of this chapter. Such writings illustrate the prisoner's ability to construct and maintain counter-publics beyond the prison walls by propagating the beliefs held by their authors (which, very often, were the very beliefs for which they had been incarcerated). The forms that best suited such a function were the letter, the treatise, and the polemic. The letter in particular, and some treatises, were usually written in the first instance with a single reader or limited readership in mind; but, as the next chapter will show, these writings were easily adapted by editors to suit a general readership. And although polemics were usually explicitly addressed to a single opponent, they were the ideal form through which to engage with a public audience on the most controversial doctrinal issues at debate within the public realm.

Polemic written by prisoners covered a range of doctrinal issues, including the existence of Purgatory and the sacrament of baptism. But the most popular topic, and one which overwhelmingly dominated this genre of prison literature, was the sacrament of the altar. Examples include the Henrician evangelical John Frith's *A christen sentence and true iugement of the moste honourable Sacrament of Christes body [and] bloude*, probably the earliest polemic on the subject to emerge from prison in 1532 (it was published later, in around 1548); *A treatyse made by Johan Lambert vnto kynge Henry the.viij. concerynge hys opynyon in the sacrame[n]t of the aultre*, written in 1538 shortly before Lambert's trial, which was presided over by Henry VIII; and the Catholic Cuthbert Tunstall's *De veritate corporis et sanguinis domini nostri Jesu Christi in eucharistia*, written during his imprisonment for concealment of treason, in the reign of Edward VI.[12] The person to write the most polemic on this topic during his incarceration, however, was Stephen Gardiner, who wrote, amongst others: a refutation of Peter Martyr Vermigli's *Tractatio de sacramento eucharistiae* entitled *In Petrum Martyrem Florentinum malae tractationis querela sanctissimae eucharistiae*; his *Explicatio[n] and assertion of the true Catholique fayth*, replying to Cranmer's *Defence of the true and catholike doctrine*; an answer to John Hooper's *Oversight and Deliberacion upon the Holy Prophete*

___

the Market: Books as Gifts in Sixteenth-Century France', *Transactions of the Royal Historical Society*, 5th series, 33 (1983), 69–88 (87).

[12] John Frith, *A christen sentence and true iudgement of the moste honourable Sacrament of Christes body [and] bloude* (London, [1548?]); John Lambert, *A treatyse made by Johan Lambert vnto kynge Henry the.viij. concerynge hys opynyon in the sacrame[n]t of the aultre as they call it, or supper of the lorde as the scripture nameth it* ([Marburg, 1545?]); Cuthbert Tunstall, *De veritate corporis et sanguinis domini nostri Jesu Christi in eucharistia* (Paris, 1554).

Jona entitled *A Discussion of Master Hopers oversight*; and his *Confutatio cavillationum*, replying to Cranmer's *An Answer unto a Craftie and Sophisticall Cavillation*.[13] Gardiner's polemics in particular demonstrate that prisoners were not cut off from the public realm of debate, for a number of the texts that he went about refuting – including those of Peter Martyr, Cranmer, and Hooper – were published while he was in prison, which tells us both that he had access to texts being produced and circulated within the public realm, and that he was anxious to ensure that the growing support for Protestant doctrine within the public realm was systematically countered.

The transmission of such texts in the public realm demonstrates that, in the same way that prison communities are not coterminous with place, neither are counter-publics bounded by prison walls. As the last chapter has shown, network theory is key to understanding how counter-publics are constituted outside the prison: each node can be said to represent an individual site of resistance; and groups of nodes connected by ties represent spheres in which proscribed thoughts can be expressed and transmitted.[14] However, network analysis was not available to early modern prisoners as a means of conceptualising how the dissident ideas they were propagating might take root within the public realm. This chapter explores the alternative ways that incarcerated writers imagined counter-publics outside the prison. Inevitably, the way that writers imagine such spheres, and the potential extent of their influence, depends to a certain degree on their own experiences of dissident communities, and on the message they wish to project to their readership. The three figures being examined here show this diversity clearly, by representing counter-publics in terms of both social models and spatial loci: an unspecified but unified, and apparently growing, community of evangelical 'brethren' (John Frith); an interior space into which the individual can privately resort to practice his or her dissident beliefs (John Fisher); and an extensive but known network of co-religionists, reachable and therefore conceptualised through the carriers of letters and other writings (John Bradford).

---

[13] BL, Arundel MS 100, fols. 1r–182v (Stephen Gardiner, *In Petrum Martyrem Florentinum malae tractationis querela sanctissimae eucharistiae*); Stephen Gardiner, *An explicatio[n] and assertion of the true Catholique fayth* (Rouen, 1551); TNA, SP 10/12, fols. 2r–65r (*A Discussion of Master Hopers oversight*); and *Confutatio cavillationum* (Paris, 1552), published under the pseudonym Marcus Antonius Constantius.

[14] See Albert-László Barabási, *Linked* (New York, 2003), 39–64.

John Frith and the 'brethren'

The challenge that faced the Henrician prisoner John Frith in the Tower of London was how to lead a community of evangelicals from his prison cell. One of the side effects of the legislation introduced in the late 1520s and the early 1530s to tackle heresy in England was that most of the leaders of the Reformation left England for the Continent, as Frith did himself for much of the period between 1528 and 1532; those who had not fled had abjured or been executed.[15] R. E. Fulop has argued that the reason Frith returned to England during the summer of 1531, and again in July 1532, was to provide leadership for the English congregations in the absence of other suitable candidates.[16] After his arrest and incarceration in October 1532, this task was made much harder for the young evangelical. The problem, however, was not only one of physical separation, but also the nature of evangelical communities at this time. Peter Marshall has remarked that '[a]s they emerged in the middle decades of the sixteenth century, Protestants were people with a group-narrative, a history they had had time to experience or invent'; the evangelicals of the early years, almost by definition, were not.[17] In order to appeal to this emerging community of believers – who had no shared sense of history and who were, in all likelihood, unaware of the extent of their number beyond the small circles of co-religionists they knew personally – Frith had first to construct it rhetorically in the mind of his readers.

Frith clearly took his role of religious leader seriously, producing over one-third of his works during the nine months of his incarceration, all of which had as their aim the furtherance of the evangelical cause. There were two strands to this agenda. The first concerns belief: Frith sought to educate his readers on pressing doctrinal issues, such as the controversies surrounding the existence of purgatory, the sacrament of baptism, and the sacrament of the altar. The second concerns behaviour: Frith's other prime concern was to instil communal values and behaviours in his co-religionists, which prescribed how they should interact. Both agendas are intimately bound up with the idea of creating and maintaining a unified community by emphasising shared ideology, in opposition to the beliefs of the Catholic Church, and by promoting a sense of belonging

---

[15] For instance, Thomas Bilney had abjured in 1527, and in 1531, after a relapse, was burned at Norwich; Robert Barnes abjured at St Paul's in 1526; and Hugh Latimer abjured in 1532.

[16] R. E. Fulop, 'John Frith (1503–1533) and his Relation to the Origins of the Reformation in England', unpublished doctoral thesis, University of Edinburgh, 1956), 97.

[17] Peter Marshall, *Religious Identities in Henry VIII's England* (Aldershot, 2006), 5.

through collective behaviour and mutual support. The main problem for Frith was that – at this time – the community remained dispersed. His challenge, then, was to provide the readers of these texts with a sense of membership within a *textual* community, and thus the motivation to adhere to these beliefs in the face of persecution. In order to achieve this, he employed a particular rhetorical strategy: of reporting, or otherwise implying, growth in the evangelical community. He did this by a variety of means: by explicitly referring to size; by focusing on an individual and then moving the focus outward to the individual's context within a community; or by detailing the spread of a manuscript beyond its intended audience, thereby creating a reputation of uncontainability. Such a reputation of growth for the community had the simultaneous functions of providing encouragement for Frith's co-religionists, because it helped them feel that they were part of an evolving history, while promoting anxiety amongst Frith's opponents.

Frith's rhetorical strategy is in clear evidence in *A letter ... wryten vnto the faythful followers of Christes gospell*. Mimicking the structure of the Pauline epistles, which open with a personalised greeting and words of encouragement to the Christian communities, Frith opens the main body of the *Letter*, following the prayer, with these words:

> It can not be expressed (dearlye beloued in the lord) what ioy and comfort it is to my harte to perceiue how the worde of god hath wroughte and continually worketh among you: so that I fynde no small numbre walking in the waies of the lorde, accordynge as he gaue vs commaundement, willynge that we shulde loue eche other as he loued vs. Nowe haue I experience of the fayth whiche is in you, and can testifye that it is without simulacion that ye loue not in worde and tonge only but in worke and veretie.[18]

In this preliminary passage, we see Frith responding to news of one or more (he is notably unspecific) evangelical congregations outside the prison. By reflecting news of these co-religionists back to them, he seeks to emphasise their membership within a community. To emphasise this fact, he evokes the Lord's commandment that 'we shulde loue eche other as he loued vs', saying that they do so 'not in worde and tonge only but in worke and veretie'. Most importantly, however, Frith asserts that those who have marked themselves thus as part of the evangelical community are 'no small numbre', thereby implying, although not explicitly stating, that the extent of the community of which individuals may perceive themselves

---

[18] John Frith, *A letter ... wryten vnto the faythful followers of Christes gospel* ([London?, *c.* 1548]), sig. A.iv. Subsequent references are to this edition and are given by signature number in the text.

to be a part is larger than they know. While it is possible that this assertion is an accurate reflection of the news brought to him in prison, there is also some suggestion that Frith has permitted himself some rhetorical inflation, for at the end of this letter he writes: 'Yf it please anye of our brethren to wryte vnto vs of any suche doubtes as peradueen-ture may be found in our bookes it shulde be very acceptable vnto vs, and as I truste not vnfrutefull for them. For I wyll endeuer my selfe to satisfye them in all poyntes' (sigs. A.5r–v). The promise to reply to letters 'in all poyntes' demonstrates how a textual community was imagined as working: Frith expected a certain amount of communication to pass in and out of the prison. The sense we get is of a free flow of news and advice, a community united despite physical divides. However, this promise is one that would be hard to fulfil if he imagined his letter being circulated to a large number of people. The discrepancy between the extent of the rhetorical community and the intended reader-ship, then, suggests some level of myth-making in the opening portion of the letter.

This appeal to a rhetorical community precedes the main message of the letter for a good reason. Frith wants to encourage his co-religionists to remain strong in the face of imminent persecution. By first suggesting that the readers are part of a community that is large, Frith establishes motiv-ation for action: it is undoubtedly easier to resist the pressure to conform when one has allies. Furthermore, the fact that this hardship is given as evidence of their election functions to set them apart as a group: 'al which wyll deuoutly lyue in Chryste, muste suffre persecucyon' (sig. A.2v). But this community emphasis is not only a prelude to the content of the letter; much of the guidance within the main body seeks to contextual-ise personal fear and tribulation within the Reformist cause as a whole. One important instance can be found in his reference to Paul's prison letter to Timothy, which he uses to affirm that everyone who lives his life in Christ must suffer persecution (2 Timothy 3.12). This derives from a passage that appears to have directly influenced Frith's letter in its use of personal experience to guide those outside the prison. In it, Paul enumer-ates his sufferings in Antioch, Iconium, and Lystra, before proceeding to write: 'and from them all the Lorde delyuered me. Yee and all they that wil liue godly in Christ Iesu, must suffre persecucion' (2 Timothy 3.11–12). It is easy to see from this enumeration of Paul's tests why he has provided a literary and ideological model for persecuted Christians and prisoners throughout history. What is notable about this passage, however, is the fact that its function is not self-reflective; rather, Paul uses it to illustrate a general truth that will comfort Timothy and other followers in the faith. Frith employs a very similar tactic in his *Letter*, writing that he had long had the 'speculacion' that walking after God's word would cost him his life, and that 'albeit that the kynges grace shulde take me into hys fauaure ond [sic and] not to suffre the bloudy Edomites to haue theyr pleasures vpon me, yet wyll I not thynge [sic thinke] that I am escaped, but God ysthe [sic hath] onely differed it for a season' (sig. A.3r–v). As in Paul's epistle, this is not to the purpose of self-reflection, but rather to emphasise to the recipients of the *Letter* that they should arm themselves with the same 'supposicion'. Thus the experience of the individual is used for the edification and guidance of the whole community. Within that context, the individual's suffering, in itself, is not important.

Frith also uses this strategy – of moving the focus outward from the individual to the community context – in *A mirroure. To know thyselfe*. This treatise has three chapters. The first affirms that the greatest aim in a man's life is to know himself, and that, in coming to know himself, he must be humbled by the knowledge that every good gift comes from God. From this advice to 'know thyself', we might expect the guidance in this treatise to be focused on the individual. However, in the second chapter the individual, along with his gifts, is contextualised within a community (where the emphasis remains for the third chapter). At the beginning of this chapter Frith writes that individuals should distribute their personal goods and gifts 'to the profyte of the comontye'.[19] The word *commonty* has its roots in the Old French *comuneté*, which derives from the Latin *communitatem*, meaning common fellowship. The first listed use in English of the word 'commonty' to mean a community is Wyclif, around 1380, demonstrating a historical association of the word with heretical authors.[20] Frith imagines this community through the image of the different parts of the body united with Christ as the head – an image used frequently by St Paul, and which is also found in

---

[19] [*A mirroure. To know thyselfe*] ([Antwerp, 1536?]), sig. A.6r. Subsequent references are to this edition and are given by signature number in the text. No firm date can be given because the title page and imprint are lacking from the sole copy, which is Oxford, Bodleian Library, 8° I 65(3) Art; however, the *STC* attributes it to the printer M. Crom, and dates it tentatively to 1536.

[20] The Old French form *comuneté* has in English diverged in two directions: first, associated with the adjective 'common' in all its varieties, it assumed the trisyllabic form 'commonty'; secondly, it remained in four syllables and was assimilated to the original Latin type as 'community'. The first listed use of the word *commonty* to mean a community or commonwealth is *c.* 1380, Wyclif *Serm. Sel. Wks.* II. 350 'Ellis þe comynte wolde not stonde' (*OED*, *commonty*, etymology). See also *MED*, *communite*, *n*, 4.a., which lists: *c.* 1425, *Wycl.Serm.*(Bod. 788) 2.75: 'Þe Chirche, þat is comunte of Cristene men. *c.* 1475 (? *c.* 1400), *Wycl.Apol.* (Dub. 245) 27: 'As al men of a comynte berun punisching for þe defaut of two or on'.

the work of John of Salisbury and medieval scholastic thought[21] – which
necessarily implicates each individual in the salvation of his fellow man.
For example, Frith says that if God has given you the gift of sight, and you
perceive a blind man about to fall in a hole, you are bound to guide him
out of danger, 'or els yf he perish there in / where I myght haue delyuered
hym / hys bloude shalbe requyred of my hande' (sig. A.5r). The duty that
the individual has to the communal body is thus expressed as a legal
obligation, with penalties imposed upon those who do not uphold such
values. The notion of a law itself has a social dimension, for it signals the
body of rules which a particular state or community recognises as binding
on its members or subjects.

The general effect of the move from the first to the second chapter,
then, is to subsume the individual within the community. The individual
is essentially eliminated in the process of establishing unity. This is
underlined by the composition history outlined in the preface. In it, Frith
tells the reader that the treatise was originally intended for a single reader,
'a faythfull frende' (also anonymous), but that he realised it might prove
equally edifying for 'Christes flocke' (sig. A.3r). It is unclear whether this
composition history is real or not, but the decision to provide this narrative
at all is telling because it means that once again we have this conscious
scaling up, moving from one to many. Subtly this movement implies the
growth of the community as the reader deduces that Frith is seeing a
wider demand for this personally addressed work. It also suggests that Frith
intended this text to have a large-scale influence; that his interest was
not only in serving individuals but producing a text that could be utilised
by a general readership as needs changed. His canny recognition of
the need for such a text pre-empts the print publication of this work three
years after his death, and it is possible that he had this very kind of
publication in mind when he wrote the preface. This rapid publication
marks the *Mirroure* apart from the *Letter*, which was not printed
until around 1548, when it was placed in a volume along with a reprint
of the *Mirroure* and an instruction on how to die (and possibly only to
justify a second printing of them). Publishers probably felt that the *Letter*
was less suitable for publication because it was so clearly intended for a
small audience, containing as it does an invitation to the recipients to
write to Frith. Moreover, while this text dealt only with the internal
unity and behaviour of the evangelical congregation, the *Mirroure* also

---

[21] See 1 Cor. 12.12–24; Rom. 12.4–5; Eph. 4; and John of Salisbury, *Policraticus*, ed. C. C. J. Webb
(Oxford, 1909), vol. 1, 281–3.

tackles public debates and controversies, thereby demonstrating its suitability for a broad readership.

One example of Frith's engagement with such controversies is his treatment of the debate between the Catholic doctrine of good works and the Reformed belief in justification by faith alone:

> Furthermore the most gloryous gyftes concerning our soules / come from God euen of his mere mercy and fauoure which he sheweth vs in Christ and for Christ / as predestinacyon / elecyon / vocacyon and iustificacion: and al be it M. More with his paynted poetrye and craftye conueyance do cast a myst before youre eyes / that you myght wander out of the ryght waye endeuoringe him selfe to instructe you that God doth predestinate and chosen vs before the beginnynge of the worlde / because he knewe before that we shulde do good workes / yet wyll I sette you vpon a candell whych shall shyne so bright / and so clerely dyspell his myste and vayne poetrye that you shall planely perceaue hym daunsinge naked in a nette / which not withstandinge thinketh hymself to go inuisible. (sig. A.4ʳ)

Frith distinguishes the evangelical community from those believing in the doctrine of good works by designating Reformed beliefs as the 'ryght waye'. This delineation, however, does not prevent engagement with those outsiders, such as Thomas More, who had been given permission by Bishop Tunstall to read the proscribed texts of the Reformers in order to refute their doctrine. The image of More dancing in a net might be seen as a motif of dispute between William Tyndale and More. Tyndale had originally used the idea of More dancing in a net in *An answere vnto Sir Thomas Mores dialoge*, published in 1531, to imply that More's arguments were like a net that failed to cover their false foundations. More had then replied in *A Confutation of Tyndale's Answer* that Tyndale did not even have a net to cover his nakedness.[22] Frith involves himself in this pamphlet war by using the same metaphor ('you shall planely perceaue hym daun-singe naked in a nette'), which suggests that he wished to be party to the polemical exchange between the Reformers and the establishment. His involvement also alerts us to the fact that his work is not intended for the closed community of the *Letter*'s readers, but rather is aimed at engage with the public realm more holistically.

The movement of the *Mirroure* from its reported single reader to a general readership is a narrative that is repeated in the history of Frith's *A christen sentence and true iugement of the moste honourable Sacrament of*

---

[22] See William Tyndale, *An answere vnto Sir Thomas Mores dialoge* (Antwerp, 1531), sig. Ar–v; *CW*, vol. VIII, 176–7.

Christes body [and] bloude. However, in this instance, it was reputedly against Frith's wishes.[23] According to the composition background of *A christen sentence* that is given in Frith's reply to More, *A boke ... answeringe vnto M. mores lettur*, this short text began as a conversation between Frith and an unnamed 'christen broder', who asked Frith to write it down because his answer was too long to retain in memory.[24] Frith says:

> I was loth to take the mater in hande / yet to fullfyll hys instant intercession / I toke vppon me to touche this terrible tragedie / and wrote a treatise / whyche beside my paynfull impresenment / ys lyke to purchase me moste cruell deth ... Notwishstondinge to say the truthe I wrote yt not to the intent that yt shuld haue byn published[.] For then I wolde haue touched the mater more ernestly / and haue writyn / as well of the spirituall eatynge and drynkynge whiche ys of necessite / as I dide of the carnall whiche ys not so necessarie / for the treatise that I made was not expedient for all men / albeit yt weare sufficient for them whom I toke in hande to enstructe ... But nowe yt ys commen abrode and in many mens mowthes / in so moche that master more which of late hathe busied hym sellfe to medle in all soche materes (of what zele I wyll not defyne) hath sore labored to confute yt[.][25]

Frith's use of the word 'abrode' suggests that *A christen sentence* had become available in the public sphere, much in the same way that his published texts were. It is this kind of circulation that Harold Love describes with his term 'scribal publication': this text may not have been published in the sense that we use the word now, that it was printed and sold, but it was subject to a chain of copying by private individuals, a chain which could have taken the text to a significant audience and clearly explains how Thomas More came to obtain copies.[26] He goes on to express two reasons why he had not wanted his text to be made available in such a way. The first is that he did not want his opponents, especially the authorities holding him, to be aware of him writing heretical doctrine, because it would provide them with evidence that would condemn him. Later in the preface to his *Boke*, Frith reports how he was summoned by Bishop Gardiner, who had become aware of *A christen sentence* through More's response to it. Secondly, he was concerned that the content would not be edifying for Protestant readers beyond the closed circle of his intended

---

[23] It is not entirely certain whether the *A christen sentence* was written before or during Frith's imprisonment, but N. T. Wright argues that since it received a reply from More dated 7 December 1532, it was probably written in October or November that year, when Frith was already imprisoned. See N. T. Wright, ed., *The Work of John Frith* (Oxford, 1983), 54.

[24] John Frith, *A boke ... answeringe vnto M. mores lettur* (Monster [i.e. Antwerp], 1533), sig. A.2r.

[25] Ibid., sigs. A.3v–A.4r.

[26] See Harold Love, *Scribal Publication in Seventeenth-Century England* (Oxford, 1993), 36, 43.

readership; it was written for a known group of people, of whom he could assume a certain basis of knowledge.

Another reason why Frith may not have wanted it circulated was the fact that its doctrine sat in disagreement with that of other Reformists. Tyndale had written to his friend, advising '[o]f the presence of Christes body in the Sacrament, medle as litle as ye can, that there apeare no diuision among vs. Barnes will be whote against you'.[27] Robert Barnes was already known as a strict Lutheran on the question of the presence of the Lord in the Supper. In 1530 he had published (under the Latin name Antonius Anglus) his *Sententiae ex doctoribus collectae, quas papistae ualde impudenter hodie damnant* (Sentences collected from the doctors, which the papists condemn very impudently today). This book, containing a preface by Luther's colleague Johann Bugenhagen, was set out in the style of a medieval sentence collection and sought to establish nineteen points, including: 'In sacramento altaris est verum corpus christi' (in the sacrament of the altar is the true body of Christ).[28] Barnes believed in a local, but emphatically real ('verum') presence of the glorified body of Christ in the bread and wine. Frith, by contrast, believed that the body was not present, and the bread and wine were merely a remembrance of Christ's last supper. Tyndale was essentially trying to enforce a form of censorship that allowed Reformists to promote a united front. It is easy to see why Frith would have wanted to keep his text under wraps.

As with the *Mirroure*, Frith need not have included this publication history, but he seems to have been acutely aware of the power of such narratives to construct rhetorical communities. In explaining how *A christen sentence* was not suitable for general circulation, the preface to Frith's *Boke* demonstrates how the following text might meet a broader evangelical readership's needs: it addresses Frith's opponents by refuting More's reply point by point, as was the style of polemic at this time; and it provides a more systematic discussion of 'spirituall eatynge and drynkynge' in order to instruct and edify those sympathetic to the evangelical faith. More important for this argument, though, is the fact that the comparison between the original text and the new one postures the scaling up of the readership in a manner very similar to that in the *Mirroure*, with one important distinction: where the expansion of the readership of the

---

[27] *TAMO* (1563), 577.
[28] For a discussion of Barnes's theology concerning the sacrament of the altar, see Carl R. Trueman, *Luther's Legacy: Salvation and English Reformers, 1525–1556* (Oxford, 1994), 156–204, and Carl R. Trueman, '"The Saxons be sore on the affirmative": Robert Barnes on the Lord's Supper', in *The Bible, the Reformation and the Church*, ed. W. P. Stephens (Sheffield, 1995), 290–307.

Mirroure had been intended by Frith, the wider circulation of *A christen sentence* had been (at least according to Frith) against his will. Of course, the true extent of the readership that *A christen sentence* reached is difficult to estimate, and the narrative of dissemination may not be entirely accurate, but the story makes a powerful statement about the uncontainability of this text in particular, and Frith's writings in general.[29] Because extended circulation means additional readers, this narrative necessarily implies the growth of the evangelical community. Interestingly, however, it may not have been Frith who spotted the ability of manuscript circulation to evoke a rhetorical community, for the text made by More in response to *A christen sentence* (which Frith in turn refuted in his *Boke*), called *A Letter . . . impugnynge the erronyouse wrytyng of John Fryth*, already demonstrates this imaginative process.

According to the martyrologist John Foxe, More managed to gain a copy of Frith's text through one William Holt, a tailor who feigned friendship with an evangelical.[30] Such covert measures would seem to suggest the limited availability of *A christen sentence*; the fact, then, that More felt the need to refute Frith's text is in itself worth remark. That More thought this scribally published text dangerous enough to deserve a response suggests the power he believed it to have, and the extent of the circulation he deemed it possible of gaining. This anxiety over the text's dissemination is expressed in the opening pages of the letter, in which he tells the nameless friend who sent the first copy of the text that he has 'ben offred synnes a couple of copyes mo in the meane whyle . . . whereby men may se how gredly that these newe named bretherne wryte it out, and secretly sprede it abrode'. As in Frith's preface to the *Boke*, we see use of the word 'abrode' to describe the availability of *A christen sentence*. While the *Oxford English Dictionary* does not define any explicitly negative connotations for *abroad*, it seems to connote ideas of 'treason being abroad in the land'. As demonstrated by another use of the word by More, and one by John Gwynnethe (discussed below), people often used it during this period in a pejorative sense, to suggest something that should not be

---

[29] One might draw a comparison with Thomas More's preface to his *Dialogue Concerning Heresies*, in which he tells how a 'secrete sure frende' sent to him a messenger to question the credence to be given to some matters. A dialogue then takes place between More and the messenger, but after the messenger has left, More doubts his ability to remember the whole discussion and thus decides to write it down. Having written an account of the dialogue, More then fears his text will be copied and circulated in a misrepresentative form amongst the evangelical community. In order to forestall the production by these 'shrewde apostates' of corrupt versions of his text, More produces a printed version of the *Dialogue Concerning Heresies*. *CW*, vol. VI, 21–2.

[30] *TAMO* (1563), 554.

abroad, but is – although not necessarily in the open. The fact that More is aware of three copies of this treatise confirms that the text was being copied, and leads him to suggest that there exists an organised network of evangelicals working together to produce and disseminate texts: 'the deuyll hath now taught hys disciples, the dyuysers of the heresye, to make many shorte treatises, whereof theyr scolers may shortly write out copyes, but in theyr treatises to put as much poysen in one wryten lefe as they prented before in fyftene'. He imagines this model of dissemination as a canker spreading through a body, or a fire laying waste to towns and countries, and fears the effect if it is true that Frith has numerous other texts circulating 'huker moker' within the closed community of the brethren.[31] There is a notable tension in these fearful words between the public and the private: although More stresses that the texts are only circulating amongst the brethren, he is anxious that it will lay waste to the whole country or body. This exhibits his awareness that the Reformers often experienced community only textually; rather than being a weakness, the fact that the individuals were dispersed across the nation meant that heretical beliefs were covering much greater geographical distances. This is a perfect example of Mark Granovetter's observations about the strength of 'weak ties' that was discussed at the beginning of Chapter 3.

In his *Letter . . . impugnynge the erronyouse wrytyng of John Fryth*, More has essentially begun to write this chapter for me: he presents a fictional narrative of dissemination which attempts to explain how these texts were getting out of the prison, and how they were then rapidly spreading. In many ways, the manner in which More imagines the evangelical community and its activities is as important in the task of creating alternative power structures as is the doctrine contained in Frith's texts. In his preface to *A Boke . . . answering unto Master Mores Lettur*, Frith emphasises the uncontainability of his text; but More had already gone one step further by representing a method through which the evangelicals might disseminate this and other texts so rapidly. By recording the networks he feared, More contributed a myth of organisation to this powerful reputation. He created a convincing picture of how communities might function, and which accurately pre-empted the processes used by the Marian martyrs, such as Nicholas Ridley and John Bradford. This was much more tangible for a reader than Frith's image, for instance, of his co-religionists preventing their blind friends from falling into holes. This myth still has currency with many historians who argue that the 'Christian brethren' (*brethren* being a

---

[31] *CW*, vol. VII, 233.

term used both by Frith and More, above) referred to an 'organised wing
of Lollardy' engaged in the financing and printing, the selling and dissemination of reforming books.[32] That there were individual activists who
became involved in the purveying of such books and enlisting the services
of printers and merchants is very clear. But, as Anne Hudson aptly notes,
what is less certain is that the term 'Christian brethren' designates a
recognisable group, let alone an organisation: contemporary usage of the
term is vague and unhelpful.[33] What is significant, however, is the pre-
occupation, both contemporary and present, with the relational networks
of brotherhood and friendship that facilitate dissemination.

     After writing this letter, More quickly tried to stop it from being
published. This may be because he realised that in attacking Frith
he was actually contributing to the public image of the evangelical community.[34] Regarding his decision to suppress the text, he wrote in his
Apology: 'And for bycause that hys boke was not put abrode in prent /
I wolde not therefore lette myne runne abrode in mennes handes. For as
I haue often sayde, I wolde wysshe that the comon people sholde of suche
heresyes neuer here so myche as the name.'[35] As demonstrated by the
association of the word 'abrode' with 'prent', there is an attempt in this
passage to suggest that the influence of Frith's text would be limited
because it was not printed. This is contrary to the effective manner in
which More represented the heretical communities copying and disseminating Frith's text in his *Letter . . . impugnynge the erronyouse wrytyng of John
Fryth*, and where the same adverb ('abrode') had been used to suggest the
notion of scribal publication. It appears that More may have realised
that his narrative of dissemination could make 'the comen people' anxious.
By first suppressing this original text and then issuing a statement of
Frith's limited influence, it seems that More hoped to undo any help he
may have given Frith in establishing a reputation of uncontainability for
his prison texts.

     The narratives of dissemination imagined by More suggest that dis-
course on heretical topics was made possible through the dispersed nature

---

[32] A. G. Dickens, *The English Reformation*, 2nd edn (London, 1989), 70, 93; William A. Clebsch, *England's Earliest Protestants, 1520–1535* (New Haven, CT, 1964), 252.

[33] Anne Hudson, *Lollards and their Books* (London, 1985), 482–3.

[34] See James Simpson, *Burning to Read: English Fundamentalism and its Reformation Opponents* (Cambridge, MA, 2007), 260–83, where he argues that, by engaging in polemic with his evangelical opponents concerning their literalist interpretations of scripture, he turned into a replica of them, engaging in 'punishing versions of early modern reading and writing' (261).

[35] *CW*, vol. IX, 122.

of heretical textual communities. It does not really matter whether the rhetorical community reflected reality: to evangelicals, it functioned as a testament to small victories; to Catholics and the establishment, it created the fear that heresy was uncontainable. The nature of textual communities meant that, once abroad, the writings and the ideas contained therein continued to spread. A statement to this effect can be found in John Gwynnethe's *A declaracion of the state*, which was published in 1554, twenty-one years after Frith's death. Responding to Frith's 'booke which he made against the veritee of the holy sacrament of the Altare', Gwynnethe admits that he did not realise 'that the venim of Frithes booke wolde haue spredde so farre abrode, as the lamentable experience therof doth presently declare'.[36] The sentiments and vocabulary are very familiar: it is no surprise to see the term 'abrode'; and the word 'venim' is reminiscent of More's reference to the written leaf carrying 'poysen', and the image of canker spreading through the body. The fear in this text, like More's, is that there is no way of restraining such doctrine. Frith had been contained in the Tower, but his texts nevertheless found their way out and sometimes far beyond the expected circle of readers, even to his enemies. The power that these texts were perceived to have suggests that the fierce legislation of the 1530s not only failed to centralise authority, but, conversely, forced into existence counter-publics, which were not only limited to the prisons but infiltrated the whole realm.

John Fisher and Elizabeth White

Both the kind of writing that John Fisher embarked upon from his prison cell and these works' intended readerships were markedly different from those of the early Reformer, Frith. While Frith had sought to rally a dissident community, and involved himself in polemical exchanges with figures representing orthodoxy, Fisher wrote almost exclusively for single readers and eschewed polemic (despite his frequent forays into religious and political controversies prior to his incarceration).[37] The writings that he produced instead were letters addressed to individuals such as Thomas Cromwell and Thomas More; a meditation probably written initially for

---

[36] John Gwynnethe, *A declaracion of the state* (London, 1554), A.2r–v.
[37] His last piece of polemic was a refutation of Richard Pace's *Praefatio in Ecclesiasten recognitum ad Hebraicam veritatem* (London, 1527), which survives in one manuscript copy, TNA, SP 6/5, fols. 46r–83v.

personal use, but later sent to More for his edification;[38] and two
devotional guides, called *A spirituall consolation* and *The wayes to perfect
Religion*, written for his half-sister Elizabeth White, nun of Dartford
Priory. From these differences it is clear that the impact that Fisher sought
to make beyond the prison walls was also distinct from that of Frith.
The explicit aim of the two guides he wrote for his sister, for example, was
to instruct her in meditative techniques. This particular choice of writing
has usually been interpreted as a retreat into medievalism under the
pressure of incarceration.[39] However, the intensely private and inward
form of devotion that the two spiritual guides set out also fulfilled a
secondary function, of providing his Catholic sister with a covert way to
continue practising her faith under the increasingly hostile conditions
within the public realm. Thus these writings should not be seen as a
retreat into the past, but rather as a direct response to contemporary
events, particularly the various Acts of Succession passed in the 1530s and
the Treason Act of 1534, which together made it a treasonous offence even
to suggest that the king was a tyrant, usurper, or heretic.

   The claim that Fisher retreated into medievalism derives from the
observed continuity between his two treatises for Elizabeth and the medieval tradition of spiritual guides. As has been noted by R. W. Chambers,
'[i]t is not fanciful to see, in the Anglo-Saxon version of St Benedict's *Rule*
adapted for nuns, the beginning of a literature which ends with the English
work addressed by ... Fisher to ... Elizabeth White'.[40] What unites these
works is the tradition of men writing spiritual guides for women in the
vernacular. However, Fisher's use of this genre of writing is not as
backward-looking as it initially seems, as spiritual guides continued to be
popular well into the sixteenth century. A brief overview of printed books
in the latter years of the fifteenth century and the first three decades of the
sixteenth century will show that, not only did presses print the most

---

[38] The poem was attributed to Thomas More by one Robert Parkyn in his commonplace book
(Oxford, Bodleian Library, MS Lat. th. d. 15). However a draft of the meditation complete with
revisions in Fisher's hand survives in the National Archives (TNA, SP1/93, fols. 99r–102v). E. E.
Reynolds reasons that Fisher must have sent a fair copy to More, who passed it on to his son John,
who, in turn, gave it to Robert Parkyn, curate of Adwick-le-Street (which is near Barnburgh, the
Yorkshire home of John More). See E. E. Reynolds, *Saint John Fisher* (Wheathampstead, 1972), 261.

[39] The perception of Fisher as an essentially conservative churchman has been challenged by Brendan
Bradshaw, 'Bishop John Fisher 1469–1535: The Man and his Work', in *Humanism, Reform and the
Reformation: The Career of Bishop John Fisher*, ed. Brendan Bradshaw and Eamon Duffy
(Cambridge, 1989), 1–24.

[40] R. W. Chambers, 'On the Continuity of English Prose from Alfred to More and his School', in
Nicholas Harpsfield, *The Life and Death of Sr Thomas Moore, Knight*, ed. E. V. Hitchcock, EETS
OS 186 (London, 1932), xciii.

popular medieval examples of this genre, monks and other spiritual men continued to write such guides well into the 1530s.[41] Fisher was adopting a form of writing that was still alive and well, but he did not imagine the broad readership that print publication could bring. Rather, and like many of his predecessors, such as Richard Rolle, Walter Hilton, and Richard Whitford, he wrote for a single female reader engaged in a solitary life of devotion.[42] He was not concerned with the corporate body of believers, but, with the individual's private experience of God. As Sarah Beckwith aptly puts it, such devotion 'concerns the unmediated inner self and its relationship to the unmediated transcendent God'.[43] It is this inherently asocial tendency in the genre that is vital to Fisher's project.

The asocial impetus of Fisher's works is evident from the very beginning of the first guide, now known as *A spirituall consolation*. The main body of the text constitutes a 'fruiteful meditacion', which should be practised when Elizabeth feels herself 'most heauie and slouthfull to doe any good worke'. At such times, she should imagine herself as a person suddenly 'taken and rauyshed' by death.[44] In the prefatory exposition of how Elizabeth should use this meditation, Fisher instructs her 'neuer reade thys meditation but alone by your selfe in secrete maner, where you maye be most attentyue therevnto' (369). Fisher stresses the importance of Elizabeth's physical withdrawal into a private space during meditation through *perissologia*, or more specifically, *synonymia*: he does not think it adequate to instruct Elizabeth to read this treatise 'alone', but adds 'by your selfe' and 'in secrete maner'. The effect of this rhetorical device, which is essentially tautological and dogmatic, is one of profound isolation. Fisher's reasoning for this is that it will allow her to concentrate, presumably by removing distractions. But we should also note that, in withdrawing,

---

[41] For a sixteenth-century example of such a guide, see Richard Whitford's, *A dayley exercyse and experience of dethe* (London, 1537), which, according to its preface, was originally written *c*. 1517 (sig, A.iv). For examples of printings of medieval versions, see *This tretyse is of loue and spekyth of iiij of the most specyall louys that ben in the worlde* (Westminster, 1493), which is a modernised version of the *Ancrene Wisse*; and the four versions of Walter Hilton's *Scale of Perfection*, published in the years 1494–1533 (*STC* 14042, 14043, 14044, and 14045).

[42] Richard Rolle's *Ego dormio* was written for a nun of Yedingham Priory; his *Form of Living* was apparently written for Margaret de Kyrkby, a young woman recluse probably at the beginning of her enclosure as an anchoress; *The Commandment*, also by Rolle, was written for a nun of Hampole; book 1 of Walter Hilton's *Scale of Perfection* is addressed to an anchoress; and Richard Whitford's *A dayley exercyse* was written originally for 'Dame Elizabeth Gybs', the Abbess of Syon.

[43] Sarah Beckwith, *Christ's Body: Identity, Culture, and Society in Late Medieval Writings* (London, 1993), 12.

[44] *English Works of John Fisher, Bishop of Rochester (1469–1535): Sermons and Other Writings, 1520–1535*, ed. Cecilia A. Hatt (Oxford, 2002), 368. Subsequent references to Fisher's works will be given by page number in the text.

Elizabeth would remove herself from any mediating figures or structures, such as that imposed by corporate worship and prayer. This implies that Fisher believes that in order to come close to God in contemplation, the religious figure really does require a private space.

That the meditation is for the medication of the individual soul is also emphasised by the manner in which the subject of death is treated. Cecilia Hatt suggests that by addressing an event that is common to all, Fisher involves the wider community.[45] However, this commonplace concerning death ignores the actual experience of reading this meditation. In fact, the notion of death's universality is notable only in its absence from Fisher's discussion. What Fisher requires from Elizabeth is that she imagine the fear and desperation that would beset the dying person if she had not had time 'to repent mee and amende my lyfe' (370). The important feature of this method of meditation is empathy, something that is impossible without a sense of identification; and one cannot identify with the anonymous masses. Accordingly, Fisher writes the meditation itself in first person, identifying fully with the dying person: 'Alas, alas, I am vnworthily taken' (369). By prioritising the individual experience of death over the universal, Fisher implies that, at the moment of death, all other people become irrelevant, and you are answerable to God alone.

It is tempting to see this treatise as an indication that Fisher spent his last days in meditation on death.[46] The topic would certainly have been apt, and there is one supporting autobiographical passage in the statement of the dying man that '[n]eyther buildyng of Colleges, nor makyng of Sermons, nor giuing of almes, neyther yet anye other manner of buzynesse shall helpe you' (375). The specific relevance to Fisher, who had a significant role in the establishment and organisation of Christ's College and St John's College, and was famous for his preaching, is indubitable.[47] But the short-sighted notion that this is a mode of self-expression or veiled autobiography ignores the very purpose of the text: to instruct Fisher's sister. Hatt is more cautious in her interpretation, suggesting that this interpolation may have been included by Fisher as reassurance for Elizabeth that her brother was aware of the nearness of death and actively engaged in preparing himself to meet it.[48] What this implies is a kind of

---

[45] Ibid., 356.

[46] Brad Gregory suggests such a biographical reading in his *Salvation at Stake: Christian Martyrdom in Early Modern Europe* (Cambridge, MA, 1999), 257.

[47] Richard Rex, 'Fisher, John [St John Fisher] (c. 1469–1535)', *ODNB* (Oxford, 2004), www.oxforddnb.com/view/article/9498 [accessed 18 December 2012].

[48] Hatt, ed., *English Works of John Fisher*, 360.

parallelism between the situation of Fisher and Elizabeth. Through the implication that he is using the isolation of the prison cell to meditate on his death, he provides a model for Elizabeth on how to withdraw and turn her mind inwards, towards her soul. Fisher's model emphasises physical withdrawal and eliminates the social context of human experience in order to come close to God.

This asocial impetus is also true of Fisher's second treatise, *The wayes to perfect Religion*, which proposes a remove, not into a private space, but into the self. As has already been discussed, in *A spirituall consolation* Elizabeth is instructed to remove herself and read this meditation, devising in her mind 'all the conditions of a man or woman sodaynlye taken and rauyshed by death: and thynke with your selfe that yee were in the same condition so hastily taken' (368). While it asks for some inward imagination and empathy, the subject matter remains external to her in the form of a text she must read. In *The wayes to perfect Religion*, Fisher instead asks Elizabeth to internalise ten considerations of why she should love God: 'trulie imprint them in your remembraunce' (399). The verb *imprint*, with its connotations of print publication, suggests a process through which the text of Fisher's treatise is written into Elizabeth's memory. In this manner, she does not require any external materials through which to come close to God.

In the same way that Fisher disposed of the text, he also dispenses with the physical space of remove. At the end of *The wayes to perfect Religion*, Fisher provides Elizabeth with seven short prayers, one for each day of the week. Each is an appeal to Jesus to change her inner attitude towards him, such as: 'O blessed Iesu make me loue thee intierlie', and 'O sweete Iesu giue me a natural remembraunce of thy passion'.[49] Fisher explains that he has provided these short prayers because then 'you may in your heart shortly pray what companie so euer you be amongest' (399). Using the device of *hyperbaton*, Fisher inverts the normal syntactical order of the components 'in your heart' and 'shortly pray' (we would more normally expect it to take the form, 'you may shortly pray in your heart'). Such an inversion functions to place the 'heart' at the greatest possible distance from the social context invoked by the phrase 'what companie so euer you be amongest'. This relegation of the social context to the end of the sentence suggests how the heart may become a place of remove, as

---

[49] As Eamon Duffy has noted, these prayers are very similar to the series of petitions in the form of a 'song' to the Holy name at the end of Rolle's *Ego dormio*. See Eamon Duffy, 'The Spirituality of John Fisher', in *Humanism, Reform and the Reformation*, 205–32 (212).

emphatically distant from outside influences as that private space in the first treatise. The notion is that, through brief inward reflection, Elizabeth may withdraw into a private communication with God without those around her either noticing or suspecting. This process – by which Elizabeth might alienate herself from her social context – has a certain dissident power. By doing away with outward observance, no clues remain as to what is going on within the mind. For this status, we might use Greg Walker's term 'alienated interiority'.

Walker coined this phrase at the end of his book, *Writing under Tyranny*, during a passage in which he interrogates James Simpson's thesis that discursive space was centralised in the reign of Henry.[50] Walker argues that as the accepted conventions of political life and cultural exchange collapsed around them, so writers were forced to invent or rediscover new ways of writing, which could sustain and justify public writing outside the conventions of courtly counsel and beyond the direct gaze of the monarch, who had hitherto been the ultimate patron and arbiter of literary activity. Fisher's guides were not conceived of as public writings, but they might nevertheless justifiably be described as expressions of 'alienated interiority', since they expound a mode by which opposition might be exercised from within the structure to which it is opposed.[51] The notion of alienation also aptly describes the effect of the legislation of the 1530s on the Catholic Church. As Ethan Shagan has commented, 'the politics of the Royal supremacy, with its firm, bipartite division of the realm into conformists and traitors, hopelessly splintered the English Catholic majority. Those who should have been the leaders of a resisting faction instead were increasingly driven underground or into exile',[52] or else imprisoned. Fisher, indeed, must have felt himself to be part of a fragmented church, incapable of the communality demonstrated by those other figures that the authorities were attempting to expunge from the public realm, the evangelicals: the only hope of Catholicism surviving outside the prison, so Fisher's guides imply, was by individual and internalised expressions of dissidence.

This has particular resonance for his intended recipient, Elizabeth White. Henry was particularly concerned about the possibility of organised resistance to his divorce and the break with Rome, and began to exert

---

[50] For a fuller discussion of this thesis, put forward in Simpson's book *Reform and Cultural Revolution*, see the Introduction above.

[51] Greg Walker, *Writing under Tyranny: English Literature and the Henrician Reformation* (Oxford, 2005), 414–15.

[52] See E. H. Shagan, *Popular Politics and the English Reformation* (Cambridge, 2003), 59.

pressure on the English religious houses to confirm their support, imposing oaths of allegiance to be sworn by monks, friars, and nuns.[53] Those who had already been vocal in their criticism of Henry and those who subsequently refused to swear the oaths were executed, including the Nun of Kent, and the monks and nuns who had helped her, three Charterhouse priors, and three Charterhouse monks. Under such pressure, the religious overwhelmingly conformed, and we must assume that Elizabeth did too. Certain questions remain, however, as George Bernard notes: 'How far did they more actively follow royal instructions? How far did they remain attached to the papacy?'[54] These are questions that the famous monastic visitations of 1535/6 sought to answer. As the spaces of resort that nuns and monks had previously kept private were opened up to the inspection of figures such as Richard Layton, Thomas Legh, John ap Rich, and John Tregonwell, we might wonder whether White recited those prayers which, as Fisher asserted, 'you may in your heart shortly pray what companie so euer you be amongest'.[55] The inner realm was the one remaining locus of resistance for this Catholic woman.

Despite specific relevance, however, Fisher's two guides, like their medieval antecedents, also offer general edification for other Catholics. While the texts were unsuitable for rallying dissident communities against the crown, they did provide models for individuals to practise their faith within hostile circumstances, and as meditative preparation for persecution and even death. The latter is suggested by the title page provided for *A spirituall consolation* in its 1578 publication, which reads:

> written by Iohn Fyssher Bishoppe of Rochester, to hys sister Elizabeth, at suche tyme as hee was prisoner in the Tower of London. Uery necessary, and commodious for all those that mynde to leade a vertuous lyfe: also to admonishe them, to be at all tymes prepared to dye, and seemeth to bee spoken in the person of one that was sodainly preue[n]ted by death.[56]

The phrase 'to be at all tymes prepared to dye' is interesting because it contains two possible readings. On the one hand, it refers to the nature of the spiritual exercise following in that it teaches the reader to behave in

---

[53] Instructions on how to elicit these oaths can be found in *LP*, vol. vii, 665 (1), (2), (3); 921, 1024, 1121, 1216, 1347, 1594; and *LP*, vol. vii, 31. For a discussion the imposition of the oaths, see G. W. Bernard, *The King's Reformation: Henry VIII and the Remaking of the English Church* (New Haven, CT, 2005), 244.

[54] Bernard, *King's Reformation*, 244.

[55] On this invasion of private devotional spaces, see Alan Stewart, *Close Readers: Humanism and Sodomy in Early Modern England* (Princeton, NJ, 1997), 38–83.

[56] *A spirituall consolation* (London, 1578?), sig. A.1r.

such a way that one is ready for death whenever it comes; however, its wording also suggests that one ought also to be prepared to die for one's faith, which would have had particular resonance for the Elizabethan Catholic readership its editor seemed to have in mind. W. Carter, to whom the *Short-title Catalogue* ascribes the printing of this sole edition of the texts, had been an amanuensis to Nicholas Harpsfield (from whom, T. A. Birrell postulates, he inherited a manuscript of these guides)[57] before he became a printer. Fisher's text is completely in keeping with the usual kinds of texts that Carter printed, which – unlike Robert Persons's so-called 'Greenstreet House' press, which published books that were aggressively polemical, clerical, and determinedly up to the minute – were devotional, edifying, and non-polemical. Like Fisher before him, Carter recognised the value of traditional devotional genres to evoke a state of interiority, which in turn provided an alternative way for readers to imagine a locus for dissidence within the public realm. However, Carter, in printing this text and therefore disseminating it to numerous readers, anticipated this asocial stance as something that could promote a more organised and widespread form of resistance than Fisher could ever have imagined. Despite the clear differences between the intended readerships of Frith and Fisher's prison works, the methods and the aims of their instruction, it is striking that eventually (in Fisher's case, forty-three years after the work's original composition) both men's work was appropriated by publishers for the broader aims of their dissident communities.

The carriers of John Bradford's letters

The organisation of dissident communities takes time. Unlike the two previous examples, John Bradford's community of co-religionists was neither new, nor fragmentary. Following the Protestant reign of Edward VI, the Marian Protestants were strengthened by previous state support; they had had time and freedom to establish Protestant networks; and they had previous experience of persecution and models of leadership to follow.[58] The result was that the leaders who were confined to prison were served by an organised network of copyists and carriers both on the inside

---

[57] T. A. Birrell, 'William Carter (c. 1549–84): Recusant Printer, Publisher, Binder, Stationer, Scribe – and Martyr', *Recusant History*, 28 (2006), 22–42. For details of the sixteen works that Carter published, see 31–4.

[58] Thomas S. Freeman argues that Anne Askew's *Examinations* and William Tyndale's correspondence with John Frith were both important harbingers of things to come. Freeman, 'Publish and Perish', 244–5 (at note 51).

and on the outside. Bradford, who had been a respected and popular preacher during the reign of Edward, was an important hub in this network (i.e. a node 'with an anomalously large number of links').[59] This is demonstrated most clearly by the massive volume of correspondence that he wrote from prison, which forms a corpus larger than that of any other prisoner during the period. John Foxe, editor of the 'Book of Martyrs', and Henry Bull, editor of *Certain most godly, fruitful, and comfortable letters of such true saintes and holy martyrs of God,* together printed eighty-six of his letters, and a further nine were published in the Victorian Parker Society volumes of his works, seven of which had never been previously printed. This correspondence allowed Bradford to maintain and extend the connections he had formed in Edward's reign covering an impressive geographical spread from Kent to Lancashire. Unlike Frith's dimensionless but apparently expanding community, the paper trail left by Bradford and his co-religionists means that scholars can begin to reconstruct the network of Protestant influence outside the prison.

However, to the near contemporary readers of the printed versions of these letters, and scholars dependent upon Foxe and Bull's editions, the structure, organisation, and extent of these textual communities are obscured. These two martyrologists designed their publications both to glorify the martyrs produced by the Reformation, and to hold them up as examples of faith. It was the content of the letters that was valuable to these two editors: they were printed not only as evidence of the martyrs' great wisdom and leadership from within prison, but also as material that is edifying for all. As Susan Wabuda has observed, the editing of the two martyrologists 'enhanced the scriptural style of the letters, and their universal application, by removing personal or mundane details which might have otherwise distracted the reader'.[60] For example, a letter addressed to Joyce Hales following the suicide of her faither-in-law is headed by Foxe: 'A letter which he wrote to a faithfull woman in her heauines and trouble: most comfortable for all those to read that are afflicted and broken harted for their sinnes'.[61] Here, an emphasis on the content comes at the expense of the relationships that the letters actually marked. The identity of the recipient is skipped over, as is the personal and

---

[59] Barabási, *Linked*, 56.
[60] Susan Wabuda, 'Henry Bull, Miles Coverdale, and the Making of John Foxe's *Book of Martyrs*', in *Martyrs and Martyrologies: Papers Read at the 1992 Summer Meeting and the 1993 Winter Meeting of the Ecclesiastical History Society,* ed. Diana Wood, Studies in Church History 30 (Oxford, 1993), 245–258 (256).
[61] *TAMO* (1570), 1861.

specific nature of her 'heauiness'. Foxe and Bull also frequently get rid of personal greetings (which normally occupy the final passages of letters, and provide useful information for scholars of the extent of the prisoner's intended influence outside the prison) and references to the letters' carriers. While reference to carriers might be perceived as banal and unedifying – indeed irrelevant to the secondary readership of the print versions of the letters, for these texts were brought to them by publishers and booksellers – for the author, Bradford, and for the intended original recipients, the figure of the carrier was vital. This is because the carrier not only fulfilled the practical function of transferring letters between the prison and the public sphere, but also served the symbolic function of representing the uncontainability of Protestant ideas.

While the significance of individual carriers has begun to be recognised through the work of historians such as Thomas S. Freeman,[62] there is a reason why the role of the carrier in general terms has been overlooked. The communication they enable between Bradford and the recipient is perceived to take precedence over any relationship that either party may have with the carrier. This has two causes. Firstly, while the nature of the relationship between author and recipient is easy to gauge – through the content of the letter, the number of letters that pass between sender and recipient, and through a bit of biographical excavation – it is much trickier to gauge roles and relationships in the case of carriers. There are prominent figures such as William Punt and Augustine Bernher, whose significance is more clearly understood, but most frequently the carriers are nameless and our picture of the relationship between Bradford and these men must be pieced together from subtle cues in the text. Secondly, the assumption remains that the content of the letter, valuable as it is deemed, is the reason for the letter's existence: that this thing needed to be said and that the carrier was subsequently sought to make sure these words found their intended audience. The carriers are really only invoked by scholars to stress how organised the martyrs were in making sure their writings got disseminated. However, the following pages will show that when we read the letters in their original manuscript forms we find that, in some cases, it is not the carrier that is the afterthought, but rather the letter. Furthermore, in the cases where a carrier is mentioned or named, we can see that the

---

[62] See Freeman, 'Publish and Perish', 240, 242, 244, 251; Thomas S. Freeman, 'Fate, Faction and Fiction in Foxe's *Book of Martyrs*', *Historical Journal*, 43 (2000), 601–23 (604–9); Thomas S. Freeman, 'Punt, William (*fl.* 1548–1563)', *ODNB*, www.oxforddnb.com/view/article/68044 [accessed 18 December 2012]. See also Susan Wabuda, 'Bernher, Augustine (*d.* 1565)', *ODNB*, www.oxforddnb.com/view/article/2256 [accessed 18 December 2012].

letters were only a small part of the ministry that Bradford practised through these individuals. As well as delivering letters, they also lent and collected texts owned or written by Bradford, communicated verbal messages and news, and provided important fellowship for more isolated figures. Sometimes they were themselves the subject matter of the letters. From this, it becomes apparent that carriers were not merely ties connecting the nodes of sender and recipient. Instead, like the figure of Bradford himself, they are hubs: figures with large numbers of ties.

Contrary to what we may expect, the evidence in the letters shows that often it is the presence of a potential carrier that prompts the writing of a letter, and not the writing of the letter that prompts the author to seek a carrier. For instance, in a letter to his mother, Bradford signs off: 'Out of /the Tower\ of London, immediatelye after I hade red my brotheris letter the vj day of october, 1553'.[63] From the detail that the letter to his mother was written 'immediatelye after' receiving one from his brother, it is clear that the carrier had not been summoned. Rather, the opportunity to get a letter to his mother had presented itself with the carrier of his brother's letter, who must return to Manchester, where all Bradford's family lived. We can also see this opportunistic aspect of letter composition and delivery in an apology in a letter to Mistress Wilkinson. Bradford excuses the brevity and roughness of his letter with the explanation that 'presently I have litle tyme by reason of this bringars short departing'.[64] These examples make it clear that a letter had not been previously prepared; rather, they were written while the carrier waited, probably in the prison cell itself. The network or infrastructure was not built to disseminate the letter; rather, it often predated the letter.

One motivation for this apparent opportunism is a sense of duty. It appears to be the case that, once a potential carrier had presented himself, the prisoner felt almost bound to use him. This is illustrated in a letter from Bradford to one Coker, who, according to the manuscript version of this letter, lived 'at Hazeleigh by Maldon in Essex'. In this letter Bradford records that he feels compelled to write:

> For if I shold not so do hauinge so conuenient a messenger, as I might towards you incurre the susspic[i]on of ingratitude and forgetfullnes of your love token sent to me, in the tower by my good brother William Punt: so might I not satisfye the desire of thys my poore brother and frende John Searchfield, whiche cometh vnto you for helpe and comforte in this troublesome time.[65]

---

[63] ECL, MS 260, fol. 125v.   [64] ECL, MS 262, fol. 247dv.   [65] ECL, MS 260, fol. 224r.

Here, even more clearly, one can see that the content of this letter does not matter as much as the act of having written when the opportunity arose. But what is peculiar to this letter is that much of the content is concerned with the carrier himself. After introducing Searchfield as a man seeking 'helpe and comforte', Bradford gives a recommendation of his character before entreating Coker to give him shelter. So while this letter shares a similar opportunism with the other examples, it has a very different relationship with its carrier. Where one might normally expect a carrier to serve the aims of the letter – to bring about a communication between the author and the recipient – it is actually the letter that serves the aims of the carrier. It aims to make a new connection, a new friendship and relationship of comfort, between Coker and Searchfield. This glimpse suggests more complex relationships between Bradford, the carrier, and the recipient. It shows how carriers might have relationships with the authors and with the recipients of the letters, and not merely act to serve these relationships from an external position.

The other carrier mentioned in the letter to Coker of Hazeleigh is William Punt, who had carried out a delivery from Coker to Bradford. This reference to a carrier by name is telling; we might contrast it with the anonymity observed in Harington's reference to his fellow prisoners in the dedication to his *Booke of freendeship*, and the anonymity of the single readers for which Frith originally composed his *Mirroure* and *A christen sentence*. It implies a certain familiarity: he is more than just a casual carrier. And from external evidence we know this to be the case. He is mentioned again by name in a letter from Bradford to Doctor Hill: 'My brother P<unt> telleth me you wold faine haue the last parte of Seint hieroms workes, to haue the use thereof for a fortnight'.[66] And he also made several trips to the Continent in order to deliver letters from John Hooper to his wife, Anna, in Frankfurt. Bradford might have responded in an opportunistic fashion, writing letters when carriers were available, but the evidence here is that the carriers themselves were far from random, and in many cases it may have been a habitual role. The benefit for Bradford of using such individuals is that he knew they could be trusted; and we might hypothesise that the repeated visits from such figures led to deep friendships.[67] This, in turn, led to the entrusting of these figures with more significant roles than that of mere carrier.

---

[66] ECL, MS 260, fol. 203v.
[67] Punt and Bradford appear to have become very close friends, and he was almost certainly the 'W. P.' whom Bradford made co-executor of his books and to whom the martyr bequeathed two

A clear example of this can be found in the aforementioned letter from Bradford to Joyce Hales, dated 8 August 1554, following the suicide of her father-in-law. This is the earliest of the surviving correspondence from Bradford to Joyce independent of her husband. From the emotional content of this letter, his personalised guidance on the subject of election, and his touching assertion that he 'wilbe a Symon absent to carrie as I can lern youre crose', we can infer that he was already familiar with her at the time of writing. However, despite this very personal involvement, the several references to the carrier of the letter (all of which are cut by the early editors, Foxe and Bull) suggest that Bradford hoped that this third person could be the Simon *present* to Joyce. Possibly fearing that Joyce's faith might be adversely affected by her grief, Bradford clearly recognised the need for the kind of comfort that could be gained from a fellow member of the Protestant community.

The first two passages in which the carrier is mentioned contain cues for Joyce that the bringer has additional messages to give her:

> The cause why hitherto sithen /I receued\ your letters by William Porrege (which I receyved savelie, <on Sondaye was sevennyght, both your tokens>) I /have not\ sent unto you /again\, this bringer can tell you.
>
> . . .
>
> Oh that god wold hereby touch your husbandes harte so that he wold get hym beyond the sees: although by that means I shuld never more corporallie see you (as in dede I fear it) but goddes good wilbe done. I have written to hym as the bringer can tell /you\.[68]

Serving as verbal messenger as well as physical carrier, the 'bringer' can explain the reason why Bradford had taken seven days to reply since receiving Joyce's letter from William Porrege (and by implication why he did not send back a reply with the carrier), and inform her what was in the letter that Bradford had written to her husband. The emphasis on immaterial speech in this passage is further heightened by the contrast of bodily contact, or the lack thereof ('I shuld never more corporallie see you'); the person who is bodily present is the carrier. That the carrier effectively stands in for Bradford is stressed by the added intimacy introduced by the interlineated 'you' in the last line. The use of supplementary verbal

---

shirts (see ECL, MS 262, fol. 72v). For further discussion of Punt, see Freeman, 'Punt, William (*fl.* 1548–1563)'.

[68] ECL, MS 260, fol. 79v. Cf. *TAMO* (1570), 1861–3.

messages like this was commonplace in letter writing of this period.[69] But in these peculiar circumstances it may be due to anxiety that, in committing this information to paper, someone might read it who should not; it may be due to a shortage of paper or time; or it may be because Bradford felt that the spoken word is more trustworthy, more comforting, and more personal.

This of course is speculation, as is the content of these verbal messages. What is certain, however, is that these extratextual messages create lacunae in the text that force the reader to look outside the letter proper to the carrier. This hints at what kind of exchange may have gone on between Bradford and the carrier. The carrier had not just stood waiting for the document that he was to transport, but obviously had been engaged in conversation about the matter discussed therein, and indeed the content of another letter sent to Joyce's husband. There is obviously a great deal of trust that the carrier will get these details right and accurately reflect Bradford's opinions, and thereby ensure that the reception of the letter is in keeping with Bradford's intentions. This demonstrates that the community could not be kept alive purely in a textual form.

Another passage invoking the carrier, also cut by Foxe and Bull, suggests that Bradford has entrusted the carrier with another role in addition to that of verbal messenger – to provide support and aid to Joyce: 'This bringer (if you come hither) shall come for you when you will and whither you will, and now tarry with you as long as you will although I desier indede to know how you do.'[70] Whether this passage refers to Joyce literally coming 'hither', coming to London, or instead whether it means simply writing a reply, remains unclear. Whichever is the case, however, Bradford gives his word that this particular carrier will be there to help her. If it signals a journey, he will 'come for her', meet her; if it signals writing, he is a ready and willing carrier. There is the clear assurance that she will not be left unattended. Neither does she need to be lonely. The assertion that the carrier will 'now tarry with you as long as you will' tells us that, at this trying time following her father-in-law's suicide and in the midst of her doubts concerning election, she does not need to be alone. From the fact that the carrier is offered as a companion until Joyce sends him back with her reply, we might deduce that he must have been a person familiar to

[69] For a detailed discussion of the history of letter writing, see Richard Beadle, 'Private Letters', in *A Companion to Middle English Prose*, ed. A. S. G. Edwards (Cambridge, 2004), 289–306. See also *Letterwriting in Renaissance England*, ed. Alan Stewart and Heather Wolfe (Washington, DC, 2004), 121–46.

[70] ECL, MS 260, fol. 81v.

her, otherwise it might not offer much comfort. Certainly Bradford trusted this individual to be able to fulfil such a sensitive task of providing real comfort. He appears to have hoped that the carrier he sent could make the textual community a tangible and comforting reality to Joyce. In these circumstances, literary criticism, touchingly, reaches the limit of its explanatory power. These letters demonstrate that texts alone were not enough to sustain co-religionists outside the prison; that, ultimately, some real human contact is necessary to help individuals sustain their faith in the face of persecution.

At the beginning of this chapter I suggested, using Alexandra Walsham's words, that the text was a 'proxy and prosthesis' for the voices of incarcerated men and women. For Bradford, like Fisher and Frith before him, this was certainly true. However, through his references to the carriers of his letters we know that the *'bringer'* also functioned as a 'proxy and prosthesis' for Bradford. As figures who could make and maintain ties through travel and human interaction, they became hubs marked by a number of physical and verbal exchanges that must have been almost as numerous as the exchanges marked by Bradford's correspondence. In this capacity, as socially integrated figures, they provided Bradford with a way of imagining the propagation of dissident ideas outside the prison that stands in striking contrast to the methods employed by Fisher. While presumably Fisher's writings were delivered to White by a carrier (possibly by his brother Robert, who is reported to have have brought food to Fisher in the Tower),[71] the human interaction that such an exchange implies is excluded from the texts by both the absence of any metanarrative of dissemination and by the emphasis on the necessity of profound isolation in meditation. Bradford's carriers, however, allowed him to do more than simply imagine the spread of information; they also enabled Bradford to carefully manage it. Not only could he control who his letters (initially) went to, he could also control their reception through instructions given to the carriers and by shaping his writings in response to the feedback he received from these same figures. These carriers thus bring to life both the reputation of uncontainability that Frith had sought to create, and the organised networks of 'brethren' so feared by More.

---

[71] Hatt, ed. *English Works of John Fisher*, 359.

CHAPTER FIVE

Liberating the text?

In an essay on the changing nature of literary enquiry in relation to the history of the book, Leah Price suggests that a change is needed in the way that we study texts, from an approach that privileges human agency to one that takes the perspective of the book itself. To illustrate her point, she discusses late examples of it-narratives dating from the nineteenth century in which novels were narrated from the perspective of a book – often *the* book. The it-narrator of one American *History of a Bible* has particular relevance to this study because of its use of prison metaphors. Beginning at the moment when a buyer 'liberates' it from being a 'close prisoner' in a bookseller's shop, this Bible's first owners are described as 'jailors' who force it 'to sit upon a chair in the corner of the room'. One owner 'in the heat of passion locked me into my old cell, where I remained in close confinement', others 'joined in scandalizing my character; and I was again confined to my old cell'.[1] As Price points out, to be read, in this metaphor, is to be 'discharged from prison'; even the glass front of the bookcase becomes a 'prison door, whose locking and unlocking determines that narrator's fortunes'.[2] This metaphor communicates not only the idea that the *raison d'être* of a book is to be read, but, more crucially, that the word of God is shackled if it is not read and circulated in the community. This evangelical sentiment expresses the fear that St Paul's boast that 'the worde of God is not bounde' (2 Timothy 2.9; see Chapter 4 above) was no longer true in nineteenth-century America.

This chapter challenges the idea that the print publication and subsequent circulation of prison literature can unproblematically be described as a form of liberation. Print, of course, was not the only way that prison writings reached a more general audience. As the last two chapters have

---

[1] *History of a Bible* (Ballston Spa, NY, 1811), 1, 5, 6. Quoted in Leah Price, 'From *The History of a Book* to a "History of the Book"', *Representations*, 108 (2009), 120–38 (126).
[2] Price, 'History of the Book', 126; *History of a Bible*, 7.

demonstrated, networks of copiers and carriers both inside and outside the prison enabled what Harold Love has called 'scribal publication', through which prisoners' writings came to be read by a surprisingly large number of people.[3] However, there are reasons to be wary of seeing print publication as the obvious next step, in which writings went from being circulated in a restricted, semi-public sphere – or, what we have been calling the counter-public sphere – to being circulated within the Habermasian public sphere. From the perspective of the book, prison writings that were circulated through scribal networks may not have been completely liberated, but neither, for example, were the Protestant prison writings published on the Continent and smuggled into England to be sold on the black market, hidden by their owners, and circulated with the utmost secrecy. Moreover, there were also various reasons for prisoners to be wary of having their writings freely available in print. The main benefit of scribal publication for more sensitive religious and political material was that it was usually dependent upon pre-existing networks of family, friends, and co-religionists.[4] This allowed authors a certain degree of control over who their readership was, and minimised the risk of such writings reaching the attention of the authorities, although there were exceptions to this trend, such as the occasion when Thomas More obtained a copy of the original, scribal version of John Frith's *A christen sentence*. Certain texts were clearly intended to be ephemeral, such as the letters sent between More and John Fisher, which were burnt after being read. Other letters that were subsequently printed in John Foxe's 'Book of Martyrs' contained instructions that they should be burnt, but these were ignored.[5] Clearly their authors did not envisage print publication, let alone inclusion in an influential martyrology. From Chapter 4 we know that many of these letters were written in great haste when the opportunity for a carrier presented itself, but prisoners might have written with more care if they had realised what would become of such missives.

The aim here is not to try and second guess whether individual prisoners intended or desired for their prison writings to be published posthumously, but rather to highlight the differences between scribal and print publication. Print publication presupposes a different kind of relationship between the author and the reader from scribal publication. Firstly, in the making of a book, print implicates a whole range of other figures, who are interposed between author and reader, including scribes and/or printers

---

[3] Harold Love, *Scribal Publication in Seventeenth-Century England* (Oxford, 1993).
[4] Ibid., 179.   [5] See for example John Bradford's letter to his mother, LM, 454.

(in the creation of copy texts), editors, compositors, correctors, typefounders, engravers, pressmen, and bookbinders.[6] Therefore, in order to take the perspective of the book as Price proposes, we must first choose whether to align ourselves with the original text penned by the prisoner, or with the printed and bound object that we call a book, which has been acted upon by a whole range of figures besides the author. Throughout this study I have endeavoured to get as close to the original prison texts as possible, eschewing printed editions where an autograph or early manuscript is available, and trying to strip away any preconceptions we might have about these writings from subsequent publications, whether in the hard-to-ignore context of Foxe's 'Book of Martyrs', modern scholarly editions such as the *Yale Edition of the Complete Works of St Thomas More*, or biographies. My perception – that I was freeing these texts from subsequent accretions – is revealing.[7] It casts the process of editing and printing these texts as a new kind of incarceration, in which writings are hampered with a range of textual shackles. Accordingly, this chapter suggests that print publication, far from liberating prison writings, enforced new kinds of incarceration upon these texts. The three primary kinds of textual shackles that I will be considering in this chapter are the addition of paratexts, the inclusion of a text within an anthology or collection, and the constraints of time. A fourth and final form of subjection, which I touch on in passing throughout the chapter, is reading.

Gerard Genette's definition of a paratext offers itself to the metaphor of imprisonment:

> The paratext is what enables a text to become a book and to be offered as such to its readers and, more generally, to the public. More than a boundary or a sealed border, the paratext is rather a threshold, or . . . a 'vestibule' that offers the world at large the possibility of either stepping inside or turning back. It is an 'undefined zone' between the inside and outside . . . a zone not only of transition but also of transaction: a privileged place of a pragmatics and of a strategy, of an influence on the public.[8]

One of the most striking aspects of this description is the architectural imagery of the paratext, which is a 'space which both frames and inhabits the text'.[9] Unless the book is missing pages, readers must always turn past

[6] For a description of the printing process, see Elizabeth Evenden and Thomas S. Freeman, *Religion and the Book: The Making of John Foxe's 'Book of Martyrs'* (Cambridge, 2011), 16–19.
[7] Cf. Leah S. Marcus, *Unediting the Renaissance: Shakespeare, Marlowe, Milton* (London, 1996), 1–37.
[8] Gerard Genette, *Paratexts: Thresholds of Interpretation*, tr. Jane E. Lewin (Cambridge, 1997), 1–2.
[9] Helen Smith and Louise Wilson, 'Introduction', in their *Renaissance Paratexts* (Cambridge, 2011), 7 (and throughout).

the title page,[10] and sometimes a preface, before they can get to the author's text. But what do these thresholds do? As Genette points out in the final sentence of the passage above, paratexts are pragmatic framing devices that shape the reader's interaction with the text. Such framing may involve editors or authors explaining the reasons for composition, it may invite the reader to interpret the text in a certain way, or it may be used to argue for the text's support of a broader agenda. But while Genette, from his transhistorical perspective, suggests that the meaning and function of the paratext in this context is almost always determined by 'the author and his allies',[11] early modernists working in the field of book history have been quick to point out that textual production was a much more collaborative process in the early days of print, involving a range of competing interests. Arthur Marotti rightly stresses that, when examining the components of a printed book dating from the early modern period, such as the frontispiece, title page, dedicatory epistles to patrons, addresses to readers, or the commendatory poems, we should remember that each was 'a site of contestation and negotiation among authors, publishers/printers, and readership(s)'.[12] In the case of prison writings, which were frequently printed after the deaths of their authors, this negotiation was unbalanced in favour of the publishers and printers' interests and agendas.

The second form of textual incarceration derives from the structure of the anthology. The middle years of the sixteenth century saw the popularisation of the anthology.[13] Authors and printers alike became obsessed with the idea that one could create *the* definitive book on a subject, whether the subject was flora and fauna, medicine or theology. The result was a profusion of big books: collections of works by single authors, multi-author miscellanies of poetry, and a number of encyclopaedic chronicles and martyrologies that spliced together narrative with collected documents. Examples include the *Mirror for Magistrates*, Raphael Holinshed's *Chronicles*, Francis Bacon's *Essays* and *Apothegems New and Old*, Camden's *Remains*, George Gascoigne's *Poesies*, and Edmund Spenser's *Complaints*. Of course, the impetus to compile was not new, as is demonstrated by late medieval manuscript miscellanies, commonplace books, and

---

[10] At least after its introduction *c*.1490–1500. See Margaret M. Smith, *The Title-Page: Its early Development, 1460–1510* (London, 2000).

[11] Genette, *Paratexts*, 2.

[12] Arthur F. Marotti, *Manuscript, Print, and the English Renaissance Lyric* (Ithaca, NY, 1995), 222.

[13] On the rise of the anthology, see David Linton, 'Reading the Meta-Canonical Texts', in *Other Voices, other Views: Expanding the Canon in English Renaissance Studies*, ed. Helen Ostovich, Mary V. Silcox, and Graham Roebuck (Newark, DE and London, 1999), 21–45 (30).

Sammelbände.[14] What set the sixteenth-century anthology apart from many of its predecessors was its strong rationale, which was often expressed in the paratexts that prefaced the collection. This rationale determined what was included and excluded, the ways in which the selection of texts was presented to the reader in terms of ordering and presentation, and how individual components were edited. Such decisions could have a significant impact on how the collected writings were read and valued by a readership. When reading a series of texts from an anthology, either in the order set by the compositor or as a result of personal selections, a reader is compelled to read comparatively, making (conscious and unconscious) links and contrasts and building up a composite picture of the subject or genre defining the anthology. The long-term impact of the anthology on canon formation has received considerable critical attention. Interestingly, the terms in which this topic has been discussed have engaged with the concepts of liberty and constraint, authority and disempowerment.[15] Whereas poets and critics interested in the content of anthologies have tended to attack its closed and exclusive nature, those concerned with their form have argued for the liberating potential of the combinatory structure that allows anthologies to 'pull language out of legal frameworks and decentralise literary culture ... by their subversive deferral of a central authority'.[16] This chapter, however, will take a middle ground by suggesting that while compilers and editors of big books often attempted to close down interpretation, they could not predict the ways in which readers would 'insinuate into [their] text the ruses of pleasure and appropriation'.[17] Not all the texts discussed in this chapter are collections or anthologies, but the most influential ones are. They collect together examples of prison writing with other kinds of literature, poems, and documents – a combination which raises its own issues.

The third and final form of constraint acting upon prison writings during the process of print publication was time, or the lack thereof.

---

[14] For discussion of the anthology's predecessors, see Julia Boffey and John J. Thompson, 'Anthologies and Miscellanies: Production and Choice of Texts', in *Book Production and Publishing in Britain 1375–1475*, ed. Jeremy Griffiths and Derek Pearsall (Cambridge, 1989), 84–102; and Alexandra Gillespie, 'Poets, Printers, and Early English *Sammelbände*', in her 'Print, and Early Tudor Literature', *HLQ*, special issue, 67 (2004), 189–214.

[15] See Jeffrey R. Di Leo, *On Anthologies: Politics and Pedagogy* (Lincoln, NE, 2004), 2.

[16] Barbara Benedict, *Making the Modern Reader: Cultural Mediation in Early Modern Literary Anthologies* (Princeton, NJ, 1996), 221. Cited in Leah Price, *The Anthology and the Rise of the Novel: From Richardson to George Eliot* (Cambridge, 2000), 3. See also *Anthologies of British Poetry: Critical Perspectives from Literary and Cultural Studies*, ed. Barbara Korte, Ralph Schneider, and Stephanie Lethbridge (Amsterdam, 2000).

[17] Michel de Certeau, *The Practice of Everyday Life*, tr. Steven Rendall (Berkeley, CA, 1984), xxi.

A key issue facing editors and publishers was when such writings should be brought to press. Immediate publication was often difficult, and many publishers waited until the reign of a new monarch before they brought sensitive religious and political writings to press. By contrast, other prison writings came to press swiftly in order to meet the needs of religious communities. In the Marian period, for example, many Protestants' writings were smuggled to the Continent, where they were published and then brought back into England by colporteurs. These differing approaches necessarily led to divergent attitudes towards editing and production. Speedy publication placed significant time constraints on the aforementioned editors, compositors, correctors, typefounders, engravers, and pressmen. This could mean the difference between a beautifully presented publication, and one that was littered with typographical errors or other mistakes. Such haste also permitted less time for editorial intervention within the texts themselves – which might involve the excising of certain material or rewriting specific passages – and for the addition of extensive paratextual apparatus. Often such pressures were reflected upon in the publications' paratexts. Tina Skoen has noted that such expressions of haste began to appear in the sixteenth century, which she attributes to rapid developments in the book trade and the ongoing debates about the quality of work issuing from publishing houses.[18] Anthologies, of course, took much longer to produce than single-text publications, so even one put together in haste would require a considerable amount of time in which to take shape. For early modern printers and publishers, then, time was a constraint both on the body of knowledge that one was able to compile and the aesthetic of the finished text.[19] However, as I will suggest below, the greater the time constraints placed upon the publishing process, the less shackled prison writings were likely to become in their final print form.

In proposing print publication as a form of textual incarceration, I do not want to give the impression that prison writers eschewed print. Although the 'stigma of print' may have prevailed for some time amongst courtly writers, many prisoners clearly desired print publication.[20] But print's

[18] Tina Skoen, 'Time and Aesthetic Value in Early Modern Literary Culture' (Norwegian Research Council, Project Period 01.01.2010–31.12.2012).

[19] See Ann M. Blair, *Too Much to Know: Managing Scholarly Information Before the Modern Age* (Princeton, NJ, 2010).

[20] See J. W. Saunders, 'The Stigma of Print: A Note of the Social Bases of Tudor Poetry', *Essays in Criticism*, 1 (1951), 139–64. For a thoughtful counterpoint to this influential study, see Steven W. May, 'Tudor Aristocrats and the Mythical "Stigma of Print"', *Renaissance Papers*, 10 (1980), 11–18.

significance for them was only just beginning to emerge: the constraints and pressures detailed above were relatively new for authors in this period. These were the first generation of prison writers that faced the near inevitability of ending up in print. But as the decades progressed, prisoners' texts were increasingly shaped by existing prison literature, which was being circulated either through scribal publication or through the ever more readily available supply of printed books. This growing body of works began to define expectations of what prisoners might write. For instance, following the publication in 1530 of the heresy trials of the Lollards John Oldcastle and William Thorpe, examples of trial narratives grew exponentially.[21] What we see is a feedback loop between what was being written in prisons and what was being circulated in print in public and counter-public spheres. As a result, prisoners could be said to be writing themselves into a particular tradition of literature – their own disciplinary structure – produced in creative tension with the agendas of editors and publishing houses.

It is because of this important symbiosis that the sections of this chapter are structured around the history of print in sixteenth-century England. The date 1557 is a watershed: in this year the Stationer's Company was granted a royal charter, and two highly influential volumes were published which also happened to contain a number of prison writings: *The Workes of Syr Thomas More Knyght . . . wrytten by him in the Englysh tonge* and *Songes and sonettes, written by the right honorable Lorde Henry Haward late Earle of Surrey, and other.*[22] The first section will examine these two influential works; those that follow will look at examples of how Protestant prison writings were printed before and after the 1557 watershed. John Foxe's famous martyrological anthology, *Actes and Monuments of these latter and perillous dayes*, more commonly known as the 'Book of Martyrs' and first published in 1563, now looks like the inevitable way of publishing Protestant prison literature. However, up until the end of Mary I's reign, evangelical prisoners' writings were being appropriated by a publishing programme that was driven by the desire for rapid circulation. Following Price's encouragement to approach book history from the perspective of the book, these accounts will focus on the different kinds of textual subjection prison writings underwent in the process of being brought to press.

[21] *The examinacion of Master William Thorpe preste accused of heresye before Thomas Arundell, Archebishop of Ca[n]terbury, the yere of ower Lord.MCCCC. and seuen. The examinacion of the honorable knight syr John Oldcastell Lorde Cobham, burnt bi the said Archebisshop, in the fyrste yere of Kynge Henry the Fyfth* (Antwerp, 1530).

[22] Lotte and Trapp's *Cambridge History of the Book in Britain* breaks volumes III and IV at 1557 because of More's *Workes* and Tottel's *Miscellany*, and also because of the royal charter.

1557

In 1557 Richard Tottel published two important books: *The Workes of Syr Thomas More* (published along with Cawood and Waly), and *Songes and sonettes*. The significance of publishing More's *Workes* at this time was that the publication reframed pre-Reformation texts for the post-Reformation context, thus capturing both the upheavals and the continuities in English society at this time.[23] The importance of Tottel's other work is demonstrated more by its commercial success: after its first publication in June 1557, the miscellany of poetry was reissued in two new editions dated 31 July, and by 1587 eleven editions had been printed. Furthermore, both these volumes marked a watershed in the printing of anthologies: after their publication many copycat volumes were printed. The organising principles behind the works, however, could not have been more different. The first collected together More's English writings, while the latter clearly took its shape from the kinds of coterie manuscripts (such as the Arundal Harington manuscript and the Devonshire manuscript) described in Chapter 3. Despite the fact that *Songes and sonettes* collected together poems by numerous Tudor poets, it is now universally know as *Tottel's Miscellany*. The strong association with Tottel's name highlights two important issues that we need to consider when examining how the handful of prison poems found in this volume are presented and what their relationship to the collection as a whole was. Firstly, the moniker reflects the human desire to see an ordering rationale behind a collection. Secondly, it draws our attention to the very present hand of the editor in this volume.[24]

The preface to the *Miscellany* tells the reader that that this is a volume with an agenda:

> That to haue wel written in verse, yea and in small parcelles, deserueth great praise, the woorkers of diuers Latines, Italians, and other, doe proue sufficiently. That our tong is able in that kinde to do as praise worthelye as the rest, the honourable stile of the noble earle of Surrey, and the weightinesse of the depe witted sir Thomas Wiat the elders verse, with seuerall graces in sondry good Englishe writers, do shew abundantly. It resteth now (gentle reder) that thou thinke it not euil don, to publishe, to

---

[23] See Lotte Hellinga and J. B. Trapp, 'Introduction', in *The Cambridge History of the Book in Britain*, vol. III, *1400–1557*, ed. Lotte Hellinga and J. B. Trapp (Cambridge, 1999), 1.

[24] Steven W. May, 'Popularizing Courtly Poetry: Tottel's Miscellany and its Progeny', in *The Oxford Handbook of Tudor Literature, 1485–1603*, ed. Michael Pincombe and Cathy Shrank (Oxford, 2009), 418–33, persuasively argues that Tottel was editor, rather than Nicholas Grimald, John Harington, or Thomas Churchyard.

the honor of the english tong, and for prosit of the studious of Englishe
eloquence, those workes which the vngentle horders vp of such tresure haue
heretofore enuied the.[25]

Tottel makes the point that both the Latin and the Italian tongues have a
canon of renowned poets. His aim is to show English readers that their
native tongue has produced poems as praiseworthy 'as the rest'. As such,
Tottel proposes that this anthology will begin to establish an English poetic
canon to rival its Continental competitors. At the top of the bill is Henry
Howard, the Earl of Surrey, and Thomas Wyatt the elder; here, at least, the
'sondry good English writers' remain nameless (within the collection,
however, forty poems entitled 'Songes written by Nicolas Grimald' follow
on from the sections dedicated to Surrey and Wyatt, but the rest remain
anonymous). In order to bring these poets the kind of recognition necessary
to establish such a canon, Tottel explains how he has had to extract these
poems from the 'vngentle horders vp', the owners of courtly manuscripts
who circulated them within limited social networks. In so doing, Arthur
Marotti argues, Tottel inaugurated 'the fashion for publishing anthologies
that disseminated privately circulated, mostly courtly, poetry to a wider
public'.[26] Tottel's boast and Marotti's gloss suggest that Tottel should be
viewed as a figure who opened up closed literary spheres, liberating texts that
had been locked away. But running against this is a counter-narrative. By
establishing a canon based on 'Englishe eloqunce', he is creating a collection
that is exclusive, comprising works that he or his editor deemed 'wel written
in verse'. He does not care about where they were written (e.g. prison), so
long as they meet the requisite standards. Such deferral to a central authority
is what makes it *Tottel's* miscellany.

We cannot know how Tottel decided what went in and what stayed out
of the volume because it remains unclear on which manuscript or manuscripts the anthology is based.[27] However, there is evidence of what editing
needed to be done for the selected poems to meet his poetic standards.
In order to present Wyatt and Surrey's verse at its best, he subjects it to
metrical correction – most noticeably in Wyatt's section. The word 'correction' here is useful: it reflects the editor's action of 'setting right' lines where
the metrical feet are irregular, but also communicates the idea of 'correcting
[the lines] by disciplinary punishment'.[28] As I argued in Chapter 2, within

[25] *Songes and sonettes, written by the right honorable Lorde Henry Haward late Earle of Surrey, and other,*
ed. Richard Tottel (London, 1557), sig, B.iv.
[26] Marotti, *Manuscript, Print,* 212.   [27] May, 'Popularizing Courtly Poetry', 421.
[28] *OED*, correction, *n*, 1.a and 4.a.

the strictures of metrical verse Wyatt made room for the kind of creativity
and plurality that interests Michel de Certeau so much. Wyatt, of course, is
famous for his uneven meter. Critics have puzzled over the system, or lack
thereof, behind his long-lined verse. For example, a manuscript version of
his prison poem, 'Syghes ar my foode', reads:

> Syghes ar my foode, drynke are my teares;
> Clynkinge of fetters suche musycke wolde crave;
> Stynke and close ayer away my lyf wears;
> Innocencie is all the hope I have.
> Rayne, wynde, or wether I iudge by myne eares.
> Mallice assaulted that rightiousnes should have.
> Sure I am, Brian, this wounde shall heale agayne,
> But yet, alas, the scarre shall styll remayne.[29]

Although the first few lines obscure this, it appears that the underlying
meter is iambic pentameter. The only line that completely adheres to this
strictly is the closing one; however, the second halves of lines four, six, and
seven do also fall into this pattern. Aside from that final law-abiding line,
one of the startling things about the poem is the series of stressed syllables
that open all the other lines, and which add a certain sense of drama and
desperation to Wyatt's laments about the physical and mental state of
imprisonment. Other departures from the iambic pentameter include the
missing foot in the opening line (unless the *es* in 'foode and 'drynke' are
meant to constitute separate syllables), and the extra syllable in lines six
and seven. Whether or not one wishes to interpret these metrical departures as intentional aesthetic decisions which give the verse a sense of
authenticity and emotion, or to believe that Wyatt simply struggled with
the composition of longer-lined verse, there is a more crucial issue to
consider. De Certeau rightly interprets the rules of meter and rhyme as
'a body of constraints stimulating new discoveries, a set of rules within
which improvisation plays' – and so, whether Wyatt's deviations are by
accident or design, we can interpret them as an expression of autonomy
and freedom.[30]

However, in Tottel's hands, this poem changes shape. As I have
signalled in the extract below, words are added and moved, changing the
meter of the finished poem:

[29] BL Harley MS 78, fol. 27r.
[30] De Certeau, *Practice of Everyday Life*, xxii. Compare this with Greg Walker's argument in the final
chapter of *Writing under Tyranny: English Literature and the Henrician Reformation* (Oxford, 2005),
422–32.

Syghes are my foode: _my_ drink are my teares.
Clinking of fetrers _would_ such Musick craue,
Stink, and close ayre away my life _it_ weares.
Poore innocence is all the hope, I haue.
Rain, winde, or wether iudge _I_ by mine eares.
Malice assault_es_, that righteousnesse should haue.
Sure am _I_, Brian, this wounde shall heale again:
But yet alas, the skarre shall still remain.[31]

Wyatt's lines, like unruly subjects, are here disciplined – but not always
very successfully. The addition of 'my' to line one brings up the syllable
count, but it is still one short of ten. Line three of the Harley manuscript
version has ten syllables if you pronounce 'ayer' with two; however, Tottel
clearly pronounced it with one only because he changes the spelling and
adds an extra word to make the line scan correctly (which also makes the
second half of the line conform to iambic meter). He corrects line six to
the present tense, to make it conform to the rest of the poem. These are all
minor changes that affect phraseology only. However, the addition of the
word 'poore' to the beginning of line four is more problematic because it
subtly changes the line's meaning. The original, with its opening stress on
the first syllable of 'innocencie', emphasises Wyatt's guiltlessness (even if
the word choice is slightly ungainly). Tottel's version of the line, by
contrast, makes a statement about the uselessness of such innocence,
which it suggests has become diminished or tainted. There is some
evidence that Wyatt would have been displeased with such tampering
because in another prison text found in the same manuscript as 'Syghes
ar my foode – 'Wyatt's _Defence to the Iuges after the Indictment and the
evidence_, which was written in response to the accusation of treason made
against him in 1541 – exhibits a concern with proper speaking and
reporting. Changing even a single syllable 'either with pen or word', he
argues, can change the entire meaning and effect of an utterance.[32]

In subjecting Wyatt's prison poem to such revisions, the editor places it
back within the 'body of restraints' that Wyatt had originally eschewed in
favour of his own metrical design. However, it is important to remember
that almost all of Wyatt's poems underwent this kind of subjugation, and
even more violent forms of reshaping, as with the series of _rondeaux_ that
were reformatted as sonnets, titled 'Request to Cupide for reuenge of his

[31] Tottel, _Songes and sonettes_, sig. L.4r.
[32] _The Life and Letters of Sir Thomas Wyatt_, ed. Kenneth Muir (Liverpool, 1963) 196. For further
discussion, see Seth Lerer, _Error and the Academic Self: The Scholarly Imagination, Medieval to
Modern_ (New York, 2002), 41–3.

vnkinde loue', 'Complaint for true loue vnrequited', and 'The louer sendeth sighes to mone his sute'.[33] As such, this universal correction provides a kind of equity: by pushing all Wyatt's poems into these legal frameworks – both his prison poem and his courtly verse – we see the irrelevance of the poems' origins to their editorial treatment. Indeed, the only thing that marks this poem apart from Wyatt's other verse is the title added to it: 'Wiate being in prison, to Brian'.

In fact, the titles that Tottel added to each poem – an innovation at this time – can be seen as another form of constraint placed upon on the verse, encasing the poems within specific, prescriptive readings. Tottel acknow-ledges the origins of one other prison poem, Surrey's 'So cruell prison', which is titled: 'Prisoned in Windsor, he recounteth his pleasure there passed'; 'My Ratclif, when thy retchlesse youth offendes' also hints at a prison context with the title 'Exhortacion to learne by others trouble'.[34] Like Wyatt's 'Syghes are my foode', then, these are turned into occasional poems. However, other possible prison verses by Wyatt and Surrey are not given such specific titles. A pair of sonnets that feature the same scar metaphor found in 'Syghes are my foode' and Wyatt's *Defence* (and therefore might reasonably be proposed as prison verse) are entitled 'The louer describeth his restlesse state'.[35] Similarly, Surrey's poem 'When Windsor walles' is headed 'How eche thing saue the louer in spring reuiueth to pleasure'.[36] There are two kinds of constraint working on this poem. Firstly, the title forces the poem into the mould of a generic poem of the love-as-imprisonment variety. Secondly, the addition of this particular title shows how anthologising poems can lead to interpretations that are coloured by surrounding poems. In this case, 'When Windsor walles' sits in the midst of a run of twelve poems (beginning with the first poem and with only one interruption) about the behaviour and emotions of the lover, including 'Description of the restlesse state of a louer', 'Complaint of a louer, that defied loue, and was by loue after the more tormented', and 'Complaint of a louer rebuked'.[37] One must wonder whether Tottel had already ordered the poems in this way and was thus affected by his titling of the preceding nine poems, or whether his choice of title was a calculated move in order to establish a theme. The other prison poem by Surrey in the volume is 'The stormes are past', which was reported by his son to be his final work. This is headed with the words *'Bonum est mihi quod humiliasti me'* (It is good for me that you have

---

[33] Tottel, *Songes and sonettes*, sigs. G.4v, H.1r, and H.2r.   [34] Ibid., sigs. B.2v–3r and C.2v.
[35] Ibid., sig. K.1v.   [36] Ibid., sig. B1r.   [37] Ibid., sigs. A.3r, A.4r and A.4v.

humiliated me (so that I may learn your justification)), a title drawn from
Psalm 118, which appears to be authorial based on the facts that it is unlike
any other title in the volume, and that Surrey produced verse translations
of the Psalms during that final imprisonment.[38] Greg Walker has noticed
the tense interplay between the penitent humility of the title and the sense
of noble self-worth with which it concludes.[39] What is significant is that
Tottel allows this interplay to occur without providing it with an over-
prescriptive framework, or with one that turns it into depoliticised and
generic verse. Rather, the reader is allowed to play with these ideas for
himself – a rare moment of liberty in this overly constrained volume.

   Of course, readers will always find space to insinuate themselves,
however restrictive the editor tries to make the text through the addition
of paratexts and silent editing. As de Certeau has noticed, 'the wandering
eyes of a reader, the improvisation and expectation of meanings inferred
from a few words', turn the text into something that is 'habitable, like a
rented apartment. It transforms another person's property into a space
borrowed for a moment by a transient'.[40] The power of the reader to
disregard even the most manipulative editorial techniques goes some way
to explaining why – despite the fact that only two poems are explicitly
identified as prison poems but given no special status in the volume – a
significant number of scholars have been keen to suggest that the anthology holds a much larger debt to the sixteenth-century prison than providing the odd poem. Marotti, for example, writes:

> While in prison, particularly in the Tower of London, as Ruth Hughey has
> suggested, some individuals actually compiled collections of verse such as
> the main manuscript on which Tottel's Miscellany (1557) was based or a
> large portion of the similar anthology began by John Harington of Stepney,
> the Arundel Harington Manuscript.[41]

As I suggested in Chapter 3, there is very little to prove this assertion except
for the fact that poets within the volume (Wyatt, Surrey, Grimald, and
John Harington) happened to be in prison at some point during their
lifetimes. A much more likely context for collection and exchange was the
court. As a result of dwelling on the shared experience of incarceration,
other critics have also been keen to detect a motive for the inclusion of

---

[38] Ibid., sig. C2r.   [39] Walker, *Writing under Tyranny*, 412–13.
[40] De Certeau, *Practice of Everyday Life*, xxi.
[41] Marotti, *Manuscript, Print*, 4. See also Ruth Hughey, *John Harington of Stepney: Tudor Gentleman;
His Life and Works* (Columbus, OH, 1971), 16–21; Ruth Hughey, *The Arundel Harington Manuscript
of Tudor Poetry*, ed. Ruth Hughey (Columbus, OH, 1960), vol. 1, 44–6; and Marcy L. North, *The
Anonymous Renaissance* (Chicago, IL, 2003), 173.

prison poems. Examining the context for the compilation of the volume – which was published in the month when Mary's campaign of burnings reached their peak, when the country was about to embark on an unpopular war in France, and with concerns about the succession (Mary was, at that time, 41 and childless) – Amanda Holton has argued that such poems were included partly because they were 'attractive models for meditation on political discontent'.[42] Thus we can see that even without editorial cues to interpret this as a text with prison origins, through the process of scholarly reinterpretation the habitable text has been restyled as a prison construct. However, the poems of Wyatt and Surrey are not the only works that have been forced back into the prison by scholars as a result of their publication. More's Tower works, collected in Tottel's other 1557 publication, have suffered from an analogous fate, but one caused directly by the compilation and editing of the anthology.

Whereas the *Miscellany* is frequently twinned with Tottel's name, his role in More's English *Workes* is often overlooked. Instead, attention usually focuses on More's nephew William Rastell, who sponsored and possibly masterminded the latter collection. Tottel was one of the three printers (the others being John Waly and John Cawood) who came together for the production of More's English *Workes*, which was completed and dedicated to Mary I in April 1557. However, this was not the first work by More that Tottel had printed. Indeed, one of Tottel's earliest known publications, produced when he was still in his early twenties, was his 1553 edition of *A dialoge of comfort against tribulacion*.[43] This was the very first publication of More's *Dialogue*, printed eighteen years after his death; it was also the earliest opportunity at which this prison writing could have safely come to press in England, and it appears to have been rushed through Tottel's printing-house as soon as the Catholic Mary Tudor ascended the throne, for it was completed on 18 November 1553, scarcely five months later. This haste is reflected in the quality of the publication. As Germain Marc'hadour and others have noted, the paper is poor, the typeface rather crude, and the Latin quotations are often misspelled.[44] Moreover, Tottel

---

[42] Amanda Holton, 'Introduction', in *Tottel's Miscellany: Songs and Sonnets of Henry Howard, Earl of Surrey, Sir Thomas Wyatt and Others*, ed. Amanda Holton (London, 2011), xv.

[43] This work will hereafter be referred to as *1553*. On 12 April of that year he was also granted a monopoly on the printing of law books pertaining to the common law, and he printed three such works before the year's end. See H. J. Byrom, 'Richard Tottel – His Life and Work', *Library*, 4th series, 8 (1927–8), 199–232.

[44] Germain Marc'hadour, 'Three Tudor Editors of Thomas More', in *Editing Sixteenth-Century Texts*, ed. Richard J. Schoeck (Toronto, 1965), 59–71 (60).

added virtually no paratextual apparatus: there is neither preface nor marginal references. This may suggest a kind of immediacy, a lack of editorial layers and the original text – an essentially liberated text. However, as Louis Martz and Frank Manley have shown in their scholarly introduction to the Yale edition of the *Dialogue*, the manuscript version that Tottel used may have been corrupt, or the haste with which a copy-text was made from the manuscript may have introduced the various errors and mangled passages that pepper this version.[45] With these particular qualities, *1553* stands as an important contrast with the English *Workes*.

Whereas the time constraints on Tottel's first foray into publishing More's writings resulted in an inferior text, the great folio of More's *Workes* was clearly put together with care. A book of this size was costly to produce, and each individual text appears to have been afforded a great deal of attention. Rastell's usual practice for the *Workes* was to send to Tottel and his colleagues the separate editions of a given work that he (or his father) had published in the years 1529–34 (or, in the case of the Tower works, collected in manuscript). One would have been selected as the basis for the copy-text, which would have been cross-referred with any other available editions. For example, a detailed comparison of the 1553 *Dialogue*, the version found in the *Workes*, and MS C.C.C. D. 37 in the Bodleian Library (which forms the basis of the Yale edition) led the editors Martz and Manley to suggest that the version of the *Dialogue* to appear in the 1557 anthology is a conflation of MS C.C.C. D. 37 and *1553*. Book 1 follows *1553* very closely, but the publishers seem to have leaned more heavily on the manuscript version thereafter (possibly as more of the errors and mangled passages in *1553* became apparent).[46] This attention to detail is a sign of the careful design behind the *Workes*. The timing of its publication, contents, organisation, and its paratexts suggest the esteem in which its producers wished it to be held. But the editors also provide a prescriptive – perhaps restrictive – reading context for More's collected Tower works, which occupy the final 319 pages of the volume.

The biggest constraint placed upon the Tower works is the rationale of the collection. The first thing to note about the volume is that it is a collection of More's *English* writings. In contrast to the picture of More's literary output that one might derive from his Latin *Opera omni*, published in Louvain in 1565, reading More's English works alone gives a very specific sense about the man and his literary output. For, apart from the English version of his *History of Richard III* and a handful of

[45] *CW*, vol. xii, li.   [46] Ibid., lv.

verses, what we get is a volume of work that is overwhelmingly religious in nature and dominated by polemical literature. As Rastell writes in his preface, addressed to Mary I:

> [H]is workes be worthy to be hadde and redde of euerye Englishe man, that is studious or desirous to know and learne, not onlye the eloquence and propertie of the English tonge, but also the trewe doctrine of Christes catholike fayth, the confutacion of detestable heresyes, or the godly morall vertues that appertaine to the framinge and fourminge of mennes maners and consciences, to liue a vertuous and deuout christen life.[47]

According to Rastell, the value of this collection derives from the benefit that English readers would derive from it. These works would instruct readers in 'the eloquence and propertie of the English tonge'. For Rastell, More's writings are the pinnacle of English literature, but their importance lies in their ability to teach others to write well, and in their provision of religious instruction. Knowing More's works, we must assume that Rastell imagines the polemic serving the function of confuting 'detestable heresyes', and his Tower works fulfilling the role of 'framinge and fourminge of mennes maners and consciences, to liue a vertuous and deuout christen life'. In his emphasis on how the texts should be received, Rastell's preface neatly demonstrates Genette's description of paratexts as a transactional zone or threshold: 'a privileged place of a pragmatics and of a strategy, of an influence on the public' (*Paratexts*, 2). If the reader approaches More's prison writings through the threshold that Rastell has outlined here, then he or she will read them as instructive texts, thus opening up the possibility of the texts 'framinge and fourminge' his or her manners and conscience. The language of correction is telling: Rastell asserts that the ideal reader will be disciplined and shaped by the text. In this way, More's pre-Reformation works are represented as having an ongoing influence, over eighteen years after they were first penned. At the same time, however, Rastell's presentation of the volume as an instructive collection attempts to narrow and constrict the way in which the writings will be approached. In his account of the rationale behind the collection of these works, the aim is not the celebration of More's life; instead the volume is shaped by the ideal reader's life, which will be improved as a result of reading the collected works.

Importantly, this 'framinge and fourminge' of the reader is also represented by Rastell as serving a larger national agenda. He outlines at length the necessity of this publication, suggesting that, had the individual works

---

[47] Thomas More, *The Workes of Syr Thomas More Knyght* (London, 1557; *STC* 18076), iir.

not been collected and printed in one volume, they might 'in time percase perish and vtterly vanish away (to the great losse and detriment of many)'.[48] For one, he suggests the loss of More's works would have been to the 'detriment' of those taken in by Protestant doctrine; he asserts that the collected works 'shall much helpe forwarde youre Maiesties most godly purpose, in purging this youre realme of all wicked heresies'.[49] Thus the correction of individual readers is represented as advancing Mary's programme of Protestant persecution, which by this point in her reign had brought about more than one hundred and eighty burnings.[50] By asserting the relevance of these pre-Reformation texts for a post-Reformation context, Rastell is undertaking two kinds of appropriation. Firstly, he is appropriating the content – which fought the first wave of evangelical heresy in the later 1520s and 1530s – for the religious struggle of the 1550s. Secondly, by virtue of being the collector of the works ('I dyd diligently collect and gather'), he claims them as his own to offer as a gift to his monarch, which sought not only to curry royal favour and patronage for Rastell and his associates in their printing endeavours, but also to associate him with this powerful figure in the minds of readers. In so doing, More's prison writings – which were written within a counter-public sphere, during a time when he was regarded as an enemy of the state – were effectively adopted to support and speak on behalf of the monarch. This seems like the ultimate form of liberty for such works. But in order to achieve this status, they needed to be reframed with Mary's 'godly purpose', which almost totally eclipses the fact that the true organising principle behind them is that they were all written by More.

While discussion of More the man and martyr is noticeably lacking in Rastell's preface, the collection of prison writings at the end of the volume, and the addition of paratexts, act to recontextualise these works within the biography of their author. This discrepancy between the approach taken in the volume's preface and the textual apparatus added to the individual texts may be explained by the expected conventions of the dedication, but it could also be attributed to the division of labour required in producing the volume. As well as Tottel, Waly, and Cawood, Thomas Paynell – a former monk and prolific translator – served an

---

[48] Ibid., iir.
[49] Ibid., iiv.
[50] See Eamon Duffy, *Fires of Faith: Catholic England under Mary Tudor* (New Haven, CT and London, 2009), 128–9.

editorial role as compiler of the index. Whoever was behind the headings and annotations to More's Tower writings was keen to establish their prison context: each of these texts, including every individual prayer and instruction, is prefaced with the information that it was written 'while he was prisoner in the tower of London'.[51] The emphasis on place and occasion ('while') creates a sense of temporal boundedness as well as physical incarceration. But what is most striking about this framing of the texts is the way these paratexts pull against the content. As I argued in Chapter 2, in his *Dialogue, De Tristitia Christi*, and each of his prayers and instructions, More studiously avoided personal identification as well as any detail that might bring their author either pity of glory – particularly his status as prisoner. Instead, More transformed personal experiences, fears, and insights into material that would be edifying for a general readership. In so doing, he wrote himself out of the prison: as de Certeau remarks, 'tactics do not obey the law of the place, for they are not defined or identified by it'.[52] The headings to each prison writing, however, place them within the very context More had sought to escape. The resulting compulsion to read these texts biographically is one that these writings have rarely escaped since this publication. In this way we can see how the paratexts have encouraged a form of interpretative incarceration.

One of the most striking examples of how the biographical context produces potentially misleading interpretative traditions can be found in the introduction to Mary Basset's translation of More's *De Tristitia Christi* in the *Workes*:

> A woorke of trouth full of good and godly lessons, whiche he began beyng then prisoner, and coulde not atchieue and finishe the same, as he that ere he could goe thorow therwith, (eauen when he came to thexposicion of these wordes, Et incecerunt manus in Iesum) was bereaued and put from hys bookes, pen, inke and paper, and kepte more strayghtly than before, and soone after also was putte to death hymselfe.[53]

The paratext implies that the reader cannot fully appreciate what this text has to say without knowing the conditions under which it was written. In providing this apparently trustworthy biographical account, the composition of *De Tristitia* is thus given a special drama and poignancy by the suggestion that More was interrupted by the authorities just as he was

---

[51] See, for example, ibid., 1139, 1254, 1350, 1405, 1408.
[52] De Certeau, *Practice of Everyday Life*, 29.
[53] See also More, *Workes*, 1350. See also 1404, where *De Tristitia* ends and the same reading context is once again repeated.

writing the words '*Et incecerunt* [sic] *manus in Iesum*' (And then they laid hands on Jesus), which also encourages the reader to draw a parallel between More's execution and that of Christ. There is, however, reason to doubt the veracity of these claims. I would tend to agree with Richard Marius' suggestion that the closing lines of the treatise sound 'very much like a real ending and not an unexpected fracture', albeit a very dramatic one.[54] The abrupt nature of this ending may be an intentional device: *aposiopesis* is a figure of speech where a sentence is deliberately broken off in order to give an impression of unwillingness or inability to continue, and can be used to convey extreme emotion, modesty, or guardedness.[55] However, the paratext prevents us from attributing this intense closure to More's artistry. Instead, it closes down interpretation of the text in pursuit of the editors' agenda, which would appear to be the elevation of More's reputation as a persecuted and Christlike figure. The implicit call for More's martyrdom fits with the broader activities of his circle in the 1550s. During these years the family, with the encouragement of Cardinal Pole, commissioned Nicholas Harpsfield to write More's biography, casting him as a blessed saint; and Rastell also began an account of his uncle's life.[56]

The paratexts show the editors' and publishers' shrewd understanding of the 'perverse imprimatur' that imprisonment bestowed upon More's works.[57] However, the editors may have applied this powerful stamp of approval a little too freely. The figure behind the paratexts would have us believe that More's *Treatise on the Passion* was penned 'whyle [More] was prisoner in the tower of London'.[58] In fact, the editors framed this tract as part 1 of *De Trisitia*: 'Syr Thomas More wrote no more in englishe of thys treatice of the passion of Chryst. But he (still prisoner in the tower of London) wrote more therof in latine (after the same order he wrote thereof in englyshe:) the translacion wherof here foloweth.'[59] The text that follows is Mary Basset's translation of *De Tristita*. However, it is now largely agreed that the *Treatise on the Passion* could not have been written in its

---

[54] Richard Marius, *Thomas More: A Biography* (London, 1984), 487.

[55] On this topic, see Gavin Alexander, 'Sidney's Interruptions', *Studies in Philology*, 98 (2001), 184–204.

[56] Harpsfield's biography remained unpublished until the twentieth century, when Elsie Vaughn Hitchcock edited it: Nicholas Harpsfield, *The Life and Death of Sr Thomas Moore, Knight*, ed. E. V. Hitchcock, EETS OS 186 (London, 1932). However, William Roper's 'notes' on his father-in-law's life, which acted as the basis for Harpsfield's biography, were printed in 1626 as *The mirrour of vertue in worldly greatnes. Or The life of Syr Thomas More Knight, sometime Lo. Chancellour of England* (Paris [i.e. Saint-Omer], 1626).

[57] Gerard A. Hauser, 'Prisoners of Conscience and the Counterpublic Sphere of Prison Writing: The Stones that Start the Avalanche', in *Counterpublics and the State*, ed. Robert Asen and Daniel C. Brouwer (New York, 2001), 35–58 (38). See introduction for discussion.

[58] More, *Workes*, 1270.   [59] Ibid., 1349.

entirety in the Tower; neither does *De Tristita* read like a continuation of this text. In a letter to John Harris, which More sent from Willesden, a parish adjoining London, he talks about the correction of an inaccurate passage in *The Treatise on the Passion*.[60] This means that the work must have been started before More's incarceration, and based on the fact that he was already editing his draft, we can assume that the treatise was at a progressed stage of the composition.[61] Similarly, Marc'hadour has also suggested that *The Treatise on the Blessed Body* was also begun outside the Tower.[62] More may have been prolific in his prison cell, but it is hard to believe that he would have had the leisure to write all of the pieces attributed to him in the *Workes* – many of them expansive – during the fifteen months of his imprisonment, when he was forced to hide his writing activities from his keepers.

But why were these two writings ascribed to More's time in prison? Rastell and the other editors working on this portion of the volume may have genuinely believed that they were prison works. For one thing, the subject matter seems to fit. *The Treatise on the Passion*, in particular, is a meditative work on the death of Christ, which, like *De Tristitia*, owes a strong debt to medieval devotional works such as Thomas á Kempis's *Imitatio Christi* and Pseudo-Bonaventure's *Meditationes Vitae Christ*. Like the other Tower works, it provides a striking generic contrast to the polemical literature that More had penned in the late 1520s and early 1530s. However, grouping this work and More's *Treatise on the Blessed Body* with his other prison works has had far-reaching effects on the critical reception of More's writings: for even though the dating of the *Treatise on the Passion* has now been corrected, this patterning introduced the idea that More changed the way he wrote when he was imprisoned. Generations of scholars have interpreted More's final fifteen months as the most spiritual and edifying period of his life, during which time he turned away from the confutation of heretics and looked to the salvation of his own soul. The only problem with this narrative is the fact that More began to write meditative literature before his incarceration, and, as Peter Marshall has pointed out, these meditative works continue to condemn heresy, albeit in a less virulent or specific manner than his polemical works.[63] As such, the *Workes* editors' keenness to label More's writings as prison

---

[60] See *Selected Letters*, ed. E. F. Rogers (New Haven, CT, 1961), 185–6.
[61] Joseph Delcourt, *Essai sur la langue de Sir Thomas More* (Montpellier, 1914), 371.
[62] Germain Marc'hadour, *Thomas More et la Bible* (Paris, 1969), 72–3, 80.
[63] Peter Marshall, 'The Last Years', in *The Cambridge Companion to Thomas More*, ed. George M. Logan (Cambridge, 2011), 116–39 (125).

works has encouraged overly schematic readings. Specifically, it has fostered the assumption that the strait space of the prison turned More's gaze inwards to his soul.[64]

The editors' drive to find and print prison writings might also have led them to compose a prayer from More's annotations in his prayer book.[65] Amongst what are described in the *Workes* as 'instruccions, meditacions, and prayers' is this piece:

> A deuoute prayer, collected oute of the psalmes of Dauid, by sir Thomas More knighte (while he was prisoner in the tower of London) whereunto he made this title following.

> Imploratio diuini auxilij contra tentatione; cum insultatione contra daemones, ex spe & fiducia in deum.[66]

There is a strong yet tantalising relationship between this cento prayer – which is composed from verses collected from Psalms 3, 5, 7, 4, 9, 12, 15, 16, 15, 17, 21, 24, 25, 27, 29, 36, 32, 33, 35, 37, 38, 39, 41, 45, 50, 61, 62, and 66 – and Thomas More's prayer book (now held in the Beinecke Library at Yale). The prayer contains many of the passages bearing More's marks and annotations in his Psalter, but not all of them: none of the annotated verses following Psalm 66 are included, and certain verses between Psalms 3 and 66 are also omitted.[67] Garry Haupt has questioned whether More made up this prayer or whether it was constructed by one of the editors going over the prayer book.[68] The ambiguity concerning the origins of this prayer can be detected in the heading above: while it makes clear that the 'deuoute prayer' is 'by Thomas More', the statement 'collected oute of the psalmes of Dauid' is a subclause, leaving it unclear whether this collection was undertaken by More or by another person. Moreover the word 'collected' may be revealing: it is the same word used by Rastell in his preface to describe how he gathered together printed texts and manuscripts by More before he began the project of publishing More's *Workes*; and, both as a noun and as a verb, it is a word more often associated with early modern editors than with authors.[69] There is an

---

[64] See for example G. R. Elton, 'The Real Thomas More', in *Reformation Principle and Practice: Essays in Honour of Arthur Geoffrey Dickens*, ed. Peter Newman Brooks (London, 1980), 21–31; Marius, *Thomas More*, xxii–iii, 3–43, 465, 470–1, 479; and Peter Ackroyd, *The Life of Thomas More* (London, 1998), 356–60.

[65] For further discussion of the prayer book, see Chapter 2 above.

[66] More, *Workes*, 1408.

[67] See *Thomas More's Prayer Book: A Facsimile Reproduction of the Annotated Pages*, ed. Louis L. Martz and Richard S. Sylvester (New Haven, 1969).

[68] *CW*, vol. xiii, cxlv.   [69] See More, *Workes*, iir.

element of design and selection involved in the final prayer. The verses are not simply copied out in systematic numeric order, and variations show a feel for thematic development. But this is not beyond the capabilities of a good editor. Furthermore, the passages that have been highlighted in More's prayer book between Psalm 3.2–4 and Psalm 66, but which were not included in the prayer, seem to follow a certain pattern. Haupt suggests that they may have been excluded on the basis of two principles: firstly, that they 'express a longing for the punishment of enemies', and, secondly, that they are 'inappropriate to More's situation in its later phases'.[70] What he does not notice, however, is the way that this fits in with the broader editorial trends in the *Workes*. Like the addition of biographical paratexts, the first principle pulls directly against More's own impetus towards an ecumenical perspective in his writing and annotations. Similarly, the second principle seeks to strengthen the idea that prison marked a rejection of writing that signalled religious opposition, and was instead concerned with the benefit of the individual soul. The expression of desire for the punishment of enemies would undercut this narrative.

It is the narrative that emerges from the paratexts and organisation of the volume – of More in the Tower, writing a certain kind of literature, and eschewing other activities – that distinguishes this volume from Tottel's other 1557 anthology. *Tottel's Miscellany*, by contrast, only labels two of its eight likely prison poems, and these are scattered between love poems. Despite these differences, though, both anthologies effectively authorise and elevate the status of prison writings by combining them with writings produced within the courtly sphere. For *Tottel's Miscellany*, it matters only that the works are each 'wel written in verse'; the conditions of their composition are irrelevant. In the *Workes* one might argue that More's Tower works gain credibility by virtue of being placed alongside his earlier polemics, which had been written at the behest of the Bishop of London, Cuthbert Tunstall. However, the addition of a biographical frame to More's prison writings, the false attribution of writings as Tower works, and the possible construction of new works from his notes suggest that Rastell and the editors working under his guidance perceived these texts to be highly influential and authoritative. Most importantly, placed at the end of the volume, they are given the final say on how More is represented.

---

[70] *CW*, vol. XIII, cxlii.

Foxe's forebears

Before the 1557 anthologies, the selection of published prison literature was narrow. Aside from Wyatt's and Surrey's Psalm paraphrases, and Tottel's 1553 edition of More's *Dialogue* (discussed above), the only printed prison writings were Protestant and proto-Protestant books.[71] Before 1557 – and following the publication of the two Lollard trial narratives of William Thorpe and John Oldcastle in 1530 (see above) – just over two-dozen publications containing Reformist prison writings were published. These came to press piece-meal, normally in single-text editions, or collected with one or two other works, and they were usually published relatively soon after their authors' deaths, some with notable speed. This meant that, apart from a small flurry of publications at the beginning of Edward's reign when the printing laws were relaxed, many of the Reformist prison writings to be published before 1557 were printed during the same reign in which the author had been imprisoned and executed. These publications, therefore, pose a direct contrast to More's *Workes*. More's texts had been held back until Mary's reign, when, collected together with his other English writings, they could be sold as a volume that actively supported the monarch's religious policies as well as furthering the careers of Rastell, Tottel, Cawood, and Waly. By contrast, the Reformist prison works that came to press in the reigns of Mary and Henry would have been perceived as direct threats to the throne: the trial narratives and doctrinal treatises were designed to encourage resistance to the religious authorities. As a result they were published by and for underground and exiled evangelical communities: after the works were smuggled out of the prison, they usually made their way to Protestant communities in exile on the Continent. During these years we see imprints from presses in Antwerp, Wesel, and Emden as well as a range of false imprints designed to protect the identities of the groups behind such publications. What More's *Workes* and the published Protestant prison writings had in common, though, was that they were each published to serve a religious agenda.

The individuals behind the early publications of Protestant prison writings clearly saw the printing press as tool of the Reformation. Indeed, for centuries scholars have perceived a direct link between the Reformation

---

[71] Thomas Wyatt, *Certayne psalmes chosen out of the psalter of Dauid* (London, 1549); and Henry Howard, Earl of Surrey (misattributed to Thomas Sternhold), *Certayne chapters of the prouerbes of Salomon drawen into metre by Thomas sterneholde* (London, 1550). The latter was later reprinted with the correct attribution. See the title page of *STC* 12631.

and the rise of the printing press.[72] However, as Thomas Freeman has persuasively argued, in the reign of Mary I, Protestants relied far more heavily on the written word, as opposed to the printed word, as a means of communicating with and leading their communities: scribal publication and the use of carriers and copyists proved to be effective ways of disseminating ideas with relative safety, as the last two chapters have demonstrated. But despite the ease with which Protestant exiles on the Continent acquired their co-religionists' prison writings, and the numerous presses available there, surprisingly few prison writings were printed during the reign of Mary I. While the project that led to Foxe's 'Book of Martyrs' brought to light hundreds of letters, trial narratives, and treatises by Protestants, only ten were printed during Mary's reign.[73] Indeed, certain leading religious figures in the exile community – especially Edmund Grindal, John Foxe, and Heinrich Bullinger – actively prevented texts from coming to press. This was not only to protect the prisoners and their associates while they lived, but also because Grindal had already conceived of a collection of martyrs' writings that would eventually lead to the publication of Foxe's famous martyrology. Texts were therefore hoarded so that their first appearance would be in this volume, in a more satisfactory edited form. Despite this broad trend, however, the works that did find their way into print before 1557 show how in these early years Protestant leaders, editors, and publishing houses were still negotiating what role print might play in religious reform, and experimenting with the ways in which prison writings might best serve their own religious, political, and economic ends. What we see in this period is the emergence of two editorial positions on how prison writings should be published. The first approach was to publish quickly, and is typified by the publications of John Frith's works in the 1530s, and the publications coming out of the Hill/Ctematius press in Emden in the reign of Mary I. The second approach was the martyrological approach, which would culminate in Foxe's mammoth history of persecution, but which had its roots in the prison writings published by John Bale in the 1540s.

Not all of John Frith's prison writings came to press immediately, but four prison writings were printed within four years of his death, and two were reprinted before the end of Henry's reign. The first was his *Boke* . . .

---

[72] The classic study propounding this relationship is E. L. Eisenstein, *The Printing Press as an Agent of Change: Communications and Cultural Transformations in Early Modern Europe* (Cambridge, 1979).

[73] Thomas S. Freeman, 'Publish and Perish: The Scribal Culture of the Marian Martyrs', in *The Uses of Script and Print 1300–1700*, ed. Julia Crick and Alexandra Walsham (Cambridge, 2004), 235–54 (235, 250).

answeringe vnto M. mores lettur, which also contained his final writing,
'The Articles wherefore John Frith dyed which he wrote in Newgate the
23 day of June the yeare of our lorde 1533'. Although it bears a false imprint,
it was published in Antwerp at some point in 1533, which means that the
text travelled from Frith's pen in England, through the hands of at least
one carrier who brought it to the Continent, via an editor, compositors,
correctors, typefounders, and pressmen, before emerging as a printed text,
all in under nine months.[74] Given the speed of this journey, it is perhaps
not surprising that it does not have a preface and the marginal annotations
are limited to references to Bible passages and figures such as 'Adam' and
'Moses'. However, it is not entirely utilitarian and bears illuminated
initials. The lack of paratexts, however, might not be solely attributed to
the pressures of time: the second edition, which appeared in 1546 from
another press – and which appears with a different typeface and illustrated
initials – also lacks a preface or other textual apparatus. It is unclear
whether this was due to a shortage of money or to lack of foresight
regarding the value of these texts to establish Frith's reputation as a martyr.
However, based on the preface to the 1536 publication of Frith's *An other
boke against Rastel named the subsedye or bulwark to his fyrst boke*, it would
seem that the teams behind the early publications placed a much higher
value on the text's instructive value than they did on its authorship or the
conditions under which it was written.[75]

The preface to the *Bulwark* makes only a passing mention of the fact
that Frith wrote this text in prison, and it does not explicitly seek to praise
the man and his martyrdom. Instead, it focuses on the value of the text to
the 'Crysten reader', clarifying its relationship to Frith's earlier work,
A disputacion of purgatorye (with which it may have been issued), praising
its sound doctrine and criticising the beliefs of those who support the
Catholic doctrine of purgatory, especially John Fisher and Thomas More,

[74] *A boke made by Iohn Frith prisoner in the tower of London answeringe vnto M. mores lettur* bears the
imprint: 'Imprinted at Monster: Anno 1533 by me Conrade Willems'. It is now normally attributed
to the press of H. Peetersen van Middelburch in Antwerp. The rates at which compositors and
press-men worked was highly variable, depending (among other things) on the number of books in
preparation, the number of printing presses in use, and the use of skeletons. It is therefore difficult
to make any calculations about a standard production time for books. For further discussion, see
D. F. McKenzie, *Making Meaning: 'Printers of the Mind' and other Essays*, ed. Peter D. McDonald
and Michael F. Suarez (Amherst, MA, 2002),19–42.
[75] The *Bulwark* does not bear an imprint, but it is usually attributed to John Mitchell's press in
Canterbury and dated around 1535 or 1536. Three other works lacking an imprint but assigned to
Mitchell on typographic grounds are: William Tyndale's *Obedience of a Christian Man*, his *Parable
of the Wicked Mammon*, and John Frith's *Disputacion*. See Janet Ing Freeman, 'Mitchell, John
(d. 1556)', *ODNB*, www.oxforddnb.com/view/article/18841 [accessed 18 December 2012].

two of the individuals against whom the *Disputacion* had been written. The ultimate seal of approval, however, comes in the preface's final lines, when its author delivers the information that John Rastell, the opponent to whom the *Bulwark* was addressed, was subsequently convinced by Frith's arguments in this volume and converted to the reformed faith:

> he was well content to counte his natural reason folyshnes and with harty thankes geuen to god becam a chylde agayne and sucked of the wysdome which cometh from aboue and saueth all that be noryshed therwith in the which he contynued to his lyfes ende with the honour and glorye of God to whome be prase for euer. Amen.[76]

For the writer of this preface, the value of this text derives from the 'wysdome' it contains. The primary aim is to meet the needs of a readership rather than to celebrate its author. The writer of the preface does, of course, provide a little biographical context, but interestingly it is the biography of the intended reader – Rastell – rather than that of the author. This echoes Frith's own approach in his prison writings, which barely ever give biographical information, focusing instead on guiding his community of co-religionists outside the prison.

The evangelical impetus behind this work and its print publication echoes some of the sentiment found in the nineteenth-century it-narrative *History of a Bible*, which was discussed at the beginning of this chapter: that the *raison d'être* of a book is to be read, but, more crucially, that if it is not read and circulated in the community, then it is shackled. This is equally true of the publications coming out of Emden in the reign of Mary I, several of which, interestingly, incorporate descriptions of the texts' material journeys into their prefaces. As suggested earlier, there was a particular press in this city that bucked the trend towards scribal publication in this period: that of Giles van der Erve (Ctematius) and Nicholas van der Berghe (known in England under his Anglicised name, Nicholas Hill). Of the ten prison writings printed during Mary's reign, five were published by the Hill/Ctematius press for Protestant exiles working out of Emden, including John Scory (the Emden congregation's leader), John à Lasco, and John Olde. These were Nicholas Ridley's *A brief declaracion of the Lordes Supper* (1555), Ridley and Latimer's *Certein godly, learned, and comfortable conferences* (1556), *The examinacion of the constaunt martir of Christ, Iohn Philpot* (1556?), *An Apologie of Iohan Philpot written for spitting upon an Arrian* (printed in the same volume as the examinations), and

---

[76] Frith, *Bulwark*, sig. A.4r.

Thomas Cranmer's *Defensio verae et catholicae doctrinae de sacramento corporis & sanguinis Christi seruatoris nostri* (1557), which was printed in two variant editions. We can thus see that Emden's exile congregation honoured the memory of the recent martyrs, Ridley, Philpot, and Cranmer by publishing *in extensio* accounts of their doctrines and trials.[77] The speed with which they responded to these deaths is probably best illustrated by Ridley's *A brief declaracion of the Lordes Supper*, which bears a title page dating it to 1555 as well as the statement that it was written 'a litel before he suffred deathe for the true testimonie of Christ' on 16 October 1555, indicating a journey from pen to print within around five months, or less, taking into account the Julian Calendar, which ran from 25 March.

The short preface that was added to this text by John Olde sought to glorify the author much more than the preface to Frith's *Bulwark*. What is striking about this preface, however, is the imagery surrounding the text. Olde opens by emphasising the importance of the fact that Ridley chose not only to state verbally his beliefs regarding the sacrament of the altar, but that in order 'to leaue a sure monument and loue token vnto his flocke . . . he hathe regestred it by his owne penne in this forme ensuyng, and sealed it vp with his blood'.[78] Olde implies that Ridley, merely by dint of writing, demonstrated his desire that his teaching on this topic should be made available to his 'flocke' after his death. More interestingly, though, he sets up a tense relationship between the martyr's death and the status of the text: Ridley's death only gains meaning as a result of his text being read, and, conversely, the text only achieves this bloody form of validation as a result of his martyrdom. In order to establish the status of this text, Olde invokes two other forms of writing: the monument and the legal document. The use of the word 'monument' – which pre-empts the title of Foxe's martyrology – signifies a written document or record (left behind), but it also plays on the multiple meanings of this word to denote a sepulchre, funerary monument, or enduring marker.[79] By twinning

---

[77] Van de Berghe was a long-term London resident who had during the latter part of Henry VIII's reign established a publishing house, which flourished under Edward VI. His command of the English language and of printing made possible 'the development of a fruitful collaboration that saw Emden quickly emerge as the undisputed centre of production of vernacular exile literature' (Andrew Pettegree, *Marian Protestantism: Six Studies* (Aldershot, 1996), 12–34 (23)). Between 1554 and 1558 the Hill/Ctematius press turned out twenty-eight editions in English or Latin, originated by members of the exiled churches and mostly intended for clandestine distribution back in England. See also Andrew Pettegree, *Emden and the Dutch Revolt: Exile and the Development of Reformed Protestantism* (Oxford, 1992) 87–108.

[78] *A brief declaracion of the Lordes Supper* (Emden, 1555), sig. A.IV.

[79] John N. King, *English Reformation Literature: The Tudor Origins of the Protestant Tradition* (Princeton, NJ, 1982), 438.

literary texts and mementoes of death, Olde suggests that the publication of this writing functions to honour Ridley's recent death. The language of legal documents ('regestred', 'this forme ensuyng', 'sealed'), however, pulls against the image of monuments. It has a greater sense of verifiable authenticity than a funeral monument, which is necessarily built by somebody else, even if it may have be designed by the deceased, and is used to emphasise that it has been printed by Olde in its original form. That the only person to have exerted their will upon the text is Ridley himself is stressed by the image of his martyr blood sealing up the text. This disquieting image evokes the red wax seals which were used at this time to secure documents, and which were often embossed with a symbol to show the provenance of the document or the identity of its sender. The implication is that this seal has remained unbroken, and the metaphor therefore serves to assure the reader that this text has not been tampered with by subsequent editors. Although there is no authorial manuscript to verify Olde's claims, we can probably take his word at face value. Given the speed with which the text emerged, the editors would have had little time in which to thoroughly rework it, in the way we will see that Foxe did, and it has scant marginal annotations, comprising biblical references and short synopses of the argument at irregular intervals.[80] Nevertheless, that the lack of editorial intervention needs to be stated is unnerving, and suggests the norm may have been otherwise.

In Olde's preface to Ridley and Latimer's *Certein godly, learned, and comfortable conferences* (discussed in Chapter 3 above), we find another metaphor that embeds a kind of it-narrative concerning the journey of the text from pen to press: 'these their scrolles and writynges wer by goddes good prouidence preserued, and as it wer, raked out of the ashes of thauthors'.[81] As with the metaphor of Ridley sealing up his *Brief Declaration* with blood, so the image of Ridley and Latimer's works being raked out of their ashes suggests that the martyr's body and the status of his text are inextricably linked. They are figured almost as the afterlives of the martyrs, as phoenixes rising out of the flames. As such, their survival is hailed as a kind of miracle. Even though Olde is only speaking figuratively when he describes these writings surviving the flames, the physical detail of

---

[80] This is not to say that the Emden editors did not undertake to correct and add to the martyrs' texts where they thought it was necessary. As Pettegree has shown, they silently introduced a number of corrections into Cranmer's citations in his *Defensio verae et catholicae doctrinae de sacramento corporis & sanguinis Christi seruatoris nostri* (Emden, 1557). See Pettegree, *Marian Protestantism*, 31.

[81] Nicholas Ridley, *Certein godly, learned, and comfortable conferences, betwene the two reuerende fathers, and holy martyrs of Christe, D. Nicolas Rydley ... and M. Hughe Latimer* (Emden, 1556), sig. A1v.

raking, and the emphasis on the material quality of the texts as parchment or paper and ink ('scrolles and writynges'), emphasise their propensity to destruction: these are ephemeral objects. Their survival, therefore, must be attributed to 'goddes good prouidence'. By implicating God in the process of their transportation from England to the press in Emden, Olde gives these printings of these works the gold seal of approval. Are we to infer that, since he makes such a point about God preserving these works untouched, God has also protected this work from editorial interventions? It is impossible to say.[82] The *Conferences* are, however, framed by more paratexts than Ridley's *Brief Declaration*. Compared to the half-page preface Olde added to the first publication, the *Conferences* have a seven-page preface, more frequent marginal references (biblical passages, synopses, and an indication of the speaker), and a five-page 'conclusyon to the Reader', also by Olde. Each paratext is concerned with how the text will serve its readership. In the preface Olde writes that he 'would not suffer [his readership] any lenger to want these small treatises, and yet no smal treasures'.[83] This is a clear statement of the press's publishing policy: to make the martyrs' writings available as quickly as possible. By likening the texts to treasure, he implies that those who have access to such texts but are not publishing them are hoarding something that is potentially very valuable to the whole Protestant community: he sees the value of the *Conferences* alike for those 'suche as are in the schole of the crosse, as also good ... for them which ... do yelde vnto the wicked worlde'.[84] In other words, this is relevant both for those who are willing to undertake persecution for their beliefs, and for those who have not yet converted to the formed faith. As with the preface to Frith's *Bulwark* and Rastell's preface to More's *Workes*, Olde's paratext is about shaping how the reader approaches the text. At the end of the preface he adds a prayer:

> God graunt that the admonicions of these and other godly martyrs maye so warne vs, their doctrine so instruct vs, and theyr example so confirme vs in the true knowlage and feare of God, that flyeng and abhorring Idolatrye, and supersticion, we maye embrace true religion and pietie ... Amen.[85]

---

[82] A manuscript version of Ridley and Latimer's *Conferences* does survive in Foxe's papers at the British Library (Lansdowne MS 389, fols. 147r–170v). However, it appears to have been copied from the Emden publication or a Strasbourg edition from the same year. Crossed out on fol. 147r, in what appears to be the same hand that copied out this text, are the words 'printed 1556'. It contains the preface 'To ye readre' by John Olde (which also appears in the Strasbourg edition); the same marginal annotations (although some of them in abbreviated forms); but, like the Strasbourg edition, it lacks Olde's conclusion.

[83] Ridley and Latimer, *Conferences*, sig. A2r.   [84] Ibid., sig. A1v.   [85] Ibid., sig. A4v.

This prayer essentially asks God to oversee the final leg of the text's journey from writer to reader. Just as God's providence ensured the miraculous survival of these writings, so Olde now asks him to ensure that the reader is receptive to Ridley and Latimer's 'doctrine'. Olde's concern that the reader gets the most out of the text can also be seen in his provision of a 'A conclusion to the Reader'. While the preface had clearly spelled out the use of the text to provide both schooling and admonition, Olde makes sure that the reader has not forgotten this message after reading the text. He writes that, after reading the *Conferences*, the reader has a choice about how he or she should act: either 'to abyde paciently thy most mercifull louing heauenly fathers rodde vnder Christes crosse, in confessing the truthe with these holy martirs, to thy eternal saluacion, or to slyde backe into the filthie soile of popishnesse'.[86] Despite his efforts to guide the reader in fruitful reading, this comment expresses Olde's recognition of the reader's liberty either to be changed by the experience of reading a text, or to continue unaffected.

The evangelical agenda, however, sometimes required a more active editorial role, or so certain editors believed. While Olde attempted to guide the reader, his paratexts can hardly be described as restrictive. Such an approach to publishing – which prized speed and accessibility – sits in direct contrast to the martyrological approach, which we see taking form in the publications of controversialist John Bale in the 1540s. In the years 1544 to 1548 Bale published four or five prison writings, all of which might be described as part of the literary culture of the heresy trial: *A brefe chronycle concernynge the examinacyon and death of the blessed martyr of Christ syr Iohan Oldecastell* (1544), *The first examinacyon of Anne Askewe* (1546), *The lattre examinacyon of Anne Askewe* (1547), *A treatyse made by Johan Lambert vnto kynge Henry the.viij. concerynge hys opynyon in the sacrame[n]t of the aultre* (1548?), and possibly also *A brife and faythfull declaration of the true fayth of Christ made by certeyne men suspected of heresye in these articles folowyng* (1547). Four of the above are trial narratives. This not only demonstrates the rising popularity of this genre during these years, but also Bale's particular interest in the form. One of the appeals of this genre for Bale was its instructiveness. As I suggested in Chapter 1, it acted as a confession of belief and provided a model of how a true Protestant should behave when being examined. The dialogic form of trial narratives, however, might also have contributed to his interest in them. A number of critics have noted that the dramatic interplay between examiner and

[86] Ibid., sig. F.4r–v.

defendant would undoubtedly have appealed to the playwright in Bale. The inherent drama of this form allowed him to cast the adversarial dispute between interrogator and defendant as part of a universal and eternal battle between the true church and its persecutors, an interest that we see most clearly in his 1547 publication, *The Image of both Churches*. It is through Bale's handling of these texts that we can see the contrast between the editorial policy of the Hill/Ctematius press, for instance, and Bale's more interventionist approach.

The most apparent sign of this approach can be found in Bale's paratexts. Oldcastle's account of his examination is not a sixteenth-century text, but it is the first trial narrative (that we know of) that Bale published, and it sets the tone for those that follow. To it he added a lengthy preface of around twenty pages: the reader is thus forced to wade through a significant volume of Bale's arguments, or else turn several pages, before he gets to Oldcastle's account of his trial. In the opening passage Bale locates the proto-Protestant martyr within a long tradition of those who 'haue eyther dyed for theyr naturall contreye or daungered theyr lyues for a common welthe'. The body of examples he chooses is notably inclusive: he lists classical figures from Scipio to Theseus; then a host of Old Testament figures such as Moses and Judith; and a list Catholic martyrs, old and new, including 'Iohan Fysher / Thomas More / Fryre Forest / Reynoldes / and the Charterhouse monkes which suffred here in Englande / with an infynite nombre more'. Bale, however, sets the Catholics up as false martyrs, against whom he contrasts another group of individuals:

> What is than to be thought of those godlye and valeaunt warryours / which hath not spared to bestowe theyr most dere lyues for the veryte of Iesus Christ agaynst the malygnaunt mustre of that execrable Antichrist of Rome the deuyls owne vycar. Of whose gracyouse nombre a verye specyall membre and a vessell of Gods eleccyon was that vertuouse knyght syr Iohan Oldecastell.[87]

Those who rejected papal authority are thus heralded as true martyrs. Implicitly this includes all those Reformers who had been put to death in the preceding decade; but, importantly, Bale paints this as part of a longer history that is continuous with the persecution of Lollards in the late fourteenth and early fifteenth centuries.

He goes on to lament the lack of an English history unpolluted with 'Romyshe lyes' and writes:

---

[87] *A brefe chronycle concernynge the examinacyon and death of the blessed martyr of Christ syr Iohan Oldecastell the lorde Cobham, collected togyther by Iohan Bale* (Antwerp, 1544), sig. A.2r–v.

I wolde wyshe some lerned Englyshe manne (as there are now most excellent fresh wyttes) to set forth the Englyshe chronycles in theyr ryght shappe / as certen other landes hath done afore them / all affeccyons set a part. I can not thynke a more necessarye thynge to be laboured to the honour of God / bewtye of the realme / errudicyon of the people / and commodite of other landes / next the sacred scripture of the Byble / than that worke wolde be.[88]

Here we see him proposing a large publishing project: 'to set forth the Englyshe chronycles in theyr ryght shappe'. In this period the phrase 'set forth' was often used in prefaces to books, not just to describe the act of writing, but (as the word 'forth' suggests) the process of publication.[89] In the light of this, the words 'ryght shappe' seem to suggest an editorial process, as if Bale imagined some other motivated editor taking the existing (Catholic) English chronicles and altering their shape – by filing away faults and adding previously overlooked material – to form a new, reformed kind of history.[90] Indeed, as with the word 'correct', discussed above, the verb 'shape' had a corrective meaning in the late Middle Ages: 'to deliver (a judgement), appoint (a penalty); condemn (a person) to punishment'.[91] Coupled with the word, 'right', we are again faced with the idea of editing as a form of punishment or incarceration that is imposed upon written history in order to make it good and true. But why put such an appeal in the preface of his edition of a Lollard trial narrative? The combination of features – the placing of Oldcastle within an ongoing tradition of martyrdom, and the call for an English chronicle that will be second only to 'the sacred scripture of the Byble' – promotes a new attitude to prison literature. Bale clearly believed that isolated works would not provide an adequate answer to the 'Romysh' account of history. What was needed was a Reformed rewriting of English history. In this way we see how, for Bale, the framing of prison works was as important as – if not more important than – the texts themselves. Consequently, we might posit that his appeal was, ultimately, answered by Foxe's 'Book of Martyrs'.

Two years later, in 1546, Bale published *The first examinacyon of Anne Askewe*. Here we begin to see just how important this framing had become. This text, along with the account of her second examination (published in 1547), has attracted considerable critical interest in recent years, much of

---

[88] Bale, *Oldcastell*, sigs. A.8r–v.   [89] *OED, set, v.¹*, 5.
[90] Cf. Bale's dedication to Edward VI in *The Laboryouse journey and serche of Johan Lelande for Englandes antiquitees* (London, 1549), sigs. A.2r–A.6r, with its account of English history being stripped clear of Popery.
[91] *OED, shape, v.*, 23.

which has focused on the sizeable paratexts that Bale added. For example, in the *First examinacyon* we have Bale's seventeen-page preface to 'the Christen readers', extensive glosses which are inserted within the main body of the text, and Bale's nine-page 'Conclusyon'.[92] In both the preface and the glosses, Bale seeks to situate Askew within a history of martyrdom. He links her typologically with the martyrs of the early church, especially Blandina, a young female martyr from second-century Gaul whom Eusebius of Caesarea had described. Blandina had been young and innocent, and so too was Anne; Blandina's spirit had never wavered under torture, and neither did Anne's; Blandina had confidently rebuked the pagan priests for their errors, and Anne from the stake spoke bluntly to Nicholas Shaxton (a bishop who had recanted his Reformist beliefs). This typological approach seeks to frame Askew's prison writing in two ways. Firstly, within her own biography; the text is lent its authority by her godly behaviour and martyrdom. Secondly, the text is framed within martyrological history; it stresses the validity of her actions by drawing analogies with an attested martyr. Bale thus claims the history of the early church for the Reformed faith, justifying this new faith through patterns of persecution that stretch across the millennia. Askew's writing is thus encased in a historical and teleological narrative.

The glosses, however, are perhaps the most interesting and unusual of the frames added to this text. They are sizeable, and are formatted in such a way that it becomes debateable whether we can call them glosses at all. Because they interpose between extracts from Askew's texts rather than sitting in the margins, it appears as if Bale himself is an interlocutor. On each page the reader sees blocks of text headed either by the name 'Anne Askew' or 'Johan Bale' – the only difference is that Askew's portions are printed in a slightly larger font. All the sections following Askew's name open with a question from one of her interrogators, which she answers, always seeming to get the last word. This is followed by Bale's commentary on the question–answer sequence preceding it, which seeks to stress the virtues of Askew, the Christlike nature of her suffering and the doctrinal value of her answers to her interrogators, and to cast her questioners Christopher Dare, Stephen Gardiner, and Edmund Bonner as satanic villains. Damning Dare's questioning techniques, he writes: 'All craftye wayes possyble, sought thys quarellynge qwestmonger, or els the deuyll in hym, to brynge thys poore innocent lambe to the slaughter place of

---

[92] See *The first examinacyon of Anne Askewe lately martyred in Smythfelde, by the Romysh popes vpholders, with the elucydacyon of Iohan Bale* (Marburg [i.e. Wesel], 1546).

Antichrist'.[93] In the same way that Bale expands on the villainy of Askew's questioners, so he also builds upon her answers. Thus modest answers given by Askew become chances to preach reformed doctrine to the reader:

Anne Askewe.

Fiftly he asked me, what I sayd concernynge confession? I answered hym my meanynge, which was as Saynt James sayth, that euerye man ought to acknowlege hys fautes to other, and the one to praye for the other.

Johan Bale.

Thys confession onlye do, the scripture appoint us, Jac. 5. as we haue offended our neybor: But yf we have offended God, we must sorowfullye acknowlege it before hym. And he (sayth Saynt Johan, 1, Johan. 1. hath faythfullye promysed to forgeue vs our synnes, yf we so do, and to clense us from all vnryghtousnesse. If the lawe of truthe be in the prestes mouthe, he ys to be sought vnto for godlye counsel, Mala. 2. But yf he be a blasphe-mouse hypocryte or superstycyouse fole, he is to be shourned as a most pestilent poysen.[94]

This answer is typical of Askew's answers, which are brief and often equivocal (if she answered at all). The statement that 'euerye man ought to acknowlege hys fautes to other' could be taken to refer to the Catholic doctrine of confession, if the reader interprets the 'other' as a priest. However, equally the statement could refer to evangelicals' eschewal of confession. From her words, however, Bale draws out a much lengthier and explicit doctrinal argument on this topic, making it clear that priests did not have the power to absolve – only God did. Through this interplay we might be reminded of Ridley and Latimer's second *Conference*, in which Ridley imagined what his responses would be to a fictional interrogator, and Latimer added his own elucidatory comments (see Chapter 3 above). However, whereas Ridley and Latimer's text was produced collaboratively, and passed back and forth between the two men, Bale made his additions after Askew's death. There is every possibility, of course, that Askew would have approved of Bale's expansive commentary, rooted as it is in biblical citation. However, his elucidatory approach pulls directly against the rhet-orical strategies that Askew employs against her interrogators. Her answers are designed to create ambiguity in order to avoid self-incrimination; but this also means that her answers are open to misinterpretation by subse-quent readers. Bale's aim is to provide unequivocal doctrinal instruction. In other words, where Askew opens up meaning, Bale closes it down.

---

[93] Ibid., sig. A.5v.   [94] Ibid. sig. A.5r.

This raises the question: where is the emphasis in this publication? Is it on the original text, or on Bale's paratexts? On the one hand, a paratext is, by definition, an 'accompanying production'.[95] Bale's glosses would be meaningless without the text on which he comments. Furthermore, a framing structure, or 'threshold' as Genette has it, usually draws attention to what is inside it: Askew's text is surrounded on all sides, with Bale's commentary appearing above and below her text, as well as marginal annotations to either side (in the margins on this page are keywords: 'Phaysees', 'The sprete', 'Mockers'). The more elaborate the frame, the more attention we tend to pay to the artwork inside it. On the other hand, Bale's paratextual commentary has inserted itself into the space normally set aside for the text proper. By the late 1540s, printers were well able to print texts with commentary surrounding the text, but Bale chose not to. Instead, the page is formatted such that it becomes impossible to read Askew's words as a continuous piece of prose. In this way it resembles the format of commentaries on classical and pseudo-classical texts for school-boys, such as Aesop's *Fables*, the *Distichs of Cato*, and Virgil's *Eclogues*, which earlier in the century were arranged in this interrupting fashion. Might Bale be evoking this old educational practice, casting himself as an instructor? Looking once again at the extract above, we are made to wonder whether Askew's text merely functions as a hook on which Bale can hang his own instructive material. Many critics have felt that while Askew appears to have successfully evaded the framing narrative of confession and condemnation that her male accusers tried to impose on her discourse, Bale brought her back, textually, into a rehearsal of the same male-controlled discourse.[96] Thomas Betteridge neatly sums this up, describing Bale's editorial voice 'speaking from a position beyond, and *enclosing*, the other voices of the text'.[97] By enclosing Aske's text with paratexts, Bale also narrows the reader's interpretative role. This book, then, both visually imprisons Askew's text and attempts to shackle the reader to boot.

The paratexts, however, may not be the only area in which Bale's influence is felt. Because his commentaries are headed with a name, there seems to be a transparency about the nature of his editorial interventions in

[95] Genette, *Paratexts*, 1.
[96] See Thomas S. Freeman and Sarah Elizabeth Wall, 'Racking the Body, Shaping the Text: The Account of Anne Askew in Foxe's "Book of Martyrs"', *Renaissance Quarterly*, 54 (2001), 1165–96 (1166).
[97] Thomas Betteridge, *Tudor Histories of the English Reformation, 1530–83* (Aldershot, 1999) 80, my emphasis.

the text. The assumption, which has been made by a number of scholars, is that the text and paratext are detachable, that the removal of the latter would leave the reader with Askew's original text.[98] But there is reason to believe that Bale might also have silently edited the content of the portions of the text ascribed to Askew. We know that he edited the account of Oldcastle's examination, which was discussed above. Where the 1530 edition of this text (probably brought to press by George Constantine, although Bale credits it to William Tyndale) has the words 'I beleue verely that the moste blessed sacrament of the altare is very Christes body in forme of bread, the same body that was borne of the blessed virgin',[99] Bale's version reads, 'I beleue in that sacrament to be contayned verye Christes bodye and bloude vndre the symylytudes of breade and wyne'.[100] The Lollard position on the Eucharist was subtly different from that of the Protestants (which of course was a hotly contested issue in the period): the most common Lollard position was 'that material bread remained in the host'.[101] But as D. Andrew Penny remarks, 'although it appears likely that some Lollards developed an appreciation for the commemorative aspect of the Eucharist, one would probably be wise to resist the temptation to equate this with the full Zwinglian or signification sense'.[102] Bale's addition of the words 'vndre the symylytudes of breade and wyne' anachronistically makes Oldcastle's statement adhere to the doctrine of the Swiss Reformer, Ulrich Zwingli: the word 'symylytudes' communicated the idea of the bread having an allegorical function, merely signifying the body of Christ. There are three issues that might arouse our suspicion that Bale edited Askew's text in a similar way. Firstly, Thomas Freeman and Sarah Elizabeth Wall have pointed out that Adriaan van Haemestede printed Askew's examinations in his 1559 Dutch martyrology, but that this version contains a passage not present in Bale's publication. This suggests that Bale may have deleted material from Askew's text.[103] The second feature to arouse suspicion involves a phrase that Anne reputedly used in a letter to an anonymous friend to describe the Eucharist: 'The breade and wyne were left vs, for a sacramentall communyon, or a mutuall

---

[98] See for example Elaine V. Beilin, *Redeeming Eve: Women Writers of the English Renaissance* (Princeton, NJ, 1987), 31.

[99] Oldcastle, *The examinacion of Master William Thorpe* ... (Antwerp, 1530) sig. H.4v.

[100] Oldcastle, *Brefe chronycle*, sig. C.2r.

[101] J. F. Davis, *Heresy and Reformation in the South-East of England, 1520–1559* (London, 1983), 27–8.

[102] D. Andrew Penny, *Freewill or Predestination: The Battle over Saving Grace in mid-Tudor England* (Woodbridge, 1990), 9.

[103] Freeman and Wall, 'Racking the Body', 1170.

pertycypacyon of the inestymable benefyghtes of hys most precyouse deathe and bloud shedynge.'[104] These particular words are compatible with Anne's sacramentarian beliefs, but, as Leslie Fairfield has observed, the specific words 'mutuall pertycypacyon' raise a small question. They happen to be the words that Bale himself used rather frequently in speaking of the Eucharist, and which otherwise do not seem to have been especially common. We must ask: did Bale put his own words in Anne's mouth?[105] The final question concerning Bale's veracity stems from a detail in Anne's account of her first examination. On 20 March 1545 Bonner interrogated Anne on the matter of the Mass. He wrote out a statement categorically affirming the Real Presence, which he demanded that Anne should sign. According to Bale's published version of the incident, Anne affixed to the document not her signature alone, but the statement: 'I Anne Askew do beleve all maner thynges contayned in the catholyck churche'.[106] An entry in the bishop's register, however, claims that Anne signed the statement without reservations. Such a discrepancy might, once more, be evidence of Bale's voice permeating his subject's testimony.

The publishing teams behind each of the Protestant books discussed above had one motivation in common: evangelism. Their editorial policies, despite stark differences, were each determined by the desire to spread reformed beliefs. The distinctions arose from the role that the respective editors gave to the prison writings. The lack of prefaces to Frith's texts, and Olde's claims about the lack of editorial intervention, demonstrate the primacy of the author's words in these publications. The Hill/Ctematius press and editors of Frith's works valued prison writings for their intrinsic evangelical message; little reframing was deemed necessary for them to further the Protestant cause. By contrast, Bale's interventions in Askew's examinations show that he did not regard the prisoner's word as authoritative without his commentary. This suggests that he perceived himself, and not the authors of the texts he edited, as the evangelical force behind his publications. Such a perception provided a different kind of imprimatur. By interpreting his role to provide a Protestant readership with the most instructive and edifying material, Bale gave himself considerable licence to 'correct' the texts, on the one hand (by removing, changing,

---

[104] *The lattre examinacyon of Anne Askewe latelye martyred in Smythfelde, by the wycked Synagoge of Antichrist, with the Elucydacyon of Iohan Bale* (Marburg [i.e. Wesel], 1547), sig. B.3v.
[105] Leslie Fairfield, *John Bale: Mythmaker for the English Reformation* (West Lafayette, IN, 1976) 158.
[106] Askew, *First examinacyon*, sig. E.6r.

and adding material to the martyrs' writings), and to reframe them with glosses and other instructive paratexts, on the other, with the justification that it best served the needs of Reformation. In this attitude we can see the beginnings of a Protestant editorial movement that would ultimately culminate in Foxe's 'Book of Martyrs'.

The 'Book of Martyrs'

In the previous pages I have uncovered some of the different kinds of textual subjection that prison writings underwent in the process of being brought to press by examining them in their printed forms and, where possible, comparing them with manuscript versions. While some of these texts seem to bear few marks of editorial subjection, others have been placed within metrical constraints, or have been framed by prescriptive paratexts. This final section is concerned with the collection and editing of texts that led ultimately to Foxe's 'Book of Martyrs', especially the first edition of 1563 and the second edition of 1570. However, rather than following the methodology of the previous sections, I will be examining the metanarrative of subjection that can be derived from letters written about the compilation and editing of the work, and notes and marks added to the manuscripts from which it was compiled. By examining these documents, we can see a number of the editorial ideologies discussed above coming together: it narrates the editorial ethos behind the 'Book of Martyrs' in the process of its formation.

In its finished form, the 'Book of Martyrs' constitutes an account of Christian martyrdom stretching from the first century through to the end of Mary I's reign; but its emphasis is on the lives and deaths of Protestants and proto-Protestant martyrs from the fourteenth to the sixteenth centuries. The most striking structural aspect of this volume is its vast inclusion 'of seemingly heterogeneous materials, including letters, royal statutes, parliamentary acts, sermons, excerpts from medieval chronicles, transcripts of trials and depositions and interrogations, and so on'.[107] It is, essentially, an anthology of martyrological documents, including prison writings, most of which focus on the Marian period. As such, this volume was the epitome of fashion for big books in England, as demonstrated by More's *Workes* and *Tottel's Miscellany*. In addition, the framing of these documents within a cosmic narrative of persecution shows the marks of Bale's

---

[107] Benedict S. Robinson, 'Neither Acts nor Monuments', *English Literary Renaissance*, 41 (2011), 3–30 (3).

influence on Foxe – as well as an answer to his call for 'some lerned Englyshe manne ... to set forth the Englyshe chronycles in theyr ryght shappe work'.[108] However, the editorial principles that determined how the martyrs' prison writings were edited and presented in the final publication arose from a much more complex set of influences. They were shaped and continued to evolve in the light of Foxe's experience of producing two Latin martyrolgies in the 1550s; his collaborations with other collectors and editors; the publication of other continental martyrologies in the 1550s and 1560s by Jean Crespin, Adriaan van Haemstede, and Ludwig Rabus; and the emergence of further prison writings, eyewitness accounts, and documents following the publication of the first edition in 1563.[109]

Foxe's earliest foray into the genre was his Latin history of late medieval proto-Protestant martyrs, *Commentarii in ecclesia gestarum rerum* (1554), a compilation of carefully edited documents that was arranged for polemical effect. Haemstede, Rabus, and Crespin were undertaking analogous projects, which, as Mark Greengrass, Evenden and Freeman have argued, actively built upon the work of Foxe's *Commentarii*.[110] Haemstede's *De Geschiedenisse ende den doodt der vromer Martelaren* (1559) is 450 pages long and presents Protestant persecutions as part of a complete scheme that extended back to the beginnings of the Christian church.[111] The first edition of Rabus's martyrology (1552–8) comprised six hefty quarto volumes totalling close to one million words, and covered the period of the Old Testament, the Apostolic era, and the early church up to the fifth century AD, and the Lollard and Hussite martyrs of the fifteenth century.[112] Crespin compiled a series of martyrologies in French and Latin,

---

[108] The two men met at the Duchess of Suffolk's London register in the summer of 1548, and, following the exile of many Protestants to the Continent after the accession of Mary in 1552, Foxe and Bale both worked for the printer Johann Oporinus. Furthermore, Evenden and Freeman have argued that the material in Foxe's first foray into martyrology, his 1554 publication *Commentarii in ecclesia gestarum rerum*, demonstrates that Bale must have lent him the source texts for his Oldcastle's examinations, the *Fasciculi zizaniorum*, a collection of documents dealing with the early history of the Lollards, compiled by the Carmelites in the first half of the fifteenth century, as well as other notebooks of Bale's (*Religion and the Book*, 39–44).

[109] For more detailed comparisons of these martyrologies, see King, *English Reformation Literature*, 41–4; Brad Gregory, *Salvation at Stake: Christian Martyrdom in Early Modern Europe* (Cambridge, MA, 1999), 165–96; and Andrew Pettegree, 'Haemstede and Foxe', in *John Foxe and the English Reformation*, ed. David Loades (Aldershot, 1997), 278–94.

[110] Evenden and Freeman, *Religion and the Book*, 56–60; Thomas S. Freeman and Mark Greengrass, 'The Acts and Monuments and the Protestant Continental Martyrologies', in *The Unabridged Acts and Monuments Online* (Sheffield, 2011), available from www.johnfoxe.org [accessed 18 December 2012].

[111] Adriaan van Haemstede, *De Geschiedenisse ende den doodt der vromer Martelaren* (Emden, 1559).

[112] Ludwig Rabus, *Der Heyligen ausserwoehlten Gottes Zeugen, Bekennern und Martyrern ... Historien ...* (Strasbourg, 1552–8).

beginning in 1554. His 1560 Latin work *Actiones et Monimenta Martyrum*, which was just two hundred and fifty thousand words long, begins with Wyclif and Hus and comes up to date, incorporating material on English martyrs from Foxe's two Latin martyrologies; but the follow-up volume of 1564 contains a total of six hundred martyrologies (including material on several more English martyrs) and around one million words.[113] The 'Book of Martyrs', however, was bigger and more ambitious than all these texts. The volume is something that inspires awe, but the narrative of how this text came into being is perhaps more impressive still.

The original editorial project behind the 'Book of Martyrs' originated not with Foxe but with Edmund Grindal, former chaplain to Edward VI. He probably approached Foxe after reading his *Commentarii* in order to work with him on two parallel editions of a *martyrum historia* based around the prison writings that Grindal had been collecting. Located in Strasbourg, Grindal was in a strategic location to receive news and prison writings from England, as well as from a network of Protestant exiles scattered across Germany and Switzerland.[114] As his letter to Foxe dated 18 June 1557 shows, there had been a 'division of labour', with Grindal overseeing the English edition, and Foxe the Latin; but at this point the English project was beginning to stall 'because copies of the Acts, at least such as could at all be relied on, were so slowly and grudgingly supplied'.[115] Grindal had hoped to have both editions ready for publication soon after the summer of 1556, but this proved a wildly over-optimistic estimate. Foxe devoted himself increasingly to the Latin martyrology, the *Rerum in Ecclesia gestarum*, which was not finished until the summer of 1559, even though he drastically reduced his original plans for the volume;[116] and the English martyrology was never completed. Rather, the material for the English volume was subsumed into Foxe's *Rerum*, which acted as the basis for the more famous English publication, Foxe's 'Book of Martyrs'. However, because the martyrology began its life as a bigger collaborative project, there survive a series of letters that discuss the editing of the prison writings at some length.

---

[113] Jean Crespin, *Actiones et monimenta martyrum, qui a Wicleffo et Husso ad nostrum hanc aetatem in Germania, Gallia, Anglia, Flandria, Italia et Hispania* ... (Geneva, 1560); *Actes des martyrs Deduits en Sept Livres, depuis le temps de Wiclif et de Hus, jusques à present* (Geneva, 1564).

[114] Patrick Collinson, *Archbishop Grindal 1519–1583: The Struggle for a Reformed Church* (Berkeley, CA, 1979), 80.

[115] *The Remains of Edmund Grindal*, ed. W. Nicholson (Cambridge, 1843), 226. For the Latin original of the letter, see BL Harley MS 417, fol. 102r.

[116] John Foxe, *Rerum in Ecclesia gestarum* (Basle, 1559)

The letters show that Grindal's ideas about publishing were not only at odds with the policies of Hill/Ctematius press at Emden, they were in fact consciously developed in opposition to their methods. In a letter sent to Ridley by Grindal in May 1555, he says that, while the English exiles had manuscript copies of many of Ridley's works, 'It hath bene thought best not to printe them till we see what God will do with you and others from writing hereafter, which should be a greater losse to the church of Christe, than forbearing of these for a tyme'.[117] Ostensibly, Grindal is saying that, while Ridley is living, it has been deemed wise to protect him by delaying the publication of works that might incriminate him. The implication is that, once he is dead the works will come to press – which is an astonishing thing to imply, even to someone willing to martyr themselves for their cause. One of the intriguing things about this statement is the passive verb ('it hath bene thought'). It gives the impression of a decision made in consultation with others, but Grindal has chosen not to disclose who these advisors might be. Indeed, as I shall discuss below, Grindal and Foxe appear to have had a whole range of associates and editors contributing to the *martyrum historia*. However, Grindal's phrasing here means that these associates sound occluded and hidden; they are silent editors. Another thing that the letter elides is Grindal's other motivation for holding back the publication: that he wished to include certain works in his martyrology. Indeed, if it had not been for the Emden press, and the Strasbourg's reprinting of Ridley's *Conferences*, this martyr's writings would have remained unavailable until Foxe's publication of one of Ridley's farewell letters in 1559 (which acted as an advertisement for his forthcoming martyrology).[118] The Hill/Ctematius press's policy of swift printing was at odds with the general ethos of the collection. But, maybe more importantly, Grindal also disapproved of the compromises this speed would have forced upon the finished Emden publications.

He makes just this point in another letter to Foxe, concerning the *The examinacion of the constaunt martir of Christ, Iohn Philpot*, which emerged from the Hill/Ctematius press in 1556:

> With regard to the examinations of Philpot, I give you my opinion, that there are some things in them which need correction. He seems somehow to entangle himself in certain words not so well approved; as for instance, that Christ is really in the supper, etc. If the English book had not been

---

[117] Edmund Grindal to Nicholas Ridley, LM, 51.
[118] Nicholas Ridley, *A frendly farewell which master doctor Ridley did write unto all his true lovers and frendes in God, a little before that he suiffered* (London, 1559).

published, some things in it might have been modified. Then again he cites the ancients sometimes from memory, being deprived of the safeguard of books, wherein one may easily slip: as when he says that Athanasius was at the head of the Nicene council; whereas at that time, if I remember rightly, he was only deacon of the bishop of Alexandria; although in disputing he laboured more than others, and so may be said to have taken the lead. But there the controversy is concerning honour and primacy. Perhaps you also have discovered others of a similar kind, for I have adduced these for the sake of example: use your own judgment.[119]

Grindal's lament, that 'if the English book had not been published, some things in it might have been modified', tells us a lot about his editorial policy. He clearly believed the Emden press were foolish to publish Philpot's examination as they stood. Firstly, there are the minor lapses in Philpot's citation of the ancients, which were due to his lack of reference material. He proposes that his colleague correct the point of error he has noticed ('that Athanasius was at the head of the Nicene council'), and implies that there are probably more that Foxe should seek out. More crucially, Grindal expresses his dissatisfaction about the way in which Philpot engages with the controversy surrounding the sacrament of the altar. Philpot seems to come down on the side of consubstantiation, a belief in the local presence of the body and blood of Christ ('that Christ is *really* in the supper'), rather than adhering to the Zwinglian position that Christ is only present metaphorically. The problem with Philpot's statements on this topic is that they draw attention to a point of contention within reformed theology. What is interesting is that Grindal proposes 'correcting' this position: in the original Latin version of the letter the word used is '*lima*', which literally means to file or polish, and which was a common metaphor in Latin for referring to polishing or revising a literary work. As with the discussion of *correction* in relation to Tottel's metrical emendations, the word *lima* at once suggests the positive process of buffing up the texts for a wider print audience, and the more negative activity of disciplining the text with a file. Indeed, what Grindal is suggesting here is not some minimal tweaking of the text, but rather changes that represent the doctrinal position of Philpot in a very different way.

To sum up the differences between the policy of the Hill/Ctematius press and that evolving in relation to Grindal's *martyrum historia*, we might think about the aesthetic points that are frequently made today by the media regarding the desire for 'real' models by the general public, as

---

[119] *Remains*, 223; BL Harley MS 417, fol. 112r.

opposed to advertisers' reliance on air-brushed, idealised versions of womanhood to sell their products. John Olde's preface to Ridley's *Brief Declaration*, for example, sought to emphasise the authenticity of the printed text: 'he hathe regestred it by his owne penne in this forme ensuyng, and sealed it vp with his blood'. Olde thus provides a clear assertion that the text has not been tampered with. We must assumed that he was either blind to the faults in these texts – which we might assume the eagle eyes of Grindal would have caught – or else he trusted his readers to appreciate the fact that these texts, written secretly in prison, would lack the polish of more carefully prepared texts written at liberty. By contrast, it appears that Grindal wanted to represent the martyrs and their writings as flawless: without faults in their arguments, lack in their knowledge, or any deviance from the dominant doctrinal beliefs of the reformed church.

Importantly, though, Grindal and Foxe were not alone in making executive decisions about how prison writings should or should not be edited. In his letters, Grindal frequently put forward the opinions of other Protestant leaders about the content of prison writings:

> I have heard also that Master Martyr and Master Bullinger have expressed a wish, with respect to the writings of Master Hooper, that he had had time and leisure to revise them: for that, being composed suddenly and in prison, he had not written on a subject, agitated at that time by the disputations of many, with the guardedness which such an ulcerated age as ours requires. I do not arrogate to myself the part of a critic; but candidly, after my manner, communicate to you the convictions of my mind. I doubt not but that, if you publish them, you will where there is need subjoin a critical note.[120]

Here, for example, Grindal is reporting to Foxe the opinions of Peter Martyr and Henrich Bullinger on John Hooper's prison writings. It is unclear whether they acted as official advisors for the project, or whether he sought their opinion in a more ad hoc fashion. Nevertheless, we see that Grindal is keen to show that he is not imposing his singular will on the shape of the texts: 'I do not arrogate to myself the part of a critic'. Based on this letter and others, Grindal seems to have arrived at his belief that prisoners' writings could and should be improved upon in consultation with other Protestant leaders. What is also interesting about this passage is Grindal's practical consideration of how editorial additions should be made to the text ('you will where there is need subjoin a critical note').

[120] Ibid.

Here Grindal seems to be suggesting the addition of paratexts, rather than silently editing the body of the original prison writing, which he recommends elsewhere.

> Hence it is that we have now nothing but a somewhat rude quantity of matter, but yet of such sort, as may afford no despicable material for constructing a noble edifice; especially if it should be polished a little by those who possess those writings, and who also know how to add other circumstances not written, but useful for illustration.[121]

This passage, in a letter addressed to Foxe, suggests two interesting things about the editorial process behind Foxe's martyrologies. This is the first time Grindal explicitly says that it was acceptable for editors to add material to the martyrs' prison writings ('add other circumstances not written, but useful for illustration') as well as 'polish' away errors and indiscretions (*'expoliretur'* in the original). Grindal also appears to be sketching a network of editors – piece-workers who would edit the prison writings in their own keeping. Although there is no clear indication of the size of this network, or indeed of the identities of those involved, it makes sense that the huge body of Protestant prison writings – which, as demonstrated in Chapters 3 and 4, required a large and organised network of individuals to write, copy, and disseminate them – should require a similar organisation to oversee their journey into print.

One person who we know was subsequently trusted with the editing of many prisoners' letters is Henry Bull. From 1560 onwards, Bull joined Foxe in the challenging undertaking of finding and editing the documents that were left behind by the Marian martyrs. Much of Bull's work was performed in collaboration (or, at least, co-operation) with Foxe's larger and more far-reaching effort to edit and re-edit his martyrology. Annotations in Bull's hand on the manuscripts that formed the basis of this collection, such as those that read 'Restore this to mr fox', show that Foxe and Bull were sharing these documents.[122] Before the first edition of the 'Book of Martyrs' in 1563, Bull called publicly for the recovery of writings by the Marian martyrs in his preface to John Hooper's *Apology*.[123] Bull initially issued the prison writings of the martyrs in both individual editions and as collections of letters or brief pamphlets, the most important

---

[121] *Remains*, 226; BL Harley MS 417, fol. 102r.
[122] These manuscripts are now held now in Emmanuel College Library MSS 260–2 and BL Additional MS 19400. See, for example, ECL MS 260, fols. 44r–v, and BL Additional MS 19400, fol. 102v.
[123] *An apologye made by the reuerende father and constante martyr of Christe Iohn Hooper late bishop of Gloceter and Worceter* (London, 1562), sigs. A2v–A3r.

being the collection *Certain most godly, fruitful, and comfortable letters of such true saintes and holy martyrs of God*, which was issued under Miles Coverdale's name and printed by Day in 1564. Although this text was published one year after Foxe's first edition of his English martyrology, Bull's editorial practices were clearly developed in conjunction with Foxe, and indeed many of the letters in this volume worked their way into subsequent editions of the 'Book of Martyrs'.

The survival of the manuscripts used for Bull and Foxe's publications provides another layer to the metanarrative of the editorial subjection that martyrs' prison writings underwent. While Grindal's letters provide a neat summary of the principles behind the editing of these texts, the manuscripts show them in action, for they bear the marks of Bull's 'polishing' or 'filing' of the text in his very own hand. For example, on a letter to Thomas Whittle, Bull wrote: 'These ij letters of whittles wold be reade advisedly and the superfluous things lefte out, as in other letter it shalbe necessary to do the like'.[124] This is a revealing statement, which tells us not only that Bull deleted lines, added material, and rewrote whole sections of the martyrs' letters, but also that there was a clear policy ('do the like') determining what should stay and what should go. As Susan Wabuda has noticed, Bull's subtle editing tended to heighten the universal elements of the letters by emphasising the writers' intense biblicism, building upon the martyrs' desire to send comforting epistles to their followers in the style of St Paul. Among the things which Bull deemed superfluous and omitted were the items of personal information with which some letters concluded, items of personal news, greetings to family and friends, as well as references to carriers which, as discussed in the previous chapter, create intriguing ellipses that point to personal relationships, but do not edify a general readership. For example, in a letter from John Careless to Augustine Bernher there is a note added at the end after Careless had signed off, mentioning an enclosure intended for Augustine's wife, Elizabeth: 'Thoughe you woulde finde me no tokens yet I have sent you a simple one / I have sent you here a simple letter vnsealed by cause you shulde see it / Looke what is amys in it I praye you mende itt and together as it shulde goo I praye you send it I have no tyme to peruse itt nor yet this therefore beare yf aught be amyse'.[125] However, this has been crossed through, and does not appear in the printed version. There are several likely reasons for this. Firstly, the postscript refers to a letter now lost, which, like the references to extratextual messages trusted to the carrier,

---

[124] ECL MS 260, fol. 33r, crossed out.   [125] ECL MS 260, fols. 215r–216r.

creates an ellipsis in the text. Secondly, it gives the recipient, Elizabeth Bernher, permission to 'mende' the letter 'yf aught be amyse'. In so doing, it shifts the attention away from the author – the martyr – and on to the broader network of carriers and supporters and their role in the maintenance of Protestant communities in the Marian period. It also provides evidence of the kind of collaboration on prison writings described in Chapter 3; perhaps, more controversially, it shows that this collaboraton was invited from women as well as men. By cutting it here, however, Bull is glossing over the fact that these letters might not be the pure unadulterated work of the martyrs: indeed, they may have been edited by co-religionists as well as by editors like Bull himself.

Bull encouraged the readers of his letters anthology to read the martyrs' missives as repositories of universal spiritual guidance – rather than as situation-specific guidance aimed at particular recipients – by suppressing certain names and adding headings that encouraged particular readings. A classic example of this is the letter that John Bradford sent to Joyce Hales to comfort her after the suicide of her father-in-law. In Bull's anthology it is headed: 'A letter which he wrote to a faithfull woman in her heauines and trouble: most comfortable for all those to read that are afflicted and broken harted for their sinnes'.[126] Hales' name is removed, and she becomes merely a 'faithfull woman', thus preventing readers from wondering about the precise nature of Bradford's relationship with this woman. More importantly, the title (and the editing of the letter, as discussed in the last chapter) takes attention away from the specific context of her sorrow and anxiety, and turns it into a generalised piece of advice '*for all those* ... broken harted for their sinnes'. The benefit of this approach for Foxe was that these universalised epistles more easily slotted into his apocalyptic framework, stressing the continuities with the persecution of the early Christians and providing valuable guidance in the event of possible future attacks from the 'false' church and other kinds of tribulation a Protestant may undergo.

This example is also typical of one specific trend in the editing of letters to and from female sustainers of the martyrs, a systematic effort intended, as Freeman has noted, to ensure that the relationships between martyrs and their female co-religionists appeared proper. One notable example of such editing can be found in Bull's markings and annotations to a letter from Careless to Margery Cooke. The original unedited letter opens with the greeting:

---

[126] *TAMO* (1570), 1861.

> Ah my deare and faythefull lovinge syster M cooke what hyghe lawed and
> prayse, yea what contynuall humble and hartye thankes am I moste synnfull
> and wretched creature, bownde I to bende vnto all myghtye god oure most
> deare lovynge father ... Truelye I will not flatter with you, but I muste
> nedes testefye the truthe, that me thynkethe youre wordes, or rather godes
> wordes by you spoken or written, have a wonderfull power with them, or as
> that weare a marvellouse efficacye or strengthe worckynge in my harte at the
> hereynge or the readynge of them.[127]

However, in Bull's hand 'M. Cooke is crossed out and 'brother' is inserted;
and on a fragment of paper, probably pasted to this letter before coming
loose, Bull has rewritten the opening of the letter (in the form that it
appears in his printed edition):

> Blessed be god the father of all mercie, for the greate /comfort\ and
> Christian consolation which he hath so mercifully ministered vnto my pore
> afflicted hart by your meanes my moste deare and faithfull brother.

In this revision, Bull not only changes the gender of the recipient, he also
deletes the passage of praise for the wisdom of the recipient. The effect is to
make sure that the writer, Careless, is beyond reproach in his relationship
with Cooke. The original version of the letter seems to suggest Careless
derives important sustenance from his relationship with this woman. And,
while he states that his comfort derives from her wise and godly words, the
way in which he speaks about them 'worckynge in my harte' could be
interpreted as showing an emotional dependency developing on his part.
By contrast, the edited version makes it quite clear that Careless is the *giver*
of wisdom rather than the *receiver*, thereby supporting the value of the
anthology as one that edifies its readers.[128]

Editing was also undertaken to suppress any signs of factionalism. In a
letter from Ridley to Grindal, which was first printed both in Bull's
anthology and in the 1570 edition of the 'Book of Martyrs' onwards, a
large and important section criticising John Knox's opposition to the use
of the the Book of Common Prayer among the English exile congregation
at Frankfurt was removed. The first wave of exiles to settle in Geneva were
required to sign a French confession of faith before they were permitted to
establish their own congregation, and they used this as an opportunity to
'purify' their mode of worship. Desiring a liturgy more reformed than the

---

[127] Correction clip (in first folder) to ECL MS 260, fol. 240r.
[128] For detailed discussion of this topic, see Thomas S. Freeman, '"The good ministrye of godlye and
vertuouse women": The Elizabethan Martyrologists and the Female Supporters of the Marian
Martyrs', *Journal of British Studies*, 49 (2000), 8–33.

1552 edition of the Book of Common Prayer, John Knox, William Whittingham, Anthony Gilby, William Cole, and John Foxe drew up a rite based on Calvin's Strasbourg rite. But when another wave of exiles arrived in Frankfurt, they wished to adopt the 1552 Book of Common Prayer. The result was an embarrassing schism within the exile community between proponents of Genevan-style ecclesiastical reform and those who believed that abandoning the Edwardian prayer book was a betrayal of the national church.[129] In this deleted passage, Ridley laments: 'Alas that brother knoxe could not beare with our book of common praiers'. And he questions in particular his reasons for opposition to the litany, and what their biblical foundation might be, asking: 'what word hath he of the scripture and if he hath none why will he not rather folowe that that the sentence of the old auncyent writters do more alow, from whom to dissent without a warrant of goddes worde, I can not thinke it any godly wisdome'.[130] Bull, and Foxe after him, had several compelling reasons for eliding these passages. Bull was always anxious to conceal any evidence of Protestant doctrinal division. But Foxe was also a prominent supporter of Knox's position at Frankfurt and he would not have wanted his readers to know of Ridley's opposition to Knox's rejection of the Book of Common Prayer.[131]

In light of the highly interventionist nature of the editing undertaken by Foxe and his collaborators, we might ask: What makes these editors any different from censors? There is an inherent irony in Grindal and Foxe's editorial policy: they were undoubtedly doing their best to 'liberate' these martyrs' writings through print publication, but in so doing they took on the role of oppressors and captors, racking and dismembering texts in the very way that the authorities had acted on the bodies of their authors. Just as the programme of persecution and burnings had been employed in Mary's reign to purge the country of heresy, so the programme of editing overseen by these Protestant leaders was also justified by religious principle. It began as a project to produce an authoritative – indeed the *definitive* – history of persecution. As it was first conceived, it was history

---

[129] See Beth Quitslund, *The Reformation in Rhyme: Sternhold, Hopkins and the English Metrical Psalter, 1547–1603* (Aldershot, 2008), 117–19; and Bryan D. Spinks, *Reformation and Modern Rituals and Theologies of Baptism: From Luther to Contemporary Practices* (Aldershot, 2006), 44–6.

[130] ECL MS 260 fols. 114r–v.

[131] Bull and Foxe also edited out passages touching on the disputes between key protestant leaders and the 'freewillers'. See Thomas S. Freeman, 'Dissenters from a Dissenting Church: The Challenge of the "Freewillers", 1550–1558', in *The Beginnings of English Protestantism*, ed. Peter Marshall and Alec Ryrie (Cambridge, 2002), 129–56.

from the perspective of the underdog, a classic counter-public narrative arguing that such persecution was a sign that the Protestant martyrs were numbered amongst God's elect. However, as the project dragged into Elizabeth's reign, the narrative became about the establishment of Protestantism as an authorised faith, and it was associated (like Mary I's programme of persecution) with purging the realm of false religion:

> yet haue I laboured and trauayled according to my infirme habilitie, what I may, in collecting and setting forth the actes, fame and memorie of these our Martyrs of this latter tyme of the churche, whiche according as my dutie doth bynde me, next vnder the Lorde, I offer and present here vnto your Maiestie, humbly desyring, and nothing yet misdoubting, but that your highnes and singuler clemencie, likewyse followyng the steppes of that noble Constantine, with no lesse propensitie of fauoure and furtheraunce, wil accept and also assiste these my laborious trauailes to the behoufe of the churche, against the importunitie of the malignaunt.[132]

This preface, dedicated to Elizabeth I, bears some clear parallels with Rastell's preface to Thomas More's *Workes*, which was addressed to Mary I and stressed how his publication would 'much helpe forwarde youre Maiesties most godly purpose, in purging this youre realme of all wicked heresies'. Similarly, Foxe suggests how his 'Book of Martyrs' would benefit the Church of England ('behoufe of the churche'). Just as Rastell talks about supporting an existing policy, so Foxe styles himself as a Eusebius to Elizabeth's Constantine: he suggests that just as Constantine had brought Christianity to Rome, ending imperial persecution, so Elizabeth had re-established a Protestant settlement. As a result, Foxe's extensive censoring – or his 'laborious trauailes' – is justified by religious and political necessity.

Reflecting on our own experiences of reading these printed works, we might interpret the process of editing as a twofold act of oppression. Not only are the prison writings disfigured by the actions of their editors, we too become victims of their manipulations. But if we choose to interrogate, or at least notice, the ways in which editors frame prison writings with their own narratives and agendas, then we can avoid becoming the editor's accomplice and instead assist the imprisoned author in overcoming the constraints of institutional oppression. However, this liberty of the literary consumer to read selectively also introduces the possibility of insinuating our own interests and readings into these texts, manipulating them for our own ends.

---

[132] 'Prefaces', *TAMO* (1563), 8. See for comparison 'Prefaces', *TAMO* (1570), 10.

Afterword

The trope of prison writing appears in two plays that were entered into the Stationer's Register in 1605: Thomas Heywood's *If You Know Not Me, You Know Nobody, Part One* (also called *The Troubles of Queen Elizabeth*) and *Eastward Hoe*, written by George Chapman, Ben Jonson, and John Marston. The former depicts one piece of prison writing being produced while another is discovered. Princess Elizabeth is represented in the Tower of London writing to her sister, Mary I, for mercy when her keeper Beningfield finds an inscription in the margins of a Bible.

> What has she written here? *He reads.*
>
> Much suspected by me, nothing prou'd can be,
> *Finis quoth Elizabeth* the prisoner,
> Pray god it proue so, soft what book's this,
> Marry a God, whats here an English bible?
> *Sanctum Maria* pardon this prophanation of my hart,
> Water *Barwick*, water, Ile meddle with't no more.[1]

The inscription provides a clear statement of Elizabeth's innocence. But it is not the writing that shocks Beningfield in this passage, but rather the place in which it is written: an English translation of the Bible. This site of writing is used to suggest Elizabeth's devotion to Protestantism during her imprisonment.

Eastward Hoe, by comparison, represents the plots, imprisonment, and supposed reformation of two confidence tricksters, Francis Quicksilver and Sir Petronel Flash, and a corrupt usurer called Security. In one scene in the Counter, the guard, Master Wolf, describes the behaviour of these three inmates:

---

[1] Thomas Heywood, *If you knovv not me, you know no bodie: or, The troubles of Queene Elizabeth* (London, 1605), sig. E.3v.

Woolfe.... I neuer knew, or saw Prisoners more penitent, or more deuout. They will sit you vp all night singing of Psalmes, and aedifying the whole Prison: onely, Securitie sings a note to high, sometimes, because he lyes i'the Two-penny ward, farre of, and can not take his tune. The Neighbours can not rest for him, but come euery Morning to aske, what godly Prisoners we haue.

Touch. Which on 'hem is't is so deuout, the Knight, or the to'ther?

Woolfe. Both Sir. But the young Man especially! I neuer heard his like! He has cut his hayre too. He is so well giuen, and has such good gifts! Hee can tell you, almost all the Stories of the Bookeof Martyrs, and speake you all the Sicke-mans Salue without Booke.[2]

These men partake in oral practices – singing and storytelling – that use texts closely associated with the prison: the Psalter and Foxe's 'Book of Martyrs'. The devotional nature of these activities is perhaps surprising for the audience, many of whom might expect the misery of prison to confirm Quicksilver, Flash, and Security in their villainy. Instead, the prisoners claim to have been through a spiritual conversion: in a subsequent scene, Quicksilver writes and performs his 'Repentance' or 'Last Farewell', a song that narrates his conversion and atonement for past sins, and brings about his eventual release from prison.

These scenes from *If You Know Not Me* and *Eastward Hoe* are important cultural markers. They illustrate not only how prison writing as a literary form and concept had developed during the sixteenth century, but also the ways that it would evolve over the coming decades. Firstly, such scenes are testimony to the fact that, by the beginning of the seventeenth century, prison literature had become a cultural practice that was not only accepted but also recognised and valued. The depiction of a recent and much loved monarch writing in her prison cell functioned to authorise the practice as respectable. And in both plays the product is something laudable. By choosing to represent Elizabeth's inscription – 'Much suspected by me, nothing prou'd can be, / *Finis quoth Elizabeth* the prisoner' – copied into a Bible (which in Foxe is described as being engraved into a window),[3] Heywood places Elizabeth within a very particular tradition of prisoners who wrote marginalia in their books of devotion.[4] Chapman, Jonson, and Marston also represent the prison as a place that encourages devotion with their description of Flash, Quicksilver, and Security singing Psalms, and

[2] George Chapman, Ben Jonson, and John Marston, *Eastward Hoe* (London, 1605), sig. H.4r.
[3] *TAMO* (1570), 2334.
[4] See examples by Thomas More and Lady Jane Grey in Chapter 2 above.

Quicksilver penning his 'Repentance'. Even if we are not meant to take this religious conversion at face value, the play makes the point that prison writings were attributed a certain authority and sincerity that Quicksilver might feasibly exploit. Indeed, as the popularity of modern-day cinematic parodies such as the *Scary Movie* franchise have shown us, a tradition needs to be well established before it can be lampooned.

As both plays demonstrate, one of the key publications that made prison literature widely available for parody and appropriation was Foxe's 'Book of Martyrs'. Heywood used the martyrology as a source for his history play, and *Eastward Hoe* suggests that it was so popular that 'devout' prisoners like Quicksilver were able to recite stories from it from memory. It is therefore unsurprising that so many writings by religious prisoners in the century following its first publication owe a clear debt to this tome. The most pervasive influence of Foxe can be observed in the ongoing popularity of the trial narrative, which, despite having its origins in Lollard writings, came into its own in the 1540s and 1550s, before being popularised by the martyrology. Separatists, Puritans, Baptists, and Quakers alike utilised the form to distinguish themselves from the Church of England, which persecuted them for their nonconformity.[5] Like their predecessors, these texts are usually set out like dialogues and present a dramatic exchange between the cruel, corrupt, or doctrinally flawed examiners and the scripturally grounded and persuasive defendants. The form was also the clear inspiration for the trial at Vanity Fair in John Bunyan's famous prison writing, *The Pilgrim's Progress*, in which Lord Hate-good the judge charges Christian and Faithful: 'That they were enemies to, and disturbers of their Trade; that they had made Commotions and Divisions in the Town, and had won a party to their own most dangerous opinions, in contempt of the Law of their Prince [Beelzebub].'[6] The passage pitches Christian and Faithful against the law of Vanity Fair and its ruler, Beelzebub. In so doing, the exchange that follows can be understood as an essentialisation of the classic trial narrative, in which the adversarial dispute between interrogator and defendant is made to stand for the a universal

---

[5] See, for example, the examination accounts of Henry Barrow and John Greenwood, *The Writings of John Greenwood and Henry Barrow, 1591–1593*, ed. Leland H. Carlson, Elizabethan Non-Conformist Texts 6 (London, 1970), 93–234; John Bastwick's *Praxeis ton episkopon sive apologeticus ad praesules Anglicanos criminum ecclesiasticorum in curia celsae commissionis* ([Leiden?], 1636); John Lilburne's *The Christian mans triall: or, A true relation of the first apprehension and severall examinations of Iohn Lilburne* (London, 1641); *A Relation of the Imprisonment of Mr John Bunyan* (London, 1765); and the various reconstructions of trials and examinations in Joseph Besse's *A Collection of the Sufferings of the People Called Quaker* (London, 1753).

[6] John Bunyan, *The pilgrim's progress from this world to that which is to come* (London, 1678), 128.

and eternal battle between the true church and its persecutors. As such, then, this prison writing is an example of how the trial narrative, which was essentially a documentary form, was turned into imaginative and popular literature in the seventeenth century, and can be seen as an analogue not only for trial scenes in plays such as Webster's *The White Devil*, but also for modern courtroom dramas, from Harper Lee's *To Kill a Mockingbird* to John Grisham's *The Pelican Brief.*

From another perspective, the 'Book of Martyrs' provided material and motivation for Catholic prisoners who wished to dismantle the Protestant narrative Foxe had constructed. Nicholas Harpsfield's *Dialogi sex* (1566) was the first systematic attack on Foxe's martyrology (as well as another influential Protestant history, the *Historia ecclesiae Christi*, known as the Magdeburg Centuries), and it set the tone for later Catholic prison writings. A religious sonnet by William Alabaster, which may have been written while he was held under close confinement, drew on Harpsfield's attack on Foxe;[7] and Thomas Pound penned 'A challenge unto Fox the Martirmonger', which he sent to another prisoner, possibly Francis Tregian the elder. One section reads:

> Com forthe fond Fox, with all the rabble rowte
> of monstrowse martyres, in thi brainsicke booke
> compare them to, this gloriowse martir stowte
> And thow shalte see, how lothly fowle thei look
> For blacke and white, compared somewhat neere
> Will cawse them bothe, the better to apeere.[8]

Pound here condemns Foxe's martyrs as a 'monstrowse' parody of the 'gloriowse martir stowte' that he is about to describe. In setting up such a 'black and white' dichotomy, however, he necessarily echoes the Foxean opposition between the true church and the false church, albeit from the opposite perspective. Such examples suggest that, so thoroughly had Foxe's martyrology defined prison writing by this time that even those writers trying to resist this Protestant history could not quite escape its tropes and conventions.

But while *If You Know Not Me* and *Eastward Hoe* both point to the dominating influence of Foxe's martyrology, the two plays also show the diversification of prison literature as a supra-genre at the end of the sixteenth century. The former signals important continuities in prison

---

[7] William Alabaster, *The Sonnets of William Alabaster*, ed. G. M. Story and Helen Gardner (Oxford, 1959), 3.
[8] TNA, SP 12/157, fols. 105r–10v (fol. 105r).

writing across the early modern period, while the latter alerts us to the emergence of a new kind of prison writer at the end of the sixteenth century. Specifically, the prison scene in *If You Know Not Me* emphasises the ubiquity of the trope of the noble, political prisoner. Throughout the early modern period we see political prisoners emerging from the numerous plots and rebellions against the establishment, from the Ridolfi plot to the English Civil War. Their status is demonstrated by their adoption of intellectual and courtly pursuits, such as the writing of translations, epic poems, and histories. Several Royalists, for example, penned ambitious translations: Sir John Glanville produced a metrical paraphrase of the entire Psalter, and Sir Thomas Urquhart produced the first English version of Rabelais.[9] The grand scope of such tasks might be compared to Ralegh's famous tome, *The History of the World*, about the ancient history of Greece and Rome. Projects like these were time-consuming, making them a suitable undertaking for prisoners who were unsure of how long they might be incarcerated, and the skills and devotion necessary for their undertaking required their authors to be individuals with their minds set on higher things. Such writings embody Elizabeth's inscription 'Much suspected by me, nothing prou'd can be': they remove their authors from suspicion by refusing to offer written evidence of the activities and beliefs with which they are charged. Many political prisoners, of course, used their incarceration as propaganda for their cause, continuing to pen polemics from their cells, such as Edward Bagshaw, who in 1660 wrote *The Rights of the Crown in England, As It Is Established by Law*. But others embraced the power of deniability offered by literary pursuits, as in the case of Samuel Sheppard, whose Spenserian epic, *The Faerie King*, contains a usefully ambivalent allegorical representation of Charles I.[10] Such circumspection necessarily recalls the prison verse of Thomas Wyatt, and Thomas More's Tower works.

While *If You Know Not Me* participates in literary tropes with a long history, *Eastward Ho* was a play of its time, engaging with pressing contemporary concerns about a specific prison population. Debt litigation had increased markedly in London in the period 1580–1640, as market activity increased and new laws were enacted mandating the incarceration of vagrants.[11] This growing population of debt-ridden prisoners was behind

[9] John Glanville, BL, Egerton MS 2590; Thomas Urquhart, *The first [second] book of the works of Mr Francis Rabelais* (London, 1653).
[10] Samuel Sheppard, *The Faerie King*, Bodleian Library, Oxford, MS Rawl. Poet. 28.
[11] See A. L. Beier, 'Vagrants and the Social Order', *Past & Present*, 64 (1974), 3–29; Craig Muldrew, *The Economy of Obligation: The Culture of Credit and Social Relations in Early Modern England* (Basingstoke, 1998), 3, 199–271.

a new satirical literary trend. The works were much more self-reflexive than the texts of prisoners of conscience. They depicted the prison population of inmates and keepers, the conditions in which they were kept, and, by showing the prison system to be cruel and corrupt, they contained both implicit and explicit appeals for reform. One such text is Luke Hutton's *The blacke dogge of Newgate* (1596), which purports to describe the author's misdeeds (robbery and trespass) and the monstrous human who was responsible for his capture and arrest, who transforms from human to animal and back again. Hutton's emphasis on the monstrous underlines the perversion of justice, locating the real horror not in the fictitious captor's shape-shifting but in his deceit, corruption, and oppression. The corruption and avaricious nature of jailors was commented upon frequently in such writings, and especially in satires featuring prison characters, such as Thomas Dekker's portrait of 'Iaylors' in *Villainies Discovered* (1616) and in his contributions to *Sir Thomas Overburie his Wife* (1616) and Geoffrey Mynshull's *Certain Characters and Essays of Prisons and Prisoners* (1618). These texts were part of an increased agitation for official aid to poor imprisoned debtors who could not afford to pay their keep and therefore relied on charity, but they also established a tradition that anticipates the Dickensian *oeuvre*, which similarly agitated for social reform through cutting satire.[12]

One text often grouped with these early seventeenth-century satires is *The compters common-wealth* (1617), penned by the poet and 'rogue' William Fennor. After giving an account of his arrest and treatment in the Wood Street Counter, Fennor describes meeting a fellow prisoner housed in the Hole, the very lowest ward in the prison, where those who could not afford to pay for their keep were placed. As with Dekker and Mynshul's pamphlets, the exchange with this prisoner leads to a series of character portraits, of 'subtile Citizens, politicke Prodigalls, villanous Sergeants, and officious Constables and Beadles', which take up the majority of the publication.[13] However, what differentiates these portraits is the way in which this narrative represents his characters as subjects within a commonwealth. The Counter is a society in miniature, with its own social structure, hierarchies, divisions, and

---

[12] Phillip Shaw, 'The Position of Thomas Dekker in Jacobean Prison Literature', *PMLA*, 62 (1947), 366–91 (379).
[13] William Fennor, *The compters common-wealth, or A voiage made to an infernall iland* (London, 1617), 77.

corruption: in the final chapter, Fennor's companion describes how the Hole is 'as a little Citty in a Commonwealth'.[14] Like any seventeenth-century city, the Hole contains people practising various trades and is governed by a lord mayor (the steward), the twelve companies of the city (twelve senior prisoners), a constable, and a privy council. The implication of Fennor's analogy is that the misery of those incarcerated in the Hole caused them to create their own form of government.

The metaphor of the Counter as a diminutive, yet self-contained, commonwealth is a useful one for considering the status of the early modern prison and its literary output in the sixteenth century and beyond. John Foxe had described Marian prisons as 'right Christian schooles and churches', and certain modern scholars have also suggested that we should view early modern prisons as sites of culture, or Muses' habitations.[15] However, both these metaphors – the church, and the Muse's habitation – are reductive: the former takes into account only religious activities and writings; the latter ignores the vast number of illiterate prisoners in this era. And even if we consider only the educated prisoners who put pen to paper, these metaphors fail to reflect the breadth and effect of the writings that emerged from early modern jails. Fennor's notion of the prison as a commonwealth, by contrast, allows us to consider the complexities of the relationship between prison communities, their literary output, and society at large. The idea that the prison mimics the social structure, hierarchies, and legalities of the society in which it is situated reflects how prisoners tried to turn incarceration to their advantage, and to pen works that would gain them favour beyond the prison walls. One notable example, discussed earlier in this book, is John Harington's translation of Cicero's *De amicitia*, which is dedicated to Katherine Brandon and opens with a description of the collaborative process behind the book's making, as well as a plea that she will give him patronage. The key to the success of this approach is an emphasis on the correspondence between the social structures inside and outside the prison walls. Harington achieves this by describing a society of learned men teaching one another languages, lending books, and checking one another's creative endeavours – thus stressing his suitability to enter back into courtly circles.

---

[14] Ibid., 82
[15] *TAMO* (1583), 1545; Molly Murray, 'Measured Sentences: Forming Literature in the Early Modern Prison', in 'Prison Writings in Early Modern England', ed. William H. Sherman and William J. Sheils, *HLQ*, special issue 72 (2009), 147–67 (150). See also in the same issue Thomas Freeman, 'Introduction: The Rise of Prison Literature', 133–46 (143–6).

But, perhaps more usefully for this study, the metaphor of the prison as commonwealth also conjures up the idea of a state within a state, a term usually used to refer to a group that exists within a country but which does not respond to civilian leadership. Such groups might be the armed forces, intelligence agencies, or police, but the concept has also been applied to the Catholic Church before the Act of Supremacy was passed. Prison inmates, of course, could never be described as a coherent group. But as the previous pages have shown, out of the multitude that were admitted to, lived, and died in prisons in the mid-Tudor period, communities emerged that fit the definition of a state within a state. Their literary outputs created counter-publics, via which they circulated texts offering social, political, and religious alternatives to those imposed by the authorities. Some of these writers employed the tricks of the weak described by Michel de Certeau, such as John Fisher, who showed his sister Elizabeth White how to practise the devout life of a Catholic within a country that declared the king the head of its church. Small-scale statements of resistance can be traced in the love epistles sent between Margaret Douglas and Thomas Howard. And an organised and extensive demonstration of group resistance emerges from the Marian prisons, where Protestant leaders penned letters designed to encourage their fellow prisoners to remain true to their faith until death, and to provide doctrinal instruction and encouragement for those outside prison to resist conformity to Popery. In Mary's reign, prisons harboured a Protestant state in the midst of a Catholic country, just as, later, Elizabethan prisons would house a counter-public that remained loyal to the Pope, and the jails of the Commonwealth would shelter a monarchical realm.

The recognition of the early modern prison as a seat of religious and political opposition is evident throughout contemporary drama; *If You Know Not Me* and *Eastward Hoe* are just two of a plethora of Elizabethan and Jacobean plays set in prisons.[16] The function and nature of dramatic prison scenes are as various as the kinds of prisoner that existed in the early modern period. Yet, more often than not, prisons were represented by dramatists as places of dissent, resistance, and threat to social order. Kristen Deiter has demonstrated that, of the twenty-four history plays to contain passages set in the Tower of London dating from the period 1590–1624, twenty-one represent the Tower's role in rebellion against the

---

[16] On the ubiquity of the prison scene in early modern drama, see Ruth Ahnert, 'The Prison in Early Modern Drama', *Literature Compass*, 9:1 (2012), 34–47; and E. D. Pendry, *Elizabethan Prisons and Prison Scenes* (Salzburg, 1974).

sovereign.[17] The long ambivalent history of the Tower – as royal palace, fortress, royal mint, repository for the royal jewels and government records, and holding place for prisoners – played a part in this. But the fact that this trope did not emerge until the end of the sixteenth century clearly points to the centrality of the sixteenth century in its development. Prisons had always housed bodies of religious and political prisoners, but, before the 1530s, dissident prison communities did not have a corpus of literature testifying to their cause. Writing provided individual prisoners and communities with the power of record, a means of spreading their message beyond the prison walls to a particular reader or social group, to lead a movement, or to witness posthumously to that cause. Together, these individual motivations created a body of texts that made prison writing one of the most influential cultural practices in the early modern period, which left its mark not only on the literary landscape but also on the politico-religious identity of the English nation.

---

[17] Kristen Deiter, *The Tower of London in English Renaissance Drama: Icon of Opposition* (London, 2008), 79.

Bibliography

MANUSCRIPT SOURCES

Bodleian Library, Oxford

MS Rawl. Poet. 28
MS Lat. th. d. 15

British Library

Additional MS 421
Additional MS 15117
Additional MS 19400
Additional MS 26737
Additional MS 36529
Arundel MS 97
Arundel MS 100
Cotton MSS, Cleopatra E vi
Cotton MSS, Vespasian F xiii
Egerton MS 2711
Egerton MS 2590
Harley MS 78
Harley MS 416
Harley MS 417
Harley MS 422
Harley MS 425
Harley MS 2370
Lansdowne MS 389
Stowe MS 1066

Emmanuel College Library, Cambridge

MS 260
MS 261
MS 262

Parker Library, Corpus Christi College, Cambridge

MS 128

University Library, Cambridge

MS Nn.iv.43

The National Archives, Kew

SP 1/71
SP 1/78
SP 1/81
SP 1/88
SP 1/93
SP 1/110
SP 1/111
SP 1/114
SP 2/R
SP 6/5
SP 6/7
SP 10/12

PRIMARY PRINTED SOURCES

Alabaster, William *The Sonnets of William Alabaster*, ed. G. M. Story and Helen Gardner (Oxford, 1959)

Anon., *This tretyse is of loue and spekyth of iiij of the most specyall louys that ben in the worlde* (Westminster, 1493)

Askew, Anne, *The Examinations of Anne Askew*, ed. Elaine V. Beilin (Oxford, 1996)

The first examinacyon of Anne Askewe lately martyred in Smythfelde, by the Romysh popes vpholders, with the elucydacyon of Iohan Bale (Marburg [i.e. Wesel], 1546)

The lattre examinacyon of Anne Askewe latelye martyred in Smythfelde, by the wycked Synagoge of Antichrist, with the Elucydacyon of Iohan Bale (Marburg [i.e. Wesel], 1547)

Atkinson, William, and Lady Margaret Beaufort, *A ful deuout and gostely treatyse of the imitacyon and folowynge the blessed lyfe of our moste mercyful sauyour cryste* (London, 1504)

Barnes, Robert, *A Critical Edition of Robert Barnes's A Supplication Vnto the Most Gracyous Prince Kynge Henry The. VIIJ, 1534*, ed. Douglas H. Parker (Toronto, 2008)

Barrow, Henry, and John Greenwood, *The Writings of John Greenwood and Henry Barrow, 1591–1593*, ed. Leland H. Carlson, Elizabethan Non-Conformist Texts 6 (London, 1970)

Bastwick, John, *Praxeis ton episkopon sive apologeticus ad praesules Anglicanos criminum ecclesiasticorum in curia celsae commissionis* ([Leiden?], 1636)

Besse, Joseph, *A Collection of the Sufferings of the People Called Quaker*, 2 vols. (London, 1753)

Boethius, *Boetius de consolationae philosophiae: The boke of Boecius, called the comforte of philosophye* (London, 1556)

The boke of comfort called in laten Boetius de Consolatione philosophie (Tavistock, 1525)

Bradford, John, *All the examinacions of the constante martir of God M. Iohn Bradforde ... wherunto are annexed, his priuate talk [and] conflictes in prison after his condemnacion* (London, 1561)

The Writings of John Bradford, ed. Aubrey Townsend, 2 vols. (Cambridge, 1848–53)

Brewer, J. S. et al. (eds.), *Letters and Papers, Foreign and Domestic, of the Reign of Henry VIII: Preserved in the Public Record Office, the British Museum and elsewhere (in England)*, 21 vols. (London, 1862–1910)

Bull, Henry (ed.), *Christian praiers and holy meditations as well for priuate as publike exercise, gathered out of the most godly learned in our time* (London, 1570)

Bunyan, John, *The pilgrim's progress from this world to that which is to come* (London, 1678)

A Relation of the Imprisonment of Mr John Bunyan (London, 1765)

Byrne, M. St Clare (ed.), *The Lisle Letters*, 6 vols. (Chicago, 1981)

Chapman, George, Ben Jonson and John Marston, *Eastward Hoe* (London, 1605)

Chauncy, Maurice, *Passio Sanctorum Patrum Cartusiana Angliæ* (1570), in *The Various Versions of the Historia aliquot Martyrum Anglorum maxime octodecim Cartusianorum*, ed. John Clark, 3 vols. (Salzburg, 2006–7)

Cicero, Marcus Tullius, *De senectute; De amicitia; De divinatione*, tr. William Armistead Falconer (London, 1923)

Collin, Jean, *Le Livre de Amytié de Ciceron* (Paris, 1537)

Coverdale, Miles, *Biblia the Bible* (Cologne?, 1535)

Certain most godly, fruitful, and comfortable letters of such true saintes and holy martyrs of God (London, 1564)

A spyrytuall and moost precyouse pearle (London, 1550)

Cranmer, Thomas, *A Defence of the True and Catholike Doctrine of the Sacrament of the Body and Bloud of our Saviour Christ* (London, 1550)

Defensio verae et catholicae doctrinae de sacramento corporis & sanguinis Christi seruatoris nostri (London, 1553 and Emden, 1557)

Crespin, Jean, *Actes des martyrs Deduits en Sept Livres, depuis le temps de Wiclif et de Hus, jusques à present* (Geneva, 1564)

Actiones et monimenta martyrum, qui a Wicleffo et Husso ad nostrum hanc aetatem in Germania, Gallia, Anglia, Flandria, Italia et Hispania . . . (Geneva, 1560)

Cromwell, Thomas, *Life and Letters of Thomas Cromwell*, ed. Roger Bigelow Merriman (Oxford, 1968)

Dasent, J. R. (ed.), *Acts of the Privy Council of England*, new series (London, 1890)

Elizabeth I: Collected Works, ed. Leah S. Marcus, Janel Mueller and Mary Beth Rose (Chicago, 2000)

Elizabeth I: Translations, 1544–1589, ed. Janel Mueller and Joshua Scodel (Chicago, 2009)

Falkoff, Marc (ed.), *Poems from Guantánamo: The Detainees Speak* (Iowa City, 2007)

Fennor, William, *The compters common-wealth, or A voiage made to an infernall iland* (London, 1617)

Fisher, John, *English Works of John Fisher, Bishop of Rochester (1469–1535): Sermons and other Writings, 1520–1535*, ed. Cecilia A. Hatt (Oxford, 2002)

A spirituall consolation (London, 1578?)

Foxe, John (ed.), *Rerum in Ecclesia gestarum* (Basle, 1559)

Frith, John, *A boke made by Iohn Frith prisoner in the tower of London answeringe vnto M. mores lettur . . . vnto which boke are added in the ende the articles of his examinacion before the bishoppes* (Antwerp, 1533)

A christen sentence and true iudgement of the moste honourable Sacrament of Christes body [and] bloude (London, [1548?])

A letter . . . wryten vnto the faythful followers of Christes gospell (London?, 1548 or 1549)

[A mirroure. To know thyselfe.] ([Antwerp, 1536?])

A myrroure or lokynge glasse wherin you may beholde the sacramente of baptisme described (London, [1548?])

An other boke against Rastel named the subsedye or bulwark to his fyrst boke ([Canterbury?, 1536?])

The Work of John Frith, ed. N. T. Wright (Oxford, 1983)

Gardiner, Stephen, *Confutatio cavillationum* (Paris, 1552)

An explicatio[n] and assertion of the true Catholique fayth (Rouen, 1551)

Grindal, Edmund, *The Remains of Edmund Grindal*, ed. W. Nicholson (Cambridge, 1843)

Gwynnethe, John, *A declaracion of the state* (London, 1554)

Hall, Edward, *Chronicle*, ed. Henry Ellis (London, 1809)

Harington, John, *The booke of freendeship of Marcus Tullie Cicero* (London, 1550)

Harington, John (the younger), *Orlando Furioso in English heroical verse* (London, 1591)

Harpsfield, Nicholas, *The Life and Death of Sr Thomas Moore, Knight*, ed. E. V. Hitchcock, EETS OS 186 (Oxford, 1932)

Haynes, Samuel (ed.), *A Collection of State Papers . . . Left by William Cecil, Lord Burghley* (London, 1740)

Heywood, Thomas, *If you knovv not me, you know no bodie: or, The troubles of Queene Elizabeth* (London, 1605)

History of a Bible (Ballston Spa, NY, 1811)

History of Parliament Trust, *Journals of the House of Lords, Beginning Anno Primo Henrici Octavi*, vol. 1, 1509–1577 (London, 1808)

Hooper, John, *An apologye made by the reuerende father and constante martyr of Christe Iohn Hooper late bishop of Gloceter and Worceter* (London, 1562)

Certeine comfortable expositions (London, 1580)

Howard, Henry, Earl of Surrey, *Certayne chapters of the prouerbes of Salomon drawen into metre by Thomas sterneholde* (London, 1549 or 1550)

Poems, ed. Emrys Jones (Oxford, 1964)

Hughey, Ruth, *The Arundel Harington Manuscript of Tudor Poetry*, 2 vols. (Columbus, OH, 1960)

Hutton, Luke, *The blacke dogge of Newgate both pithie and profitable for all readers* (London, 1596)

James I, King of Scotland, *The Kingis Quair and other Prison Poems*, ed. Linne R. Mooney and Mary Jo Arn (Kalamazoo, MI, 2005)

John of Salisbury, *Policraticus*, ed. C. C. J. Webb, 2 vols. (Oxford, 1909)

Kempis, Thomas à, *Imitatio Christi, A ful deuout and gostely treatyse of the imitacyon and folowynge the blessed lyfe of our moste mercyful sauyour cryste* (London, 1504)

Lambert, John, *A treatyse made by Johan Lambert vnto kynge Henry the.viij. concerynge hys opynyon in the sacrame[n]t of the aultre* (Wesel, 1548?])

Leland, John, *The Laboryouse journey and serche of Johan Lelande for Englandes antiquitees*, ed. John Bale (London, 1549)

Lempriere, William (ed.), *John Howes' MS, 1582: Being a brief note of the order and manner of the proceedings in the first erection of the three royal hospitals of Christ, Bridewell & St Thomas the Apostle* (London, 1904)

Lilburne, John, *The Christian mans triall: or, A true relation of the first apprehension and severall examinations of Iohn Lilburne* (London, 1641)

Luders, A., et al. (eds.), *The Statutes of the Realm . . . From Original Records . . . (1101–1713)*, 11 vols. (London, 1810–28)

More, Thomas, *The Complete Works of Sr Thomas More*, 15 vols. (New Haven, CT, 1963–97)

The Correspondence of Sir Thomas More, ed. Elizabeth Frances Rogers (Princeton, NJ, 1947)

A dialog of comfort against tribulacion, made by Syr Thomas More Knyght, and set foorth by the name of an Hu[n]garie[n], not before this time imprinted (London, 1553)

Selected Letters, ed. E. F. Rogers (New Haven, CT, 1961)

Thomas More's Prayer Book: A Facsimile Reproduction of the Annotated Pages, ed. Louis L. Martz and Richard S. Sylvester (New Haven, CT, 1969)

The Workes of Syr Thomas More Knyght ... wrytten by him in the Englysh tonge (London, 1557)

[Mynshal, Geoffrey], *Certaine characters and essayes of prison and prisoners. Compiled by Nouus Homo a prisoner in the kings bench* (London, 1618)

Nichols, John Gough (ed.), *The chronicle of Queen Jane: and of two years of Queen Mary, and especially of the rebellion of Sir Thomas Wyat; Written by a resident in the Tower of London* (London, 1850)

Narratives of the Days of the Reformation, Camden Society, old series 77 (London, 1859)

Oldcastle, John, *A brefe chronycle concernynge the examinacyon and death of the blessed martyr of Christ syr Iohan Oldecastell the lorde Cobham, collected togyther by Iohan Bale* (Antwerp, 1544)

The examinacion of Master William Thorpe preste accused of heresye before Thomas Arundell, Archebishop of Ca[n]terbury, the yere of ower Lord.MCCCC. and seuen. The examinacion of the honorable knight syr John Oldcastell Lorde Cobham, burnt bi the said Archebisshop, in the fyrste yere of Kynge Henry the Fyfth (Antwerp, 1530)

Peter of Celle, 'On Affliction and Reading', in *Selected Works*, tr. Hugh Feiss (Kalamazoo, MI, 1987)

Rabus, Ludwig, *Der Heyligen ausserwoehlten Gottes Zeugen, Bekennern und Martyrern ... Historien*, 8 vols. (Strasbourg, 1552–8)

Ridley, Nicholas, *Certein godly, learned, and comfortable conferences, betwene the two reuerende fathers, and holy martyrs of Christe, D. Nicolas Rydley ... and M. Hughe Latimer* (Emden, 1556)

A frendly farewell which master doctor Ridley did write unto all his true lovers and frendes in God, a little before that he suiffered (London, 1559)

Robbins, Rossel Hope (ed.), *Secular Lyrics of the XIVth and XVth Centuries* (Oxford, 1952)

Robinson, Hastings (ed.), *Original Letters Relative to the English Reformation*, 2 vols. (Cambridge, 1846–7)

Roper, William, *The mirrour of vertue in worldly greatnes. Or The life of Syr Thomas More Knight, sometime Lo. Chancellour of England* (Paris [i.e. Saint-Omer], 1626)

Smith, Thomas, *Literary and Linguistic Work: Part 1, Certaigne psalmes or songes of David (1549)*, ed. Bror Danielsson (Stockholm, 1963)

Strype, John (ed.), *Ecclesiastical memorials; relating chiefly to religion, and the reformation of it, and the emergencies of the Church of England, under King Henry VIII. King Edward VI. and Queen Mary the First*, 3 vols. (London, 1721)

Thorpe, William, *The examinacion of Master William Thorpe preste accused of heresye before Thomas Arundell, Archebishop of Ca[n]terbury, the yere of ower Lord.MCCCC. and seuen. The examinacion of the honorable knight syr John Oldcastell Lorde Cobham, burnt bi the said Archebisshop, in the fyrste yere of Kynge Henry the Fyfth* (Antwerp, 1530)

Testimony, in Two Wycliffite Texts: The Sermon of William Taylor 1406; The Testimony of William Thorpe 1407, ed. Anne Hudson, EETS (Oxford, 1993)
Tottel, Richard (ed.), *Songes and sonettes, written by the right honorable Lorde Henry Haward late Earle of Surrey, and other* (London, 1557)
Tottel's Miscellany: Songs and Sonnets of Henry Howard, Earl of Surrey, Sir Thomas Wyatt and Others, ed. Amanda Holton (London, 2011)
Tunstall, Cuthbert, *De veritate corporis et sanguinis domini nostri Jesu Christi in eucharistia* (Paris, 1554)
Tyler, Royal, and others (eds.), *Calendar of Letters, Despatches, and State Papers, Relating to the Negotiations between England and Spain, 1485–[1558]*, 13 vols. (London, 1862–1964)
Tyndale, William, *An answere vnto Sir Thomas Mores dialoge* (Antwerp, 1531)
Thomas Urquhart, *The first [second] book of the works of Mr. Francis Rabelais* (London, 1653)
Van Haemstede, Adriaan, *De Geschiedenisse ende den doodt der vromer Martelaren* (Emden, 1559)
Whitford, Richard, *A dayley exercyse and experience of dethe* (London, 1537)
A werke for houshoulders (London, 1530)
Wriothesley, Charles, *A Chronicle of England during the Reigns of the Tudors, from AD 1485 to 1559*, 2 vols. (London, 1875–7)
Wyatt, Thomas, *Certayne psalmes chosen out of the psalter of Dauid* (London 1549)
Collected Poems, ed. Kenneth Muir and Patricia Thomson (Liverpool, 1969)
Wyche, Richard, 'Trial', in F. D. Matthews, 'The Trial of Richard Wyche', *English Historical Review*, 5 (1890), 530–44

SECONDARY SOURCES

Ackroyd, Peter, *The Life of Thomas More* (London, 1998)
Ahnert, Ruth, 'Imitating Inquisition: Dialectical Bias in Protestant Prison Writings', in *The Culture of Inquisition in Medieval England*, ed. Mary C. Flannery and Katie L. Walter (Woodbridge, 2013), 146–163
'The Prison in Early Modern Drama', *Literature Compass*, 9:1 (2012), 34–47
Alexander, Gavin, 'Sidney's Interruptions', *Studies in Philology*, 98 (2001), 184–204
Allen, Stuart, *Letters from Prison: An Exposition of the Prison Epistles of the Apostle Paul* (London, 1975)
Arn, Mary-Jo (ed.), *Charles D'Orleans in England, 1415–1440* (Rochester, NY, 2000)
Ayris, Paul, and David Selwyn (eds.), *Thomas Cranmer, Churchman and Scholar* (Woodbridge, 1999)
Bachelard, Gaston, *The Poetics of Space*, tr. Maria Jolas, revised edn (Boston, MA, 1994)
Barabási, Albert-László, *Linked* (New York, 2003)

Barker, Francis, *The Tremulous Private Body: Essays on Subjection* (London, 1984)

Baron, Helen, 'Mary (Howard) Fitzroy's Hand in the Devonshire Manuscript', *Review of English Studies*, 179 (1994), 318–35

Bartlett, R., '"The misfortune that is wished for him": The Life and Death of Edward Courtenay, Earl of Devon', *Canadian Journal of History*, 12 (1979), 1–28

Beadle, Richard, 'Private Letters', in *Companion to Middle English Prose*, ed. A. S. G. Edwards (Cambridge, 2004), 289–306

Beckwith, Sarah, *Christ's Body: Identity, Culture, and Society in Late Medieval Writings* (London, 1993)

Beier, A. L., 'Vagrants and the Social Order', *Past and Present*, 64 (1974), 3–29

Beier, Lee, 'Foucault Redux?: The Roles of Humanism, Protestantism, and an Urban Elite in Creating the London Bridewell, 1500–1560', in *Crime, Gender, and Sexuality in Criminal Prosecutions*, ed. Louis A. Knafla (Westport, CN; London, 2002), 33–60

Beilin, Elaine V., 'A Challenge to Authority: Anne Askew, in *Redeeming Eve: Women Writers of the English Renaissance*, ed. Elaine V. Beilin (Princeton, NJ, 1987), 29–47

Bellamy, John, *Crime and Public Order in England in the Later Middle Ages* (London, 1973)

Benedict, Barbara, *Making the Modern Reader: Cultural Mediation in Early Modern Literary Anthologies* (Princeton, NJ, 1996)

Bernard, G. W., *The King's Reformation: Henry VIII and the Remaking of the English Church* (New Haven, CT, 2005)

Betteridge, Thomas, 'The Henrician Reformation and Mid-Tudor Culture', *Journal of Medieval and Early Modern Studies*, 35 (2005), 91–110

Tudor Histories of the English Reformation, 1530–83 (Aldershot, 1999)

Birrell, T. A., 'William Carter (*c.* 1549–84): Recusant Printer, Publisher, Binder, Stationer, Scribe – and Martyr', *Recusant History*, 28 (2006), 22–42

Blair, Ann M., *Too Much to Know: Managing Scholarly Information Before the Modern Age* (Princeton, NJ, 2010)

Boffey, Julia, 'Chaucerian Prisoners: The Context of The Kinges Quair', in *Chaucer and Fifteenth-Century Poetry*, ed. Julia Boffey and Janet Cowen (London, 1991), 279–316

Manuscripts of English Courtly Love Lyrics in the Later Middle Ages (Cambridge, 1985)

Boffey, Julia, and John J. Thompson, 'Anthologies and Miscellanies: Production and Choice of Texts', in *Book Production and Publishing in Britain 1375–1475*, ed. Jeremy Griffiths and Derek Pearsall (Cambridge, 1989), 84–102

Bradshaw, Brendan, 'Bishop John Fisher 1469–1535: The Man and his Work', in Bradshaw and Duffy (ed.), *Humanism, Reform and the Reformation*, 1–24

Bradshaw, Brendan, and Eamon Duffy (eds.), *Humanism, Reform and the Reformation: The Career of Bishop John Fisher* (Cambridge, 1989)

Brigden, Susan, 'Henry Howard, Earl of Surrey and the "Conjured League"', *Historical Journal*, 37 (1994), 507–37

Buzacott, Martin, 'A Boethian Analogue for Sir Thomas Wyatt's "Who List His Wealth"', *Notes & Queries*, 31 (1984), 163–4

Byrom, H. J., 'Richard Tottel – His Life and Work', *Library*, 4th series, 8 (1927–8), 199–232

Casey, Edward S., *The Fate of Place: A Philosophical History* (Berkeley, CA, 1997)

Chambers, R. W., 'On the Continuity of English Prose from Alfred to More and his School', in Nicholas Harpsfield's *Life and Death of Sir Thomas More, Knight*, ed. E. V. Hitchcock, EETS OS 186 (London, 1932), xlv–clxxiv

Clebsch, William A., *England's Earliest Protestants, 1520–1535* (New Haven, CT, 1964)

Coffey, John, *Persecution and Toleration in Protestant England, 1558–1689* (Harlow, 2000)

Cohen, Anthony P., *The Symbolic Construction of Community* (London, 1985)
 'Of Symbols and Boundaries, or, Does Ertie's Greatcoat Hold the Key?', in *Symbolising Boundaries: Identity and Diversity in British Cultures*, ed. Anthony P. Cohen (Manchester, 1986), 1–19

Collins, 'Michael, The Antipanopticon of Etheridge Knight', *PMLA*, 123 (2008), 580–97

Collinson, Patrick, *Archbishop Grindal 1519–1583: The Struggle for a Reformed Church* (Berkeley and Los Angeles, CA, 1979)

Connor, T. P., 'Malignant Reading: John Squier's Newgate Prison Library, 1642–46,' *Library*, 7 (2006), 154–84

Cormack, Bradin, *A Power to do Justice: Jurisdiction, English Literature, and the Rise of Common Law, 1509–1625* (Chicago, IL, 2007)

Cox, Virginia, *The Renaissance Dialogue: Literary Dialogue in its Social and Political Contexts, Castiglione to Galileo* (Cambridge, 1992)

Crick, Julia, and Alexandra Walsham (eds.), *The Uses of Script and Print, 1300–1700* (Cambridge, 2004)

Cummings Brian, *The Literary Culture of the Reformation: Grammar and Grace* (Oxford, 2002)

Davis, John F., *Heresy and Reformation in the South-East of England, 1520–1559* (London, 1983)

Davis, Natalie Zemon, 'Beyond the Market: Books as Gifts in Sixteenth-Century France', *Transactions of the Royal Historical Society*, 5th series, 33 (1983), 69–88

De Certeau, Michel, *The Practice of Everyday Life*, tr. Steven Rendall (Berkeley, CA, 1984)

Deiter, Kristen, *The Tower of London in English Renaissance Drama: Icon of Opposition* (London, 2008)

Delcourt, Joseph, *Essai sur la langue de Sir Thomas More* (Montpellier, 1914)

Dickens, A. G., *The English Reformation*, 2nd edn (London, 1989)

Di Leo, Jeffrey R., *On Anthologies: Politics and Pedagogy* (Lincoln, NE, 2004)

Duffy, Eamon, *Fires of Faith: Catholic England Under Mary Tudor* (New Haven, CT, 2009)

Marking the Hours: English People and their Prayers, 1240–1570 (New Haven, CT, 2006)

'The Spirituality of John Fisher', in Bradshaw and Duffy (ed.), *Humanism, Reform and the Reformation*, 205–32

Dutschke, C. W., et al. (eds.), *Guide to Medieval and Renaissance Manuscripts in the Huntington Library* (San Marino, CA, 1989)

Edward S., Casey, *The Fate of Place: A Philosophical History* (Berkeley, CA, 1997)

Eisenstein, E. L., *The Printing Press as an Agent of Change: Communications and Cultural Transformations in Early Modern Europe*, 2 vols. (Cambridge, 1979)

Elton, G. R., 'The Real Thomas More', in *Reformation Principle and Practice: Essays in Honour of Arthur Geoffrey Dickens*, ed. Peter Newman Brooks (London, 1980), 21–31

Studies in Tudor and Stuart Politics and Government, 4 vols. (New York, [1974]–1992)

The Tudor Revolution in Government: Administrative Changes in the Reign of Henry VIII (Cambridge, 1953)

Epstein, Robert, 'Prisoners of Reflection: The Fifteenth-Century Poetry of Exile and Imprisonment', *Exemplaria*, 15 (2003), 157–98

Evenden, Elizabeth, and Thomas S. Freeman, *Religion and the Book: The Making of John Foxe's 'Book of Martyrs'* (Cambridge, 2011)

Fairfield, Leslie, *John Bale: Mythmaker for the English Reformation* (West Lafayette, IN, 1976)

Fleming, Juliet, *Graffiti and the Writing Arts of Early Modern England* (London, 2001)

Foucault, Michel, *Discipline and Punish: The Birth of the Prison*, tr. Alan Sheridan (London, 1977; reprinted 1991)

Fox, Alastair, *Politics and Literature in the Reigns of Henry VII and Henry VIII* (Oxford, 1989)

Fraser, Nancy, 'Rethinking the Public Sphere: A Contribution to the Critique of Actually Existing Democracy', in *Habermas and the Public Sphere*, ed. Craig J. Calhoun (Cambridge, MA, 1999), 109–42

Freeman, Thomas S., 'Dissenters from a Dissenting Church: The Challenge of the "Freewillers", 1550–1558', in *The Beginnings of English Protestantism*, ed. Peter Marshall and Alec Ryrie (Cambridge, 2002), 129–56

'Fate, Faction and Fiction in Foxe's *Book of Martyrs*', *Historical Journal*, 43 (2000), 601–23

'"The good ministrye of godlye and vertuouse women": The Elizabethan Martyrologists and the Female Supporters of the Marian Martyrs', *Journal of British Studies*, 49 (2000), 8–33

'Introduction: The Rise of Prison Literature', in Sherman and Sheils (ed.), 'Prison Writings in Early Modern Britain', 133–46

'Publish and Perish: The Scribal Culture of the Marian Martyrs', in Crick and Walsham (ed.), *Uses of Script and Print*, 235–54

Freeman, Thomas S., and Sarah Elizabeth Wall, 'Racking the Body, Shaping the Text: The Account of Anne Askew in Foxe's "Book of Martyrs"', *Renaissance Quarterly*, 54 (2001), 1165–96

Fulop, R. E., 'John Frith (1503–1533) and his Relation to the Origins of the Reformation in England', unpublished doctoral thesis, University of Edinburgh, 1956

Genette, Gerard, *Paratexts: Thresholds of Interpretation*, tr. Jane E. Levin (Cambridge, 1997)

Geltner, Guy, *The Medieval Prison: A Social History* (Oxford, 2008)

Gertz, Genelle, *Heresy Trials and English Women Writers* (Cambridge, 2012)

Gillespie, Alexandra, 'Poets, Printers, and Early English Sammelbände', in 'Manuscript, Print, and Early Tudor Literature', ed. Alexandra Gillespie, *HLQ*, special issue, 67 (2004), 189–214

Goff, Cecilie, *A Woman of the Tudor Age* (London, 1930)

Görlach, Manfred, *Introduction to Early Modern English*, revised edn (Cambridge, 1991)

Greenblatt, Stephen, 'Mutilation and Meaning', in *The Body in Parts: Fantasies of Corporeality in Early Modern Europe*, ed. David Hillman and Carla Mazzio (New York, 1997), 221–42

Renaissance Self-Fashioning: From More to Shakespeare (Chicago, IL, 1980; reprinted 2005)

Gregory, Brad S., 'The Anathema of Compromise: Christian Martyrdom in Early Modern Europe', PhD thesis, Princeton University, 1996

Salvation at Stake: Christian Martyrdom in Early Modern Europe (Cambridge, MA, 1999)

Habermas, Jürgen, *The Structural Transformation of the Public Sphere: An Inquiry into a Category of Bourgeois Society*, tr. Thomas Burger and Frederick Lawrence (Cambridge, MA, 1991)

Hackel, Heidi Brayman, *Reading Material in Early Modern England: Print, Gender, and Literacy* (Cambridge, 2005)

Haigh, Christopher, *The English Reformation Revised* (Cambridge, 1987)

Hamlin, Hannibal, *Psalm Culture and Early Modern English Literature* (Cambridge, 2004)

Hammer, Carl I., 'A Hearty Meal? The Prison Diets of Cranmer and Latimer', *Sixteenth Century Journal*, 30:3 (1999), 653–80

'The Oxford Martyrs in Oxford: The Local History of their Confinements and their Keepers', *Journal of Ecclesiastical History*, 50 (1999), 235–50

Hanson, Elizabeth, *Discovering the Subject in Renaissance England* (Cambridge, 1998)

Harrison, Brain A., *The Tower of London Prisoner Book: A Complete Chronology of the Persons Known to have been Detained at Their Majesties Pleasure, 1100–1941* (Leeds, 2004)

Hatt, Cecilia A., 'The Two-edged Sword as Image of Civil Power for Fisher and More', *Moreana*, 175 (2008), 67–86

Hauser, Gerard A., 'Prisoners of Conscience and the Counterpublic Sphere of Prison Writing: The Stones that start the Avalanche', in *Counterpublics and the State*, ed. Robert Asen and Daniel C. Brouwer (New York, 2001), 35–58

Head, David M., '"Beyng ledde and seduced by the Devyll": The Attainder of Lord Thomas Howard and the Tudor Law of Treason', *Sixteenth Century Journal*, 13:4 (1982), 3–16

Heale, Elizabeth, *Wyatt, Surrey and Early Tudor Poetry* (London, 1998)

Hellinga, Lotte, and J. B. Trapp (eds.), *Cambridge History of the Book in Britain*, vol. III, *1400–1557* (Cambridge, 1998)

Hillman, David, and Carlo Mazzio (eds.), *The Body in Parts: Fantasies of Corporeality in Early Modern Europe* (New York, 1997)

Hudson, Anne, *Lollards and their Books* (London, 1985)

Hughey, Ruth, *John Harington of Stepney: Tudor Gentleman; His Life and Works* (Columbus, OH, 1971)

Johnston, Norman, *Forms of Constraint: A History of Prison Architecture* (Chicago, IL, 2000)

Jones, Howard, *Master Tully: Cicero in Tudor England* (Nieuwkoop, 1998)

Kesselring, K. J., *Mercy and Authority in the Tudor State* (Cambridge, 2003)

King, John N., *English Reformation Literature: The Tudor Origins of the Protestant Tradition* (Princeton, NJ, 1982)

Knafla, Louis A., 'The Geographical, Jurisdictional and Jurisprudential Boundaries of English Litigation in the Early Seventeenth Century', in *Boundaries of the Law: Geography, Gender and Jurisdiction in Medieval and Early Modern Europe*, ed. Anthony Musson (Aldershot, 2005), 130–48

Korte, Barbara, Ralph Schneider, and Stephanie Lethbridge (eds.), *Anthologies of British Poetry: Critical Perspectives from Literary and Cultural Studies* (Amsterdam, 2000)

Lake, Peter, and Steven Pincus, 'Rethinking the Public Sphere in Early Modern England', in *The Politics of the Public Sphere in Early Modern England*, ed. Peter Lake and Steven Pincus (Manchester, 2007), 1–30

Lake, Peter, and Michael Questier, 'Prisons, Priests and People', in *England's Long Reformation, 1500–1800* ed. Nicholas Tyacke (London, 1998), 195–234

Lathrop, H. B., *Translations from the Classics into English from Caxton to Chapman, 1477–1620* (Madison, WI, 1933)

Lerer, Seth, *Courtly Letters in the Age of Henry VIII* (Cambridge, 1997)

Error and the Academic Self: The Scholarly Imagination, Medieval to Modern (New York, 2002)

Linton, David, 'Reading the Meta-Canonical Texts', in *Other Voices, Other Views: Expanding the Canon in English Renaissance Studies*, ed. Helen Ostovich, Mary V. Silcox, and Graham Roebuck (Newark, DE and London, 1999), 21–45

John Dudley, Duke of Northumberland, 1504–1553 (Oxford, 1996)

John Foxe at Home and Abroad (Aldershot, 2004)

Politics, Censorship and the English Reformation (London, 1991)

Love, Harold, *Scribal Publication in Seventeenth-Century England* (Oxford, 1993)

McConville, Sean, *A History of English Prison Administration*, vol. I, *1750–1877* (London, 1981)

MacCulloch, Diarmaid, *Thomas Cranmer* (New Haven, CT, 1996)

McKenzie, D. F., *Making Meaning: 'Printers of the Mind' and other Essays*, ed. Peter D. McDonald and Michael F. Suarez (Amherst, MA, 2002)

Marc'hadour, Germain, *The Bible in the Works of Thomas More*, 5 vols. (Nieuwkoop, 1969–72)

Thomas More et la Bible (Paris, 1969)

'Three Tudor Editors of Thomas More', in *Editing Sixteenth-Century Texts*, ed. Richard J. Schoeck (Toronto, 1965), 59–71

Marcus, Leah S., *Unediting the Renaissance: Shakespeare, Marlowe, Milton* (London, 1996)

Marius, Richard, *Thomas More: A Biography* (London, 1985)

Marks, Diane, 'Poems from Prison: James I of Scotland and Charles d'Orléans', *Fifteenth-Century Studies*, 15 (1989), 245–58

Marotti, Arthur F., *Manuscript, Print, and the English Renaissance Lyric* (Ithaca, NY, 1995)

Marsh, David, *The Quattrocento Dialogue: Classical Tradition and Humanist Innovation* (Cambridge, MA, 1980)

Marshall, Cynthia, *The Shattering of the Self: Violence, Subjectivity, and Early Modern Texts* (Baltimore, MD and London, 2002)

Marshall, Peter, 'The Last Years', in *The Cambridge Companion to Thomas More*, ed. George M. Logan (Cambridge, 2011), 116–39

Religious Identities in Henry VIII's England (Aldershot, 2006)

Marshall, Peter, and Alec Ryrie (eds.), *The Beginnings of English Protestantism* (Cambridge, 2003)

Mason, H. A., *Humanism and Poetry in the Early Tudor Period: An Essay* (London, 1959)

May, Steven W., 'Popularizing Courtly Poetry: Tottel's Miscellany and its Progeny', in *The Oxford Handbook of Tudor Literature, 1485–1603*, ed. Michael Pincombe and Cathy Shrank (Oxford, 2009), 418–33

'Tudor Aristocrats and the Mythical "Stigma of Print"', *Renaissance Papers*, 10 (1980), 11–18

Muldrew, Craig, *The Economy of Obligation: The Culture of Credit and Social Relations in Early Modern England* (Basingstoke, 1998)

Muller, J. A., *Stephen Gardiner and the Tudor Reaction* (New York, 1926)

Murray, Molly, 'Measured Sentences: Forming Literature in the Early Modern Prison', in Sherman and Sheils (ed.), 'Prison Writings in Early Modern Britain', 147–67

North, Marcy L., *The Anonymous Renaissance* (Chicago, IL, 2003)

Orgel, Stephen, 'Margins of Truth', in *The Renaissance Text*, ed. Andrew Murphy (Manchester, 2000), 91–107

Pendry, E. D., *Elizabethan Prisons and Prison Scenes*, 2 vols. (Salzburg, 1974)

Penny, D. Andrew, *Freewill or Predestination: The Battle over Saving Grace in Mid-Tudor England* (Woodbridge, 1990)

Pettegree, Andrew, *Emden and the Dutch Revolt: Exile and the Development of Reformed Protestantism* (Oxford, 1992)

'Haemstede and Foxe', in *John Foxe and the English Reformation,* ed. David Loades (Aldershot, 1997)

Marian Protestantism: Six Studies (Aldershot, 1996)

Pineas, Rainer, 'Thomas More's use of the Dialogue form as a Weapon of Religious Controversy', *Studies in the Renaissance,* 7 (1960), 193–206

Pollard, A. W., and G. R. Redgrave (eds.), *A Short-Title Catalogue of Books Printed in England, Scotland, and Ireland and of English Books Printed Abroad, 1475–1640* (London, 1926)

Potter, Lois, *Secret Rites and Secret Writing: Royalist Literature, 1641–1660* (Cambridge, 1989)

Price, Leah, *The Anthology and the Rise of the Novel: From Richardson to George Eliot* (Cambridge, 2000)

'From *The History of a Book* to a "History of the Book"', *Representations,* 108 (2009), 120–38

Pughe, Ralph, *Imprisonment in Medieval England* (Cambridge, 1968)

Quitslund, Beth, *The Reformation in Rhyme: Sternhold, Hopkins and the English Metrical Psalter, 1547–1603* (Aldershot, 2008)

Remley, Paul G., 'Mary Shelton and her Tudor Literary Milieu', in *Rethinking the Henrician Era,* ed. Peter C. Herman (Urbana, IL, 1994), 40–77

Reynolds, E. E., *The Field is Won: The Life and Death of St Thomas More* (London, 1974)

Saint John Fisher, revised edn (Wheathampstead, 1972)

Robinson, Benedict S., 'Neither Acts nor Monuments', *English Literary Renaissance,* 41 (2011), 3–30

Rostenthal, Bernard M., *The Rosenthal Collection of Printed Books with Manuscript Annotations: A Catalog of 242 Editions Mostly before 1600, Annotated by Contemporary or Near-Contemporary Readers* (New Haven, CT, 1997)

Ryrie, Alec, *The Gospel and Henry VIII: Evangelicals in the Early English Reformation* (Cambridge, 2003)

Saunders, J. W., 'The Stigma of Print: A Note of the Social Bases of Tudor poetry', *Essays in Criticism,* 1 (1951), 139–64

Sawday, Jonathan, *The Body Emblazoned: Dissection and the Human Body in Renaissance Culture* (New York, 1995)

Schuster, Louis A., 'The Tower of London: More's Gethsemane', *Moreana,* 74 (1982), 39–45

Scott-Warren, Jason, *Sir John Harington and the Book as Gift* (Oxford, 2001)

Sessions, W. A., *Henry Howard, the Poet Earl of Surrey: A Life* (Oxford, 1999)

Shagan, E. H., *Popular Politics and the English Reformation* (Cambridge, 2003)

Shaw, Phillip, 'The Position of Thomas Dekker in Jacobean Prison Literature', *PMLA,* 62 (1947), 366–91

Sheils, William J., and William Sherman (eds.), 'Prison Writings in Early Modern Britain', *HLQ,* special issue, 72 (2009)

Shepard, Alexandra, and Phil Withington (eds.), *Communities in Early Modern England* (Manchester, 2000)

Sherman, William H., *Used Books: Marking Readers in Renaissance England* (Philadelphia, 2007)

Shrank, Cathy, *Writing the Nation in Reformation England, 1530–1580* (Oxford, 2006)

Simpson, James, *Burning to Read: English Fundamentalism and its Reformation Opponents* (Cambridge, MA, 2007)

 Oxford English Literary History, vol. II, Reform and Cultural Revolution: 1350–1547 (Oxford, 2002)

Slavin, A. J., 'The Tudor State, Reformation and Understanding Change: Through the Looking Glass', in *Political Thought and the Tudor Commonwealth: Deep Structure, Discourse, and Disguise*, ed. Paul A. Fideler and Thomas Frederick Mayer (London, 1992), 229–60

Smith, Helen, and Louise Wilson (eds.), *Renaissance Paratexts* (Cambridge, 2011)

Smith, Margaret M., *The Title-Page: Its Early Development, 1460–1510* (London, 2000)

Southall, Raymond, *The Courtly Maker: An Essay on the Poetry of Wyatt and his Contemporaries* (Oxford, 1964)

 'The Devonshire Manuscript Collection of Early Tudor Poetry, 1532–41', *Review of English Studies*, 15 (1964), 142–50

Spearing, A. C., *Medieval to Renaissance in English Poetry* (Cambridge, 1985)

 'Prison, Writing, Absence: Representing the Subject in the English Poems of Charles d'Orléans', *Chaucer to Spenser: A Critical Reader*, ed. Derek Pearsall (Oxford, 1999), 297–311

 Textual Subjectivity: The Encoding of Subjectivity in Medieval Narratives and Lyrics (Oxford, 2005)

Spierenburg, Pieter, *The Prison Experience: Disciplinary Institutions and their Inmates in Early Modern Europe* (New Brunswick, NJ and London, 1991)

Spinks, Bryan D., *Reformation and Modern Rituals and Theologies of Baptism: From Luther to Contemporary Practices* (Aldershot, 2006)

Stewart, Alan, *Close Readers: Humanism and Sodomy in Early Modern England* (Princeton, NJ, 1997)

Stock, Brian, *The Implications of Literacy: Written Language and Models of Interpretation in the Eleventh and Twelfth Centuries* (Princeton, NJ, 1983)

String, Tatiana C., 'Henry VIII's Illuminated "Great Bible"', *Journal of the Warburg and Courtauld Institutes*, 59 (1996), 315–24

Summers, Joanna, *Late-Medieval Prison Writing and the Politics of Autobiography* (Oxford, 2004)

Taylor, Andrew William, 'Psalms and Early Tudor Humanism', unpublished PhD thesis, University of Cambridge, 2002

Throness, Laurie, *A Protestant Purgatory: Theological Origins of the Penitentiary Act, 1779* (Aldershot, 2008)

Tribble, Evelyn B., *Margins and Marginality: The Printed Page in Early Modern England* (Charlottesville, VA and London, 1993)

Trueman, Carl R., *Luther's Legacy: Salvation and English Reformers, 1525–1556* (Oxford, 1994)

'"The Saxons be sore on the affirmative": Robert Barnes on the Lord's Supper', *The Bible, the Reformation and the Church*, ed. W. P. Stephens (Sheffield, 1995), 290–307

Wabuda, Susan, 'Henry Bull, Miles Coverdale, and the Making of John Foxe's Book of Martyrs', in *Martyrs and Martyrologies: Papers Read at the 1992 Summer Meeting and the 1993 Winter Meeting of the Ecclesiastical History Society*, ed. Diana Wood, Studies in Church History 30 (Oxford, 1993), 245–58

Wakelin, Daniel, *Humanism, Reading, and English Literature, 1430–1530* (Oxford, 2007)

'William Worcester Writes a History of his Reading, in *New Medieval Literatures*, vol. VII, ed. Wendy Scase, Rita Copeland, and David Lawton (Oxford, 2005), 53–72

Walker, Greg, *Writing under Tyranny: English Literature and the Henrician Reformation* (Oxford, 2005)

Wall, Wendy, *The Imprint of Gender: Authorship and Publication in the English Renaissance* (Ithaca, NY, 1993)

Walsham, Alexandra, 'Preaching without Speaking: Script, Print, and Religious Dissent', in Crick and Walsham (ed.), *Uses of Script and Print*, 211–34

Zim, Rivkah, *English Metrical Psalms: Poetry as Praise and Prayer, 1535–1601* (Cambridge, 1987)

WORKS OF REFERENCE AND ELECTRONIC RESOURCES

Early English Books Online, http://eebo.chadwyck.com/home
Middle English Dictionary, http://quod.lib.umich.edu/m/med/
Oxford Dictionary of National Biography (Oxford, 2004; online, 2008), www.oxforddnb.com/
Oxford English Dictionary, 2nd edn (Oxford, 1989; online, 2009), www.oed.com/
The Unabridged Acts and Monuments Online or TAMO (Sheffield, 2011), www.johnfoxe.org

Index